The Cores of Game Design

This book considers the four essential cores of game design: Mechanics, the interactive elements that allow players to be part and interact with the game itself; Economy, the resources and numerical concepts that will enable players to evaluate and consider the options in the game, creating strategy, risk, and fun; Narrative, the textual features that enable players to create and generate meaning for the game and its parts; and the Aesthetics, the audiovisual elements that allow players to experience the game through their senses and feelings.

This book discusses all four essential cores and how to design games by using each one as a starting point. It also discusses how each one is connected and can be understood as a valuable tool to elevate a game's design. It follows a practical approach to how we can implement the game design and development process by being prototype-focused, user-centred, and lean.

This book will be of great interest to students, indie game developers, and aspiring early-career designers looking to hone their game design craft.

Yvens R. Serpa is a Lecturer and Researcher at Saxion University of Applied Sciences, Enschede, The Netherlands; Head of Computer Graphics at Audo Health Technologies, Fortaleza, Brazil; and Owner of Dagon Graphics Creative Studios.

The Cores of Game Design

Mechanics, Economics, Narrative, and Aesthetics

Yvens R. Serpa

CRC Press
Taylor & Francis Group
Boca Raton London New York

CRC Press is an imprint of the
Taylor & Francis Group, an **informa** business

Designed cover image: Yvens R. Serpa

First edition published 2025
by CRC Press
2385 NW Executive Center Drive, Suite 320, Boca Raton FL 33431

and by CRC Press
4 Park Square, Milton Park, Abingdon, Oxon, OX14 4RN

CRC Press is an imprint of Taylor & Francis Group, LLC

ISBN: 978-1-032-39751-1 (hbk)
ISBN: 978-1-032-39754-2 (pbk)
ISBN: 978-1-003-35119-1 (ebk)

DOI: 10.1201/9781003351191

Typeset in Latin Modern font
by KnowledgeWorks Global Ltd.

This book is dedicated to my godmother, Filomena Maria Serpa Calvacante, also known as Mena, by her family and friends.

*The acronym used for the Cores of Game Design, **M**echanics, **E**conomy, **N**arrative, and **A**esthetics (MENA) was chosen as a homage to her.*

May you rest in peace, Mena.

Contents

Preface

I do not know exactly when I started making games. As far as I can remember, I have always been making games. I remember it next to when I started to draw and play make-believe. Early on, I was introduced to the idea of roleplaying games you would play with dice and paper, and I was hooked. However, even before that, I remember doing paper prototypes and sketching levels for the games I played or saw people playing.

Making games has been a driver for my research and studies since then. I learned how to program by writing simple text-based games, which unlocked a world of possibilities for my ideas. While at first, programming games felt like the last frontier, I soon found out that there was more to it that was somehow unreachable.

I was born and lived all my young years in Brazil, more specifically in the city of Fortaleza. Fortaleza has always been a big city, the fourth biggest in Brazil, with about three times the size of Paris. At the same time, most of the resources and courses on game development were hardly accessible there. By that time, even reliable and stable internet connection was, and to some extent, still is not readily available for everyone. Most of the games and game-related content I could get were second-hand or generations behind current trends.

Moreover, almost all of those sources came from perspectives widely different from mine. Starting off, they were mostly in English, which I was not proficient in. They also assumed experiences and access to tools were only possible in dreams. They also spoke from the point of view of companies and established game developers that had an entire industry in their countries. Even today, Brazil's gaming industry is still in its infancy despite its high number of excellent developers and games.

As I studied those sources, I noticed that many proposed workflows and methods did not suit me or my previous experiences. And, of course, I gave them all a try. But something was off. Either I was inadequate or wrong, or those approaches were inadequate or wrong from where I was.

That feeling stuck with me, and I started to develop my own tools and approaches to developing games.

Fast-forwarding to the near future, in 2018, I was hired as a lecturer/researcher to teach in the Creative Media and Game Technologies (CMGT) Program at Saxion University of Applied Sciences, in Enschede (Netherlands). To my surprise, my colleagues and the students' experiences were quite similar to mine. Although they had their own upbringings, backgrounds, and experiences, their feelings towards the general literature on game development were similar.

Most of the projects I am involved in are small-scale projects. Even the companies I have contact with are usually on a smaller scale. It felt and still feels more as if we are indie developers. Books and sources on the theme were not really focused on our experiences. At least not in Brazil. Surprisingly, not in the Netherlands, too.

You can even research that yourself, as I did a myriad of times again and again while writing this book. Most of the books on Game Design, to use a precise term, come from the US, Canada, or the UK, written by people from those places with a background that reflects their industries and privileges. Most of those books are great, invaluable information on developing games, but they are also a result of background and experiences that the rest of the world cannot truly relate to.

That was my primary motivation for writing this book. There is still so much to talk about game design and game development that is often overlooked. Moreover, there is even more to consider about it if we accept that our backgrounds and environments shape us and change how we approach our processes.

In this book, I propose a methodology for looking at your own approach, background and experiences and finding how you can create/enhance/reflect on your own process. We do that by using what I call the Cores of Game Design, which are the main components that form a game. I present this methodology with a simple game design framework focused on playtesting and applied game design principles.

Moreover, although the title of the book focuses on the term game design, this book discusses the theme in a broader sense, as in the process of designing and developing a game, rather than only its conceptualisation and project.

Finally, before writing this book, I conducted several formal and informal interviews with professionals in the field, but with a special focus on indie developers from around the globe and from diverse communities. That helped me to assess my ideas and learn from experiences different from my own. Moreover, I tried to reach out and study a more diverse set of games and developers, including, but not limited to, marginalised communities, people of colour, LGBTQIA+, and people with disabilities. I also spoke to professionals in related creative fields for inspiration and to diversify the points of view explored in my studies.

The finalised book you have is a result of years of study, game development practice, and many lessons learned from these interviews and experiences I have been through in this journey. It helped me shape a more personal approach to game design and understand how to help others make their own.

This book does not propose an ultimate solution to designing games but should assist you in building tools and finding your own way to uncover your own process. We are all different, and our differences make the search for an ultimate solution a foolish one. Instead, I propose a practical approach to finding your own solution.

Good reading.

THANKS TO

This book would not be possible without the help of many people. Here, I want to briefly mention and thank some of them by their names.

First, my wife, Juliana Santos de Carvalho, and our cat, Morgana do Bujari, are my main support and partners for life. Second, the rest of my family, especially my mother, Maria do Carmo Serpa

Cavalcante, my brother, Ygor Rebouças Serpa, and my sister-in-law, Luana de Sousa Serpa, for their continuous support, love, and cooperation. Third, my extended family, my mother-in-law, Marly dos Santos de Carvalho, my father-in-law, Sergio Vicente Carvalho, and my sister-in-law, Monise Santos de Carvalho, for having me as their loved family member and always supporting my career and dreams.

Thanks to my friends at CMGT Saxion Enschede who helped me immensely with their teachings, cooperation, and feedback on my activities: Bram den Hond, Hans Wichman, Alejandro Moreno Celleri, Max-Michael Klostermann, Taco van Loon, Afra Willems, Paul Bonsma, Mirjam van Tilburg, Mark Boerrigter, Hester van der Ent, Mark Schipper, Yiwei Jiang, Kacper Sikora, Malik Nabil, Léontine Kamphuis, Lukas Malec, Daniel Valente de Macedo, Johannes de Boer, Iain Douglas, Joeri Constandse, Ruben Hulzebosch, and Janet van der Veen, as well as the entire CMGT team, students, and alumni, especially the active ones on our Discord Server.

Thanks to my all-time best friends from Brazil: David Costa Araújo, Eduardo Bruno Silva Lustosa, Yara Viana, Rodrigo Visco Mattos Coelho, Marília Siqueira de Lima, Victor de Sousa Rocha, Louise Moreira Brandão, Maurício Conde Ramon Oliveira, Iná Barbosa, Caroline Pontes de Castro, Diego Pattini, Edson Gustavo Santiago, Kaleo Mendes, and Argeu Alcântara, among others.

Thanks to my friends from Audo Saúde e Tecnologia (Audo Technology), especially my partners and co-creators Leonardo Augusto Pires and Milena Rosado Lapa, as well as the best teammates anyone could dream: Sinara Braga Dias, Matheus Braga Dias, Brena Kesia da Costa Chagas, Mayra Pontes Benevides, Fabrício Fernandes Feijo, Anderson Luiz Karl, Raiza Vaz de Lima Fernandes, Luigi Queiroz Menezes, and Guilherme Sales Fernandes. A special thanks to my friend Marcos Mendes for his teachings on UX Design.

Thanks to Maria Andreia Formico Rodrigues, the best teacher and supervisor any student could hope for.

Thanks to Marcelo Bastos, the amazing artist and game developer partner. Some of the illustrations in this book come from our collaborations.

Thanks to my friend Luuk Waarbroek, one of the greatest teachers, game developers and designers I have the privilege of being friends with.

Thanks to my therapist Antônio Marlon Coutinho, for helping me keep my mental health in check and being a better person.

Thanks to the IGDA Fortaleza and the amazing game developers and designers from Fortaleza, especially my friends Gabriel "Gabas", Daniel "Guarah" Feitosa, and Lucas Mamede. Also, thanks to all the amazing Brazilian developers who share their experiences on our online communities and social media.

Thanks to the entire staff of the SUPERJUMP, especially James Burns, not only for having me as one of their own but for the incredible work done, raising the international level of quality of what writing for and about games is about.

Thanks to everyone who accepted my invites for the interviews. I have learned greatly from you all.

Finally, thanks to you for reading this book. I hope it helps you and your processes.

I

The Cores of Game Design

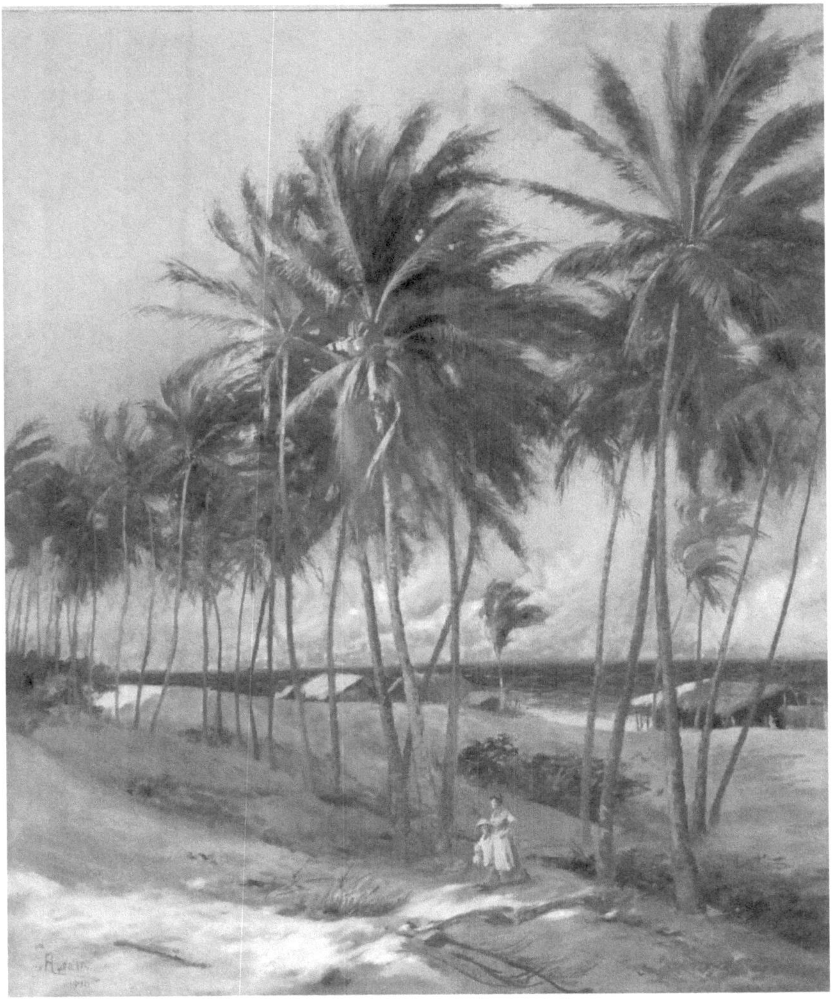

Aurélio Figueiredo – Beach in Fortaleza (1910).

CHAPTER 1

Introduction

UP TO WRITING THIS BOOK, I have been working with games for a little over 10 years. I have worked on projects of different sizes and in different roles. Every project has its own process and story. As I worked my way in this industry (and other industries related to it), I have constantly studied the process of designing and producing games. One thing that stands out is the constant urge from authors to suggest workflows. This book is not necessarily different in that regard, but instead of a strict game development workflow, it proposes a meta-approach to a game design and development workflow.

The term meta is often used in games in the context of **metagames**. In short, a metagame refers to the strategies and discussion of tactics that happen outside the game but about the game [1, 2, 3]. The metagame is a sort of game in which the players try to find the optimal way of playing the game, such as which characters are stronger in certain scenarios or which resources to prioritise to achieve the game's goal faster. Metagaming is also known as theory-crafting and is quite famous in some game communities [4].

In this book, I propose a meta-approach to game development and the design process. Let us put it as an analogy to metagames:

For example, a metagame for a tower defence game encompasses knowing which towers are better than others and in which circumstances. It is a play on finding the best decisions for how to play the game. In our case, this book proposes ways to look at the game

DOI: 10.1201/9781003351191-1

design process as a whole and find your own way of approaching it that best suits you, your needs, and your goals.

This process is supported by what I define as the Cores of Game Design, which are `Mechanics`, `Economy`, `Narrative`, and `Aesthetics` (MENA). These are the main, or core, elements that compose a game, be it digital or not:

`Mechanics` stands for the game's mechanical, interactable and playable aspects: *how the player interacts with the game.*

`Economy` stands for the resources and numerical concepts that form the strategies, risks, and values in the game: *how the player evaluates and makes decisions in the game.*

`Narrative` stands for the textual and intertextual elements in the game that the player perceives: *how the player creates, assigns and perceives meaning to and from the game.*

`Aesthetics` stands for the audiovisual elements and mood of the game in a wide range of senses and feelings: *how the player perceives and experiences the game.*

All elements in the game design process are somehow covered by the four cores, as you will see in their respective chapters and sections.

Given all the different aspects and elements in a game, you can easily find which core it belongs to by resorting to the statements that follow their definitions. If one element is related to how the player *interacts* with the game, such as Level Design, it belongs to the `Mechanics`.

The Cores of Game Design are connected. Some game elements are more easily seen through the perspective of multiple cores at once. The player's immersion can be seen as a combination of `Aesthetics` and `Narrative` cores. The player's strategy throughout the game can be understood as a combination of the `Economy` and `Mechanics` cores.

However, not all elements in the process of producing and selling games are represented by these cores. For example, the `Economy` core is often misunderstood as how we market or sell the game. Contrarily, the `Economy` core deals with in-game resources and mechanisms. This book does not cover marketing, selling, and other entrepreneurial aspects of the gaming industry, although these are important topics. Instead, the Cores of Game Design are discussed in the context of the playable experience.

More precisely, this book explores the Cores of Game Design from multiple perspectives to understand how to work and combine them to build a game design and development process.

The following subsections of this chapter will discuss how the initial concept of the cores and their validation was performed (Getting to the Core 1.1), followed by a discussion on other approaches and frameworks for game design (Other Game Design Frameworks 1.2). Beware, there are lots of food analogies from here on. Do not read while hungry!

Notation

This book uses notations to improve its readability. It is not necessary to memorise them, but it is good to be introduced to them earlier. The following notations are used throughout the book:

Cores, like `Mechanics`, are written with a different font to better contrast them to their regular forms, such as when discussing a specific game mechanic rather than the `Mechanics` core.

Variables, like the number of players or the player's health, are displayed as P and H. Whenever a variable is introduced in the text, its meaning will be explained. Do not worry; there is not a lot of math or programming in the book (except for the `Economy` sections), I promise.

To better exemplify some ideas, **Concepts Games** are presented and named such as **`Family Tree`** and **`Another Starry Sky`**. Concept games are not real games (they are not available anywhere), but they illustrate the main points of this book.

1.1 GETTING TO THE CORE

As stated previously, I have been studying and practising game design for quite some time, and in the process, I have encountered many resources on the theme. However, these resources rarely match the experiences me and my peers have. This is far from surprising, to be honest.

From my research, most of the books on the theme come from authors in the USA, Canada, and the UK. Many authors have been involved in game development for years in their industries and have built their knowledge by experiencing and being in contact with large-scale projects. Their teachings, experiences, and knowledge are of extreme value, but they do not always translate well to those who have never and might never have the same opportunities.

This is also not limited to game development and game design books; it is also the case for games themselves. As stated by Anna Anthropy in her book, *The Rise of the Zinester* [5, p. 5]:

> *The problem with video games is that they're created by a small, insular group of people. Digital games largely come from within a single culture.*

For that, while I started to work on this book, I tried to contact other designers from varied backgrounds to hear their opinions and experiences on designing games. I've sent e-mails to game studios and independent developers from across the globe. From all the e-mails I sent, only a few actually replied and followed up with an interview. Some replied, saying they were currently too busy with their own developments to participate but were kind enough to wish me luck. I am grateful to all of them. From these, 25 game designers agreed to be interviewed or to answer my questions via e-mail.

To compensate for a possible lack of their insights, I also included books such as Black Game Studies [6] and The Queer Games Avant-Garde [7] as part of my research to gain insights on experiences and processes different from my own. They will be referenced and cited throughout the book.

The interviews won't be depicted in this book, as agreed with the interviewees, and the manuscript you have in your hands does not reflect their opinions or sayings. Instead, this book presents the

Table 1.1: Current affiliation for the interviewees.

Artyom "Tricky Fat Cat" Volkov	Game Designer
Beatriz Nascimento	Marshmallow Flame
Dean Gichukie	CEO & Co-founder of Kunta Content
Ellraiser	TNgineers
Eyram Akofa Tawia	Leti Arts & Ashesi University
Fernanda Dias	Studio Pixel Punk
Gabriel "Gabas"	Rastrolabs Game Studio
Geovanni Weizenmann	Independent Game and Level Designer Level Designer Kaze and the Wild Masks
Ian Okinda	Kunta Content
Isabelle Teles	Game Designer at Hoplon
João Gabriel Guimarães	Wompa Games
Kara Stone	Alberta University of the Arts
Lawrence Fuhnwi	Kiro'o Games
Lia Fuziy	GameDev Toolkit Coordinator
Luy	Amazing Block Game Studio
Maarten Stevens	(CEO of) 8D Games
Max Musau	Jiwe Interactive
Melina Juraski	Sunblack Game Studio
Nina Freeman	Game Developer http://ninasays.so
Odongo G. Ahere	Independent Game Designer/Developer Weza Interactive Entertainment
Pat Podchara Petcharapirat	NAMSON Digital Indie Game Development Team
Pedro Savino	Founder of Orube Game Studio
Selima Heister	Gentle Troll Entertainment
Thabo Tsolo	SpaceSalad Studios
Tiani Pixel	Studio Pixel Punk

results of my studies and reflections, including what I have learned from them.

The names and affiliations of the interviewees can be seen in Table 1.1. I truly thank them for their time and patience and for sharing their knowledge and experience. Needless to say, I wholeheartedly recommend you check their work.

Additionally, during the writing of this book, I conducted workshops and lectures on the subjects presented to test, validate, and improve on them. I also applied all the techniques and concepts in my own development practice, including at least 10 solo game jams and other game development activities in the period between 2020 and 2024. Moreover, as a lecturer on Game Development and Creative Media [8], I also supervised dozens of game and creative projects every year, which helped me with many insights into these processes, especially in the context of planning, organising, and production[1].

As a result of all these experiences, the four Cores of Game Design were defined based on which processes and disciplines seemed to be recurrent in the making and design of games. As stated before, they are not perfect nor encompass the entirety of what game development means, but they are generic enough to guide the process. The cores are also based on studies on other game design frameworks, as will be explored in the following section.

Where the Cores Come From

The core of `Mechanics` is the most prevalent in Game Design literature, as many developers and designers focus on it as the main distinction between games and other media. Many of the sources on game design are actually based on mechanical game design and interaction, which is only a part of the game's experience. There are other important aspects besides mechanics, and many of them come from the other cores, such as the `Economy`.

The `Economy` core is a subject that I rarely see covered in Game Design literature directly. Instead, it is often conflated with the `Mechanics` core. However, the `Economy` comes from its own theory and is an important and separate aspect of a game. `Economy` stands for the resources and their relations within the game, which exist beyond the other cores, but are strengthened by them. There are a few books focused on `Economy` theory, though, which are the main sources used in this book for the subject [3, 9, 10].

`Narrative` and `Aesthetics` might not be the best names for what they represent, but these terms are easy enough to

[1]You can see the results of some of those projects on my website, www.dagongraphics.com.

associate with their meanings. `Narrative` stands for all elements that create meaning in the game. The `Narrative` core is commonly associated with the game's story, which is only part of the `Narrative`. The `Narrative` also encompasses theme and message, for example.

`Aesthetics` stands for all of which allows the game to be experienced. It encompasses visuals, sounds, mood, and other senses. It is what might be commonly referred to as the "artistic" part of the game[2], which in many cases can hold the game on its own.

All of the cores are explored more in-depth in their respective parts, chapters, and sections, as well as in Section 2.2, Four Cores of Game Design.

Moreover, it is important to emphasise that besides the research conducted, the four cores and their names are still arbitrary in a sense. I came up with them as a way to better guide this book and the processes proposed, but they are by no means infallible, nor should they be followed dogmatically. Feel free to use them as they fit your process. They are meant to help you, not to hold you back. Changing and creating cores is perfectly fine, as you are the only one capable of figuring out which form best suits your methods. With that, the following section explores other frameworks and how they relate to the one proposed by this book.

1.2 OTHER GAME DESIGN FRAMEWORKS

If you are familiar with Game Design literature, you might have been wondering about the terms used for the Cores of Game Design and how they relate to other known design frameworks. If you are not, do not worry; this section briefly covers them and how they are related to this book's proposal.

The most known framework for game design and game research is the MDA framework [11]. The MDA Framework stands for Mechanics, Dynamics, and Aesthetics. However, these terms are used with different meanings than the ones in this book. Mechanics stands for the components of the game in terms of data

[2]However, consider that the other cores might also represent "artistic value", such as the `Narrative` core.

representation and algorithms; Dynamics stand for the run-time interaction and reactions from the players and mechanics; and Aesthetics are the emotional responses caused by the dynamics.

The MDA Framework proposes a bidirectional path between the (game) designer and the player. The designer reaches the player through the path of Mechanics ⇒ Dynamics ⇒ Aesthetics, while the player perceives the game through the opposed path of Aesthetics ⇒ Dynamics ⇒ Mechanics. That is intended to analyse games from both a (game) designer's perspective as well as from a player's perspective.

There are plenty of criticisms and alternatives to the MDA Framework in books and literature, many of which can be found in the work of Junior and Silva [12]. Specifically, about the MDA Framework, the authors state the following [12, p. 6]:

> *Although somewhat accepted in the field mostly used in universities for analytical purposes, MDA is not in use in the games industry for helping game design work. The main issue that surrounds this framework, according to the literature, is that its concepts lack scrutiny and accuracy and can even contradict themselves in the definitions. This framework has been criticised for leaving certain aspects of the game outside its definition, such as narrative, graphics, sound, and interface of the game outside its definition, which can impact the invoked aesthetics.*

On the other hand, the MDA Framework has no conflict with the meta-framework proposed by this book (except for some name clashing). It can still be used to analyse games and work on them, but it is insufficient as a development process or methodology for producing games or game design.

To emphasise the MDA issue, just consider what you read about it so far and ask yourself how you would approach starting to design a game. Which step would you take first? Which strategy would you use to build prototypes? Those are relevant points that are not well addressed by the MDA framework.

What most of the frameworks and processes seem to agree on is that game development is an iterative process: it is repetitive. We perform the same steps over and over again until the final result is achieved. Those steps, though, vary from proposal to proposal. In essence, they can be reduced to a form of **pre-production/concept**, **production**, **test**, and **post-production**. Although this point is discussed more in-depth in Chapter 4, it is worth it to mention three major issues with this approach:

1. **Creates an illusion of a directional and continuous process** that resembles a Waterfall Methodology [13]. On it, each phase of the development is followed in order with no overlap [14], while it should be seen as a circular process without a clear distinction between phases.

2. **Assumes a game can be fully conceived in an initial phase**, often called *concept phase*, followed by continuous development steps that polish the idea. In reality, many ideas will be created and changed as the game is developed.

3. **Separate testing for production**, while both should be done in parallel, fully overlapping each other. Some studies even point out that many game studios test their products during production sprints[3], and not necessarily at the end of their cycles [15].

Tekinbas and Zimmerman present a more straightforward approach that is reduced to Prototyping, Playtesting, Evaluation, and Refinement [16], and also enforce the concept of iterative design: a cyclical and repetitive process performed on a prototype during the entire production process.

Their perspective on prototyping is not a visual one but one focused on assessing the game mechanics. The following quote comes from their chapter on the Design Process [16, p. 23]:

> *This prototype is played, evaluated, adjusted, and played again, allowing the designer or design team to base decisions on successive iterations or versions of the game.*

Although this view on the design process more closely resembles the actual practice, its disregard for visual quality and focus on

[3]We will discuss these further in Chapter 4

game mechanics is limiting. In fact, it is a very common statement in the field of game development and game design that good game design stands on top of any other aspect, such as graphics, sound, story, etc. I believe that is an oversimplification and ignores how different people act upon their own creativity.

Consider, for example, the highly popular visual novel genre [17]. In a visual novel, the game mechanic aspect is very simplified, mostly based on making decisions based on the text [18]. Should visual novelist then spend their initial time working on very fun and engaging choice-making game mechanics? It makes more sense that their game design process starts from elements of the `Narrative`, instead.

Surely, visual novelists could develop other game mechanics, but enforcing that the process should start from these mechanics is not productive. Also, visual novels commonly present some sort of `Economy` aspect[4] regarding the player's choice and mechanics in the form of puzzles [19].

Mechanics are surely a strong and important aspect of game design. They take a central point in game design processes, but they are not necessarily the first elements to be tackled. It depends on the designer. During the interviews I conducted, some designers stated that they begin their process from other points, such as a visual style, story, and even personal moments and memories.

In the famous and excellent The Art of Game Design [20], Jesse Schell also proposes a framework based on mechanics, defined as a **tetrad** as a form of defining what makes a game, and that is very similar to the Cores of Game Design presented in this book. In his view, the tetrad is composed of Mechanics, Story, Aesthetics, and Technology. Mechanics are the procedures and rules of the game and are the very essence that makes games distinct from other means of entertainment. The story is the sequence of events that unfold in the game and are enforced by the mechanics. Aesthetics are the visuals, sounds, smells, tastes, and other feelings of the game that are also enforced by the mechanics. Finally, Technology,

[4]For example, the player must have a significant number of points with a certain character to unlock more dialogue options.

in a broader sense, is the combination of materials and interactions that make the game possible.

The broader definition of Technology by Schell is important and often forgotten by other game designers and scholars, as many articles and books focus solely on digital games. Games are not bound to be digital; thus, the game design process has no reason to be strict with the digital medium.

Apart from technology, Schell's definitions of Mechanics, Story, and Aesthetics are similar to the ones presented in this book, but they are not without differences:

Mechanics for Schell are bound to rules and procedures, while I prefer the more mechanical (literal) understanding of them as the elements of interaction. Also, although implied, Schell conflates the ideas for `Economy` and `Mechanics` into one single term, while I think the separation is useful both from a study perspective as well as from a production point of view. Starting from `Mechanics` is quite different than starting from `Economy`, for example.

Story for Schell is the main sequence of events in the game, whether it is linear or not. I use `Narrative` instead as a broader term that involves more aspects than just story. For example, the `Narrative` also encompasses the game's message, ethics, and even the approach to writing for the game. The term story can be faulty, as some games might simply not have one (for example, Tetris [21]), while they still have ways of communicating their message and intent to the player[5].

Aesthetics for Schell is a combination of sensory outputs from the game, including visuals and sound. Although it is very similar to how I use the term, the main distinction is that `Aesthetics` can be a goal or a starting point for the game development process. Also, `Aesthetics` in this book are

[5]Following on the given example of Tetris, one could argue that it has no story nor Narrative at all. However, consider that the game constantly conveys information to the player which holds meaning on their own. For example, the next available block and the high score. Both of these are part of the Narrative, even though they are not connected to a broader idea of a story.

inherently responsible for the mood of the game, which is an overarching element beyond audiovisual elements.

Technology for Schell is the tangible part of the game, be it software or hardware (including elements of a board game). Although the technology used is surely a very important aspect of game development, I understand it more as a means to an end rather than an element of its own. Throughout this book, we will discuss how the choice of technology (or materials) has an important role in the development and design processes, but technology is a tool, and in many aspects, it is very interchangeable[6].

Building upon the last point of the discussion, interchangeability is an important aspect to consider. Many frameworks and discussions on game design, especially those focused on mechanics, insist that other elements (graphics, for example) can be changed without a major impact on the game, to match a desired result. This statement is only partially true.

Shooter games, for example, can be easily manipulated by changing what and who you shoot. That allows for the creation of a myriad of shooter-like games. Imagine it as if making a game is like baking a pie. For some, the mechanics are the dough that holds everything in place, including the fillings that come after. The same dough can be used for many types of fillings. For sure, if you assume this analogy, you must also understand that you can only make pies with that approach. If you want to make a cake or a lasagna, the same approach might fail (although it can still be tasty).

With that, if your creative inspiration for a game comes from other places that are not immediately mechanical, this approach will not help you.

Consider also the other way around. You can stick to one element and have others change to fit it. For example, if a more art-oriented game designer decides to make a game based on the Brazilian Neo-Concrete Art movement [22], then the `Aesthetics` elements are somewhat stable already, and the process now is to

[6]Consider the software aspect of technology, for example, the choice of the game engine is mostly a personal decision based on familiarity, experience, and preference, rather than a major impact on the game development.

find how the other cores can be used to emphasise it. Thus, mechanics are still important but are subject to change to whatever better suits the `Aesthetics`.

Mechanics are not necessarily more important than other aspects, nor should they be seen as the backbone of the development process. As we are going to discuss further, the design process can start from other aspects which should not be seen as mere building blocks or interchangeable parts. Instead, a more holistic approach in which all parts of the game are important and should be considered as reinforcing each other can lead to a more cohesive final result, as well as a more stable and coherent development process.

Finally, an important aspect of this discussion of other frameworks and approaches is a distinction between bigger and smaller teams and project scale.

This book is focused on smaller scales and smaller teams (including solo developers). As far as I could research while writing this book, most of the approaches to game development and game design are not very suitable for smaller productions, although they claim themselves to be universal.

Some books, such as The Indie Game Developer Handbook, by Richard Hill-Whittall [23], are good at explaining technical terms and aspects of game development but offer a very general approach and act very much as the title stands for: as a handbook. It is very well worth checking out for its useful information, but it has no in-depth discussion on game design.

The point of books not being directed to a smaller scale, be it indie developers, D.I.Y.s, hobbyists, and any other person or group of people developing games outside the "big industry"[24], is that it often misses the crucial point in their development: it happens on a smaller scale. Most of the time, there are no budgets nor will or plans for one. Most do not even intend to go to the market or participate in sales.

Game development can be a hobby. It is a creative activity such as writing or painting. For that, the need for a highly efficient and effective process to churn out games is not a goal and can actually kill the will to make games in the first place.

Furthermore, some people might want to have some sort of guidance in the process and learn ways in which they can improve their skills. That is the focus of this book, be it a small-scale production for an indie development studio or a hobbyist making games to play with her friends. The approaches and studies in this book were not tested for large-scale productions, although I tried to discuss its aspects with people who work or have worked in larger-scale companies besides studying other books on Game Design and Game Development, which are largely focused on those. Despite this, these approaches and studies were tested and are used by me, the teams I work with, and the teams I supervise, with varying degrees of success.

I can also be clear and honest with regard to the varying degrees of success. Making games, such as making art, is not an exact science. Applying the same steps in the same order will lead to different results. That is part of the enjoyment of making them. I also want to be clear that you should not take any of the writings of this book dogmatically. Find what works for you and use it. Whatever does not work or does not feel right, either change or discard it. You might give a chance later again for some aspects, but others might just not click with you, and that is alright.

Consider also taking the time to check the other frameworks I discussed briefly in this section. They all have their values and teachings. Some might even make more sense to you than the ones presented in this book. No matter what you choose, consider yourself and what helps you.

With all of that being said, it is time to focus ahead on exploring the Cores of Game Design and how to use them to develop games.

Book Format

This book is divided into 6 parts. This initial part, Part I, is the Introduction part, in which the main topics and concepts are presented. The following Parts, II, III, IV, and V, are dedicated to each one of the cores of game design, as follows:

II `Mechanics`

III `Economy`

IV Narrative

V Aesthetics

Finally, Part VI is the Conclusion part, in which the main takeaways from the book are discussed together with other important topics about the end of the game design process.

Although the parts are sequential, this book can be read as a form of "choose your adventure" format. Except for Parts I and VI, the cores can be read in any order, as their contents reinforce each other but do not depend directly on each other. This should allow you to read and study the cores following the order that makes more sense to your own process. If you are curious as to what you can do with the Economy core, for example, then jump right away to Part III and start reading from there.

Feel free to navigate the book in any order. It is your process.

If you prefer a guided read, you can read it sequentially. Otherwise, if you want a suggestion as to which order to read given your preferences, then consider the following orders:

Starting with Mechanics: **I → II → III → IV → V → VI**

Starting with Economy: **I → III → IV → II → V → VI**

Starting with Narrative: **I → IV → V → II → III → VI**

Starting with Aesthetics: **I → V → II → IV → III → VI**

You can see the book as making your own sandwich. Keep the bread on the extremes (Parts I and VI), and rearrange the fillings as you like. Also, do not hesitate to revisit some parts later, as the insight of some cores can help you understand better the ones you have read already.

CHAPTER 2

How to Start Game Designing

In this chapter, we explore further the aim of the game design and development process, as well as a deeper understanding of the 4 Cores of Game Design. It ends with an overview of the meta-game development framework that will be enhanced with new features in the upcoming Chapter 3, Exploring the Framework.

2.1 IS IT SUPPOSED TO BE FUN?

One commonly discussed point in games is the "fun aspect", often with the question of whether some game (or part of it) is "fun". However, defining fun is a huge challenge. Fun can hold different meanings in a myriad of contexts. Fun is also not constant. Some activities can be fun sometimes and boring at other moments. Small variations can completely ruin the fun of an experience, while others can actually enable it.

For games, this discussion goes even deeper. Depending on the context, many inside and outside game elements can have a massive impact[1] on fun. For example, playing a cooperative game with close friends might make even the dullest of games fun. Besides that, inside game elements, such as faulty gameplay and bugs, can make a game fun and entertaining, even if that was not the intention of the game's creators.

[1] These concepts are further explored in Section 5.3.

DOI: 10.1201/9781003351191-2

Many of these aspects are out of our control as game designers, and there is not much we can do about them. You can design your game to enforce some positive aspects, such as forcing a mandatory multiplayer experience, but there are plenty of pitfalls to this solution, such as restricting the game time to when players are available and limiting the experience instead of letting the players enjoy the game on their own accord.

Besides that, I firmly believe that using mandatory and restricting technical requirements as part of the game design is a very troubling approach and should be limited to a few occasions in which it benefits either the game production or is meant to protect the player from harmful experiences[2]. Besides that, fun is very subjective, as noted by Scott Rogers in his book Level Up! The Guide To Great Video Game Design [25, p. 40]:

> *The problem with fun is, like humour, it is completely subjective. You can try to skew the odds in your favour by basing your game on an existing, proven gameplay style, but more often than not, you end up with a "clone" game.*

Rogers proceeded to acknowledge that a "fun" activity in a game can be fun for the first time but boring after it is repeated for the 100th time. In fact, it is very common to see criticism towards main game mechanics getting old after a while, harming the overall experience.

Still, fun is a good objective. From my experience, most beginner game designers have fun as a goal for their games. They often do so with extra goals, such as having a positive impact on the player or using the game as a tool for self-expression.

Consider also that many games can appeal to a wider range of emotions. Visual novels, as cited before, can aim at engaging the player in a romance, reaching out to other feelings such as sadness and joy [17]. Horror games can be fun for some players, but it is hard to disagree that their main intent is to evoke fear and anxiety [26]. Educational games aim at learning experiences that should be prevalent from other aspects of the game and even to the detriment of those [27].

---

[2]For example, in online multiplayer games in which the chat and other mechanics of interactions are restricted to avoid toxic behaviour.

A similar claim is made by Gajadhar, de Kort, and IJsselteijn in their paper, Shared Fun is Doubled Fun: Player Enjoyment as a Function of Social Setting [28, p. 107]:

> *Explicitly treating player enjoyment as a multidimensional construct will give a better understanding of how player experience is shaped; for example, a digital game can induce frustration and aggression but still be experienced as a positive and challenging activity.*

Furthermore, games can be tools for empathy and sympathy, allowing players to experience the perspective of others. On the contrary, games can even oppose that and be focused on a specific target audience, ignoring players who are not familiar with their own context and experiences.

Consider, for example, games with a strong cultural background: they can be developed to teach outsiders about a certain culture and give an insight into how it is to be part of that culture, while others can instead develop the game towards the participants of that culture, with cultural elements that only those that participate on it would engage and understand [6, 7].

Moreover, the latter can be a space for innovation. Read the following quote by Bo Ruberg, on The Queer Games Avant-Garde book, on how some queer games (in the case, Curtain, by Llaura McGee (DREAMFEEL)[29]) avoid the didactic approach to achieve other objectives with their players [7, p. 10]:

> *Yet, unlike some "serious games" or "games for change", which are often didactic and heavy-handed, Curtain and many other works that emerge from the queer games avant-garde are not primarily designed to educate or elicit empathy. Instead, Curtain invites players to spend time inside an emotionally complex situation, one which is queer both in its narrative content and its interactive form.*

For that, the question of whether the game is fun or not only makes sense in a context in which fun is the game designer's objective. In many cases, it can be a byproduct of other objectives. An exergame, that is, a game focused on having the player perform exercises [30], may turn out to be fun, but that is not necessarily its main objective.

It is important, though, to ask yourself what is the **purpose of your game**. Having that in mind can help you make decisions and move on with the process, as well as understand if your game is reaching that purpose at all. It is also perfectly fine to change purposes during development. Games change all the time during development, and you should not limit yourself to first ideas and impressions. It can also happen that your final game evokes a completely new purpose that you have not foreseen.

In that sense, game development is very similar to other artistic expressions. We are constantly pouring a little bit of ourselves into the process. The final result has a piece of us that we might not have noticed or acknowledged before, but it is there in all its honesty. We might only find it out once we play the final version.

I also like to compare the process of game development to the act of doing (scientific) research. Both are like exploring a dark cavern with limited sight. Every step leads us into a new unexplored area until we find the exit. By the end, the path we took should be clear and easy to understand. The traversal of the cavern is the process of game development (or researching) because it is when we actually have our findings and make our progress. Not knowing the path is an important and crucial part of the process. If we already knew the way from the beginning, we were not developing games (or doing research); we were simply copying others and their paths. It is important to find our own paths.

2.2 FOUR CORES OF GAME DESIGN

As presented in the Introduction (Chapter 1), this book focuses on using and exploring the 4 Cores of Game Design: `Mechanics`, `Economy`, `Narrative`, and `Aesthetics`. In this section, we cover them in more detail as to what we can use them for and how they can help you find a more personalised approach to game design and game development.

Let us first do a quick recap of the 4 cores and their intent:

`Mechanics` are the interactable elements of the game, such as gameplay mechanics, level design elements, character behaviours, and others. The `Mechanics` dictate how the player interacts with the game. Any interaction, be it a button or a die roll, is a mechanic. `Mechanics` happen all the time during a game session.

`Economy` are the relations between resources and mechanisms in the game. Through the `Economy`, the elements of the game can be measured, assessed and planned by the player. The `Economy` also plays an important role in rewarding, motivating, and punishing the player. Any resource in the game, be it the player's health or the number of cards in a player's hand, is part of the `Economy`. The `Economy` is always present in games, especially if you consider the game's goal (how you win) itself as a resource.

`Narrative` are the textual and intertextual elements of the game. The term intertextuality here is used in the sense of how the texts in the game can be reinterpreted by other elements of the game (including other texts). `Narrative` is more than the story, which can even be absent in some games. Instead, it encompasses all that conveys meaning to the player, including the message, morals, and ethics of the game. `Narrative` is always present in games because, without it, the game would have no way of communicating to the player the information necessary to be playable. Moreover, games, like other art forms, are political[3], even though some might disagree or dismiss this fact.

`Aesthetics` is the mood and the audiovisual elements of the game in their many forms. Physical and mixed-reality games can go even further to reach out to other senses, such as smell and touch. The `Aesthetics` is responsible for presenting the game, as well as commanding how the player will perceive and experience it. The mood, which ultimately dictates the feelings and emotions expressed by the game, is the responsibility of the `Aesthetics`. Just the same as the other cores, `Aesthetics` are always present in games, even if the game has minimal audiovisual elements.

[3]The most common argument to dismiss the political aspect of games is to recur to more abstract games, such as Tetris or Pong. However, it is important to note that "being political" does not mean "having a political message" or taking a "political stance". Tetris and Pong are games based on conflict and competition, which are already political elements. Moreover, games do not exist in a vacuum. They are played by people, and people are political agents.

All cores are presented in games, but they should not be seen as checklists or mandatory concerns, especially from a game design role. In fact, it is common to have multiple roles in the development process that focus their work solely on one core. For example, in a development duo, one person might be more responsible for the technical implementation of the game elements (`Mechanics` and `Economy`) while the other can be more responsible for the artistic implementation (`Narrative` and `Aesthetics`).

It is important to notice that all cores can be fairly technical, and a general label of technical and artistic that divides them can be misleading.

Below, you can see two concept games, **`Family Tree`** and **`Another Starry Sky`**, that explore the idea of the cores, as well as small discussions on how the technical aspect of the core applies to them. These concept games are explored throughout the book to exemplify many of the cases in which we use the Cores of Game Design and their elements.

Concept Game: Family Tree

`Family Tree` is a concept board game in which the players roleplay as a family with a growing tree in their background. The tree grows by having players place blocks that represent roots, bark, leaves, and other tree parts on it. The tree represents the passage of time.

Each player takes the role of one or more family members, which are equally distributed among players. The goal of the game is for each player to achieve happiness with their family members. They do so by achieving objectives and goals in the game that need to be negotiated with the other players. Successfully achieving an objective or goal awards happiness points to a family member that are accumulated by the player that represents them. During the negotiations, it is possible to lose happiness points for conceding the goals and objectives of the others. However, an unhappy family has fewer chances of achieving their goals; thus, players have to balance their happiness with each other.

While the game progresses, the tree in the family backyard grows. Players take turns on its growth by placing blocks on it. The aspect and presentation of the tree are related to the overall happiness level of the family.

The game is played with blocks and cards. The cards are divided into multiple decks that represent daily affairs, goals, objectives, and important events. These cards have cartoon graphics that depict multiple varieties of families, settings, and environments. Family is also a term with multiple meanings for different people. It can be a family of relatives or a chosen family [31], for instance. The cosy and open mood of the game is part of the `Aesthetics`. It is meant to let the players lower their guard and open up for honest discussions and negotiations.

To build the tree blocks used by the players, the game developers can use a multitude of techniques, such as actual wood blocks engraved with a wood laser cut machine. Operating the wood laser cut, its software, and necessary computer files is a technical work that is part of the `Aesthetics` core.

Another less computer-centric approach is to model the tree parts manually with clay and other materials (it could also be part of the game that the players themselves mould and form their trees). Manually sculpting such pieces is also technical work, even if it is not performed on a computer or other similar machines and is also part of the `Aesthetics` core.

Mechanically, the game is played with in-game elements, such as the blocks and cards that inform the family members' goals, objectives, and other events. There are also outside game mechanics, which are the discussions and negotiation for the happiness points. Placing blocks, playing cards, negotiating, and progressing through the games are elements of the `Mechanics` core.

The cards, points, blocks, and tree growth are elements of the `Economy`. The economy is responsible for creating the strategy and dynamics of value that happen during the playthrough. For example, two players might have to negotiate their goal: a young kid wants to go to a party, but the parent needs to give up going to the gym to take them to the party. The party can reward two happiness points to the kid, but it removes one happiness point from the parent. The decision of how many points are won and lost is part of the `Economy` core.

The tree can be limited to only growing leaves once the entire family has a minimum of 20 happiness points each, which is also an `Economy` element that helps to motivate the players to gather happiness points as a group.

The example of a player (a young kid) wanting to go to a party is part of the `Narrative`. The game can tell the player that the party has a greater meaning to the kid because it is the first time the kid has been invited to one. At the same time, the gym can be the only moment the parent has on their own to relax from their hard day at work. These descriptions give more sense to the players and guide their decisions. Moreover, the text on the cards is also part of the `Narrative`. The game's box, its texts, and instructions are likewise part of the `Narrative`.

The idea of Family Tree is a game in which players discuss their own ambitions and wishes in a group rather than pursuing their individual goals in a selfish manner. Players have the conflict of pursuing their own goals and objectives but also balancing them with consenting and giving up on their own (pieces of) happiness for the sake of allowing others also to be happy. This discussion and thought about what the game is actually about, which is how to be happy in a group or community setting, is also an important aspect of the `Narrative`. It is the game's purpose and what it tries to have players think about when they play the game and afterwards.

As you read in the concept game, the cores have a more important role than simple decisions in the game development process. They are the main pieces that compose the game. Also, they support the decisions made by each other.

If `Aesthetics` goes for cosy feelings of openness, then the `Narrative` should enforce that with its tools. In fact, although we are discussing how the `Narrative` enforces `Aesthetics`, the game itself is more strongly focused on the `Narrative`, and it is where the initial process for **`Family Tree`** actually starts. As discussed in the concept game description, the main point of the game is a `Narrative` one: having players discuss happiness in a community setting.

The Mechanics for **Family Tree** involve game elements, such as blocks and cards, which are quite simple, not to take away from the main mechanic, which is talking. The event cards, for example, are only there as mechanics that force the discussions and negotiations. We could surely add other, more dynamic elements, like rolling dice for chances or using an hourglass to enforce a time frame. These additions should come by playtesting the game and checking whether they reinforce (or prevent) the game's purpose – in the sense of what we, as game designers, want to achieve.

Furthermore, the concept game used some example values for a negotiation example (Party x Gym), in which allowing the younger kid to attend the party would get them 2 happiness points and remove 1 from the parent. The relation between those numbers (2 and 1) is part of the Economy and serves to signify in concrete terms what is being exchanged. The choice of using a 2:1 ratio is not completely arbitrary. Awarding 2 happiness points to the young kid means that the event has a higher happiness value compared to what the parent loses (1). We could, for example, change the ratio to 3:1 if we decided on fostering the Narrative element that the party is the first one the kid has ever been invited to or balance the ratio to 2:2 if we want to suggest that the free and relaxing time at the gym has as much value to the parent as the party to the kid. Studying those numbers and their relations in the gameplay is a central activity in working with the Economy, and it is hard to detach it from the other cores.

The following concept game is an example of how these cores apply in a digital, single-player experience, in contrast to **Family Tree**, which is a physical multiplayer concept game.

Concept Game: Another Starry Sky

Another Starry Sky is a concept digital game in which the player must navigate a damaged spaceship by using stars and constellations to guide herself back to her home planet. The spaceship was damaged due to an unexpected collision with a rogue deserted space vessel.

Another Starry Sky is a 3D game that uses 3D models and environments to display its elements while also using 2D images to convey the protagonist and her interactions with other characters of the story.

The player can fly her ship between observation points, which are positions in the game world in which it is possible to see stars and constellations. By looking at them, the player can compare them to her own notes on celestial bodies to figure out her location and, from there, move to the next observation point.

Travelling through observation points happens in a top-down perspective in which the player must avoid obstacles (meteors, space trash, etc.) and collect bonuses (fuel) until the destination is reached.

The choice of using 3D graphics for this concept game is both a stylistic and a practical choice. Style-wise, many 3D rendering techniques can be used to achieve a nice spacey feeling, while it also makes for easier to reuse and readjust elements. Besides, from a technical perspective, since all elements mentioned in the game are static, there is no need to follow a complete and complex 3D modelling pipeline[a]. Also, notice that the `Aesthetics` decision to work with 3D models requires technical knowledge.

Besides that, the mood for the game can be a combination of a sense of contemplative stargazing and an urge to get back to safety. One can be emphasised over the other depending on what is decided to be the game's purpose.

For this game, the main focuses are the two mechanics (`Mechanics`): stargazing and flying the spaceship. The stargazing involves the player looking at the starry sky and trying to find constellations that match the notes to make an informed decision as to where to move next. Being a digital game, many visual aspects can be explored to work with this mechanic, such as highlighting possible constellations or transforming the entire aspect into a puzzle game of its own.

The flight mechanic also has space for exploration and testing. It could work as a sort of infinite-runner game, in which objects constantly come at the player, and it is not possible to stop the spaceship. Besides that, other elements, such as the spaceship fuel, could be used to activate speed-ups that reward the player with points or other useful resources, such as tips and help for the stargazing mechanic.

Besides these elements, their difficulties and related resources are commanded by the `Economy`. An easy trajectory between two observation points can have a reduced number of obstacles and a high number of bonuses. The percentage or even defined quantities for these elements are part of handling the economy. As the player approaches the end of the game, these numbers can grow to increase the difficulty.

The increased difficulty can be backed up by elements of the `Aesthetics` and `Narrative`. The environment can be warmer and friendlier as the player approaches the final destination, while the game can explain that there are more debris and obstacles closer to the player's home due to the elevated space pollution caused by greedy corporations.

As we previously discussed `Narrative` in more abstract terms for **`Family Tree`**, for this concept game, we can use an easier approach and focus primarily on the game's story and motivation. It was already established that the player needed to return home, and her main equipment was broken. The story can proceed to tell more details about the event, such as what the player was doing there in the first place and what happened to the rogue space vessel, while the player progresses through observation points.

Moreover, it can expand with side stories, such as the meaning and reasoning for the constellations that are observed by the player. There could be a Kahlo constellation inspired by the painter Frida Kahlo and her famous self-portraits [22]. That could also introduce to the `Narrative` real teaching about events in the world that could interest the player.

---

[a]Commonly, while 3D modelling, the artist needs to make the 3D model and texture it. After that, if the 3D model needs to be animated (like a character), it is rigged (in which a "skeleton" is programmed for the 3D model) and then animated.

Notice that in both concept games, the Economy does not involve money or other sorts of currency that are related to financial entities. The Economy deals with resources, and resources can be of many types, shapes, and forms, not only gold and coins.

Both games are also abstract enough in their concept form that many aspects could be changed and interpreted differently, which is perfectly fine for a concept stage. As stated previously, concepts are only initial plans and ideas which are all bound to failure and modification. You should not assume the conception phase (or the concept games) as immutable or solid plans for development. Stay open to modifying whatever needs to be modified to achieve the game's purpose better.

Don't Kill Your Darlings Just Yet

Some authors like to use phrases such as "kill your darlings" and "ideas are cheap" when discussing the open attitude towards changes in the game and the game development process. What they mean is that you should not get too attached to an element in your game that can actually undermine it.

For example, imagine that you have a very nicely drawn side character for **Another Starry Sky**, but there is no place to use it in the story. If the character indeed has no place, it is better to focus your effort on other characters that are actually part of the story. But well, if you really like the character, you can always consult with the rest of your team on how the character could be used anyway. Surely, you could draw other nice characters, but the game development process should not be entirely about "killing darlings" or "churning out ideas" to achieve a more "efficient product"; it should be about developing games. Keeping your darlings can actually help foster your motivation and engagement, even if other changes have to be made to accommodate that.

In this sense, I believe it is healthier to approach situations like that as the mechanics of **Family Tree**: negotiations and consent to reach a balanced level of happiness from the involved parties. It would be unfair to force the entire team to change their work to accommodate one of your darlings, wouldn't it? On the other hand, if there are ways to allow that without causing a major issue, then there is no reason not to do it. A happier team is surely going to produce better games, regardless of the arbitrary metric used to assess how good the game is.

Another aspect of the "ideas are cheap" concept is related to effort. While your ideas are still only written or abstract, no effort was put into making them, and they might have minor impacts on the rest of the process. But you can easily see that this is only the case for ideas that are not tightly coupled to other parts of the game. Some ideas, even if they are still on paper, can be connected to other parts of the game that were developed already. Thus, modifying them might cause major issues and repercussions.

These are points at which you can recur to the Cores of Game Design. As ideas and concepts are produced and linked, you can separate and analyse them from the perspective of which core they belong to and how they relate to other cores. The rejected side character is initially a product of the `Aesthetics`, but its implementation in the game and story is bound to impact parts of the `Narrative`, for example. If the side character has specific mechanics or systems, it will also impact the `Mechanics` and `Economy`.

To be more general, any modification is bound to impact multiple cores at once. The following section, Game Design Development Cycle, Section 2.3, presents a very simple and obvious approach to this process and how we can see the influence of the cores.

2.3 GAME DESIGN DEVELOPMENT CYCLE

When I said this book does not propose a framework for building games, I meant it. Games are created in a wide range of ways by people from varied backgrounds. There will never be a solution that works for everyone. However, there are key aspects of making games that are (almost) universally embraced, such as the iterative nature of the process and the focus on playtesting.

Obviously, iterations and playtesting only happen when the game can be played through a prototype. For that, it is necessary to have some sort of interaction (`Mechanics`) and some activity in the game—the latter I like to call a goal or objective. **Thus, to playtest, it is necessary to have at least one mechanic and one goal.** This initial mechanic can derive from all of the cores, as it is going to be expanded on their respective chapters. For now, it is easier to understand this process if we assume a simple gameplay mechanic that derives from the `Mechanics` core.

Furthermore, regardless of whether you have started the process by literally developing the mechanic or if the mechanic came later, the gameplay experience only starts as the player can interact with the game, *i.e.*, through a mechanic, even if it is just walking in a scenario or reading cards from a deck.

The other important half is the **goal**. Before diving into definitions of what a game is and if games require a goal to be games, having a goal for the prototype is very useful. The goal helps to assess a complete experience. You can even discard the goal by the end of the process if you aim at a more open or sandbox type of experience. You can alternatively decide on a different goal for each testing setup, but from experience, this tends to get confusing to players and developers. Moreover, keeping the same goal for the playtesting allows for easier iterations since changing fewer elements per iteration makes it easier to analyse the outcome separately.

The goal should be concrete and tangible, at least for the initial iterations of the game. Abstract goals are tough to achieve with just one game mechanic. For the moment, you can keep more abstract goals as part of the `Narrative` for the moment, as they are more likely to be connected to the game's message (more on that in Chapter 11).

With (at least) one mechanic and (at least) one goal, you have what I consider a **complete prototype**: it is a prototype that can be played until the end. For a food analogy, imagine that the complete prototype is one meal, including the cutlery and plate necessary to eat it.

It is important to note that a **complete prototype** is not a final game. Most of the features and other important aspects of the game will be missing. The final game is the full meal, composed of individual and connected parts, plus drinks and dessert. Learning to distinguish and separate these elements is an important learning process for game designers.

After achieving a **complete prototype** stage, we can move to the continuous process of improvement and adjustment. The

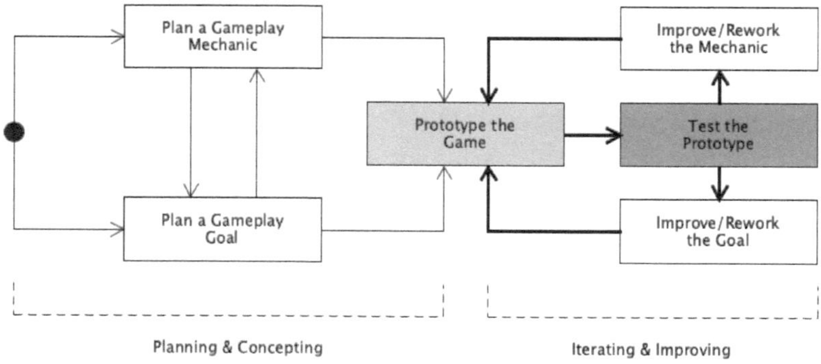

Figure 2.1: Diagram for the prototyping framework.

prototype can be enhanced with new features, others can be removed, and alterations can be made according to the results of the playtest sessions.

Figure 2.1 shows a simplified diagram of this process, dividing it into two phases: Planning & Concepting, and Iterating & Improving.

The diagram starts with either planning a mechanic and a goal and then proceeds to build the prototype. As players test the prototype, the mechanics and goals are improved, and the game is tested again. This repetitive process will continue for the entire duration of the game development.

From a `Mechanics` standpoint, the first playtest can already assess whether the game mechanic and the goal are suitable. If both mechanics and goals do not work, *i.e.*, the player is not engaged nor succeeds in achieving the goal; it is time to move back to the Planning & Concepting phase. However, if only one of them does not work, you are bound to one of the following situations:

Even though the mechanic is not good, the players still actively try to achieve the goal: The objective is compelling, but the players need better methods to achieve it.

Even though the goal is not good, the players are having fun: The goal needs to change to some of the other objectives players are engaged in and using the mechanics for.

Let us see how these cases apply to the `Another Starry Sky` game, specifically to the travelling mechanic between observation points:

The mechanic is not good: Players want to reach the next observation point, but driving the spaceship is not interesting (it is too slow, for example). Then, this aspect should be adjusted, such as increasing the movement speed.

The goal is not good: Players want to keep on driving but are not motivated to reach the next observation point or are moving towards other goals, even goals they created themselves while playing. Then, the goal should be adjusted to be either more engaging (adding more meaning to it, for example) or completely changed to match other goals the players were more interested in.

Notice, for instance, that in the second case, we might completely drop the idea of a linear travel between observation points and let the player freely travel between observation points as it might be a more engaging activity. This decision changes a considerable amount of elements in our concept but seems to achieve a more desirable experience. Additionally, it does not break with the game's `Narrative` or `Aesthetics`, making it a good candidate to change without major repercussions.

Adding new mechanics to the game can be seen either as a new start on this diagram, as if you start back at Planning & Concepting, or as part of the cycle of Iterating & Improving.

Now that we have the base diagram for prototyping and testing, we can see how the cores apply to it. There are two main ways in which we see the cores: first, as they are worked on until we reach the prototyping stage, and second, as we iterate over the prototyping stage.

As stated before, you should start your process from the core that you want. You might choose the one you are more familiar with or one that you have not experimented with before. From this choice, you start to create ideas for the game and its elements. As you reach the point in which you have at least one mechanic and one goal, you can start the prototyping process.

Let's see that with another concept game:

Concept Game: Memories by the Sea

Consider that we want to make a game based on an afternoon at the beach. Let us enumerate some elements that evoke this setting: sea, sand, seashells, seagulls, parasols, waves, etc. We are then starting from the `Aesthetics`, from a mood.

We can proceed to look for references and elements to help our creative process. We could build a moodboard[a], for example.

The game could be about spending the afternoon walking by the beach and collecting seashells. But the seashells are spread and hidden across the beach. The reason why we collect the seashells is part of the `Narrative`.

Let us say that the player is a Seashell Specialist who collects rare seashells and also engages in trading them with other specialists. We do not have a main message in the game (yet), but we have some base motivation that can guide the other elements, such as the `Mechanics` and `Economy`.

With this base, we already have a mechanic in mind: collecting seashells. If the game is digital, then we could simply have the character walk on the beach and literally interact with the seashells to collect them. With that, we also have an easy goal to work with: collect a certain amount of seashells.

The amount of seashells to complete the game is part of the `Economy`. It is always good to establish real numbers for the game's goal. It is very hard to get the correct number on the first try; for that, we simply stipulate a value and play with it. Let's use 10, for example. If the amount of seashells is too much or not enough, we can adjust on the next iteration.

[a]Moodboards will be further explored in Section 14.1.

For the **`Memories by the Sea`** concept game, we started the process at the `Aesthetics` and then moved on through all 4 cores until we reached a point in which we could start the prototyping process. This initial moment is the Planning & Concepting phase. Now, we can work on the game's initial implementation and iteration.

Mechanic – Collect Sea Shell: The player moves close to a seashell and interacts with it to collect it.

Goal – Collect 10 Sea Shells: The player must collect 10 sea shells to finish the prototype.

Now let's assume the problematic situations mentioned before, *i.e.*, either the mechanic or the goal is bad. If the collecting mechanic is not good, we can enhance it to be more dynamic, like adding time-based commands to get the shell successfully, hiding them in more interesting places, or even scrapping it and focusing the game on the trading seashell mechanic. Notice that those alternatives are mostly in the realm of `Mechanics` still since we want to tackle a `Mechanics` problem, but we could also try to approach them from the other cores. Maybe a funny animation for the seashell collection can already make it engaging (`Aesthetics`).

Alternatively, we could work on the `Narrative` of the game and emphasise other aspects, making the mechanical aspect secondary. For example, while collecting the shells, the protagonist might do small bits of a monologue, which can engage the player on their own. Therefore, the player goes through collecting the required seashells and achieving the goal but focuses on the story being told rather than on the mechanics.

After the **complete prototype** stage is achieved, the process becomes a sequence of improving the prototype by working on the cores. Just like the paragraph above suggests, the next step could be an improvement on the `Narrative`. The steps taken to create the concept for **`Memories by the Sea`** can be seen in the diagram shown in Figure 2.2.

Notice that we still have the two phases of Planning & Concepting and Iterating & Improving, but now the first phase is expanded to show which cores were worked on before achieving the second phase. Moreover, the second phase is now simplified by considering that it is a repeatable process of improvements based on the work done on each core.

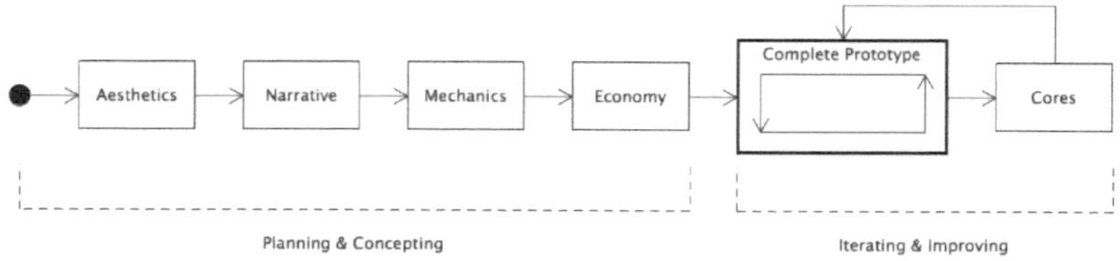

Figure 2.2: Diagram for the steps taken to achieve the complete prototype, followed by a cyclical process of improving it by working on the cores. This diagram follows the order of steps used for the concept game `Memories by the Sea`.

It is important to notice that the order presented in Figure 2.2 is not mandatory. You should follow whichever order feels more natural to your process and better help your game and your **complete prototype**. You might also decide to work on the same core for many consecutive steps until the need arises and your production moves to another core, or even to the **complete prototype** stage. However, it is very likely that you are going to work at least once with the `Mechanics` and `Economy` core since they are required to achieve the **complete prototype** stage.

For example, assume that we decided initially to spend more time working on the story and validating its aspects before figuring out which mechanic would best suit it. We would achieve the following sequence:

$$\text{Aesthetics} \Rightarrow \text{Narrative} \Rightarrow \cdots \Rightarrow \text{Mechanics} \Rightarrow \text{Economy} \\ \Rightarrow \text{Complete Prototype}$$

Or, as another example of the process after getting to the **complete prototype** stage, let us assume that some balancing was done with the goal (`Economy`), followed by the addition of a sea ambience sound (`Aesthetics`), and then a new UI label was added to show the number of collected sea shells (`Narrative` and `Aesthetics`), we would have the following sequence:

$$\cdots \Rightarrow \text{Complete Prototype} \Rightarrow \text{Economy} \Rightarrow \text{Aesthetics} \Rightarrow \\ \text{Narrative} \Rightarrow \dots$$

Notice that playtesting is not restricted to happening only after the **complete prototype** is achieved. It can happen before as a means to validate and test what is already part of the game. Surely, it will achieve other results due to the lack of one of its key aspects (mechanic or goal), but it can still give valuable insight. Moreover, after the **complete prototype** is achieved, every new step taken with the cores can be immediately tested.

The main takeaway from using the game design cores and the game design development cycle is that they do not impose order or restrictions. They are flexible to suit your development preference and the needs of the project. It is your team's decision to figure out which order is more suitable and also when the **complete prototype** should be constructed. That is why these concepts form a meta-framework: they act as a base for you to find your own framework.

CHAPTER 3

Expanding the Cycle

THIS CHAPTER DISCUSSES HOW WE CAN ENFORCE GAME DESIGN PRINCIPLES AND METHODOLOGIES DURING THE DESIGN PROCESS. First, the famous theory of Flow is presented in Section 3.1, which serves as a cornerstone for many game design decisions.

Building on the Flow theory, Section 3.2 focuses on dealing with how we teach players how to play our games. This discussion focuses on the most common difficulties: Inaptitude and Ignorance.

Section 3.3 explains a simple framework, the **Forced Action Framework**, that helps tackle the issue of Player Ignorance while also providing simple guidelines for level and tutorial design.

Section 3.4 explains the **Goal-Achievement-Reward cycle** (**GAR** cycle), which helps to motivate and teach players. The GAR cycle can be used to tackle Player Inaptitude. Due to their connection with rewards, GAR cycles are often viewed under the controversial lens of exploitative mechanics, which are also discussed.

The final section, Section 3.5, Game Design Cycle Revisited, discusses the expanded game design development cycle in light of these theories. It then presents a list of questions a game design team can use to guide their initial process.

3.1 FLOW AND BALANCE

The Flow theory, popularised by Mihaly Csikszentmihalyi [32] and Jeanne Nakamura [33], is probably one of the most used and cited psychology theories in game design [34]. Many of the books on

DOI: 10.1201/9781003351191-3

game design have at least one mention of Flow. This book will not be different in this aspect. Still, this chapter brings a different perspective on it by using other related sources to the research on Flow theory, as well as a discussion on how Flow is not restricted to players. It also happens to developers.

Starting from the beginning, Flow is an optimal and positive state of mind in which one is fully immersed and engaged in an activity [32]. The experience of being "in the flow" is quite universal and generally described as a rewarding, joyful, effortless and highly focused state of consciousness.

Furthermore, in their publication, The Concept of Flow, by Nakamura and Csikszentmihalyi [33], the authors propose the following definition for the Flow state:

> *Being "in (the) flow" is (...) the subjective experience of engaging just-manageable challenges by tackling a series of goals, continuously processing feedback about progress, and adjusting action based on this feedback. Under these conditions, experience seamlessly unfolds from moment to moment, and one enters a subjective state (...).*

There are essential aspects of this definition that deserve attention. First, it assumes a "subjective" experience, which means that it can be different in some aspects from person to person and should not be taken as an exact experience. The second important aspect is the observation about "just-manageable challenges". This segment is often used in game design discussions to justify the layout of goals and challenges in a game, often from the perspective that challenges should increase in difficulty over time according to the player's capacity. The following statements on feedback enforce this:

> *Feedback should be continuous and used to adapt the action performed.*

Thus, a simplified understanding of Flow from a game design perspective is that to achieve it, the game should have a well-balanced difficulty that accompanies the player's progression while providing clear feedback on overcoming challenges, allowing players to remain "in the flow".

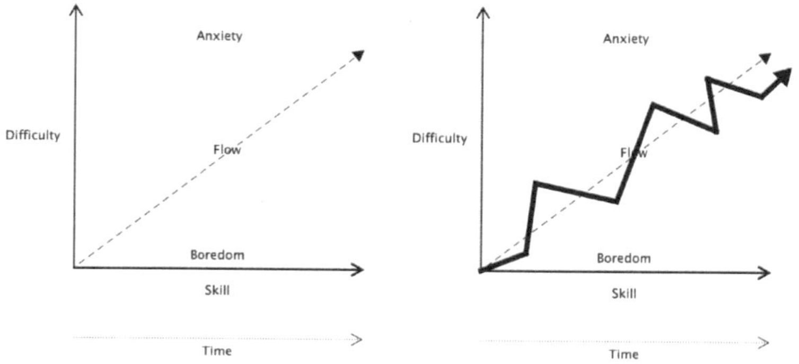

(a) Flow state diagram.

(b) Example of a flow-like experience.

Figure 3.1: Flow diagram and example case.

Figure 3.1a exemplifies staying "in the flow" as the perfect balance between skill and difficulty. If the skill surpasses the difficulty, the experience tends to boredom and apathy, which disengages from the optimal state by allowing the attention to drift away from the activity. If the difficulty surpasses the skill, the experience triggers anxiety, fear, and frustration, which can shift the attention towards insecurities and shortcomings.

In reality, especially in games, a real Flow experience resembles the thick black arrow in Figure 3.1b. The player drifts between boredom and anxiety while playing, as moments of relaxation and challenge will not always reach a perfect balance. Moreover, consider that in the context of difficulty, the player's experience might move towards anxiety due to **perceived difficulty**, *i.e.*, to how demanding a given challenge looks like rather than how difficult it is. While engaging in the challenge, the player might return to a Flow state or even descend into boredom if the task's difficulty turns out to be far easier than anticipated.

The jagged line that moves between the states in Figure 3.1b is inspired by the suggested pacing presented by Ernest Adams in his book Fundamentals of Game Design [35]. While discussing pace and balancing, Adams proposes that a good approach to a difficulty curve is to use a sawtooth shape. The sawtooth shape has an overall increasing motion, but it is done in steps that return to lower values before reaching new highs. Figure 3.2 exemplifies an ideal experience that matches Adams' proposed shape. The numbers in Figure 3.2 are the difficulty peaks along the path.

For a digital game, numbers 1 to 4 could be the end of levels 1 to 4. In this case, each new level starts in an easier setting than the end of the previous one, allowing players to relax. In the concept game **Another Starry Sky**, peak 1 could be the end of the first travel between observation points, in which the number of obstacles is higher than the start of the second travel.

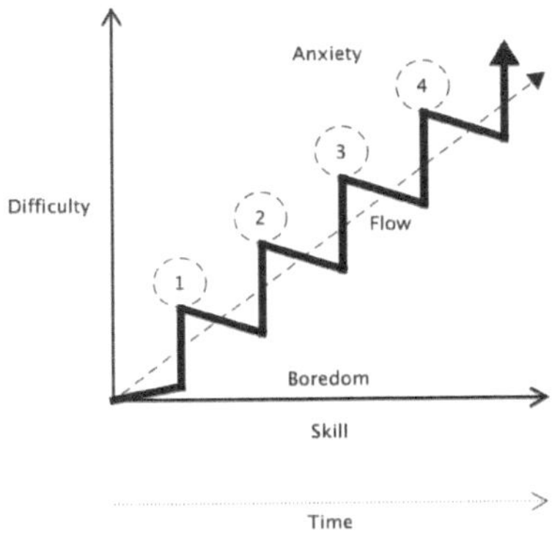

Figure 3.2: Example of the flow diagram with a sawtooth behaviour.

For a non-digital game, numbers 1 to 4 could be phases in the game or important decision moments. In **Family Tree**, these points could be the moments in which the players must decide which tree parts to grow, as this process is only achieved when a given threshold of shared points is met. That forces the discussions before reaching the growth process to be more intense as concessions have to be made to secure a balanced happiness distribution.

Moving To and Away From Flow

Moreover, the Flow state graph can be used to analyse player behaviour during playtest. As in most of the cases for prototypes, players will not be constantly (or ever) in the Flow thus, it is helpful to resort to the other areas of the graph to study what is happening:

Boredom: The player is not motivated or engaged to play the game activities.

Anxiety: The player is either engaged but struggling in the game or is demotivated due to the game's (perceived) difficulty.

Both cases can be solved in the realm of the `Economy` by balancing the experience. But the other cores can also be used: the `Mechanics` core can be used to rework or add new tools to engage and improve the experience. The `Aesthetics`, together with the `Narrative` cores, can improve the feedback aspect of the experience, which is an important aspect of Flow, to guarantee that the player has a clear idea of what has to be done and how.

Depending on the game's purpose, the `Narrative` core can be used to keep the experience in these non-Flow states. Keeping the player in a state of (near) anxiety or boredom can help deliver a message. For example, games that want to simulate real-life experiences might have boring, repetitive tasks as an integral part of their experience to move players into a state of boredom.

Remember that "being fun" is not the only possible purpose of a game, and a conscious decision to move the player away from the Flow state can be a good game design decision to reach the intended purpose.

Distortion of Temporal Experience

The difficulty increase is an important aspect of Flow. Nakamura even acknowledges that by stating that the flow experience pushes for an expansion of the goals and growth of skill [33]. As we improve in a given activity, we aim for higher and more complex goals that match our newly acquired abilities. Although this process can be seen as benign, there is a dark side to it.

One of the known effects of being in the Flow state is the distortion of temporal experience: time is experienced as it has passed faster than normal [32]. From a game design perspective, it is also our responsibility to care for the effects of the Flow state in our players. It might feel rewarding to have players spending hours engaged in our designs, but consider if, at some point, those hours should not have been spent on other healthy activities, including sleeping and eating properly. Individuals might engage in gaming, therefore, in the Flow state, to escape boredom and evade other aspects of their lives that are not as engaging, which might have harmful long-term effects [36]. With that, it is relevant to consider flow-inducing techniques in the game's development, but it is also relevant to consider when to avoid these strategies.

Development Flow

The very act of developing and designing games can lead you into the Flow state. Developers and designers are as, if not more, prone to enter the Flow as they perform their tasks. We can even use the Flow theory to discuss why it is not happening. Let us discuss the Flow graph (Figure 3.1a) in practical terms.

If your design and development process is not going well, you might be in one of two areas: anxiety or boredom. Acknowledging this can help you to decide on the next steps.

Boredom: You have the feeling that your current tasks are not engaging or challenging. They do not motivate you.

Anxiety: You have the feeling that your current tasks and activities are too hard to do or that you lack the required knowledge on how to approach them.

The boredom scenario might be the most common one during development and is often confused with anxiety. Boredom can happen due to a lack of engagement but also for reasons outside the game development, such as a loss of interest in the game's idea or a shift in motivation to other aspects of life. In some of these cases, there is no remedy. Losing interest in the process is part of the experience, and it might be more beneficial to focus your energy on other activities. You should see no shame in "giving up" on your game. If the experience is not providing you with the energy and motivation to persist, continuing it might be detrimental to your health. Moreover, any effort spent is not wasted. Even if the game is never completed, you still learn and improve your craft while working on it, and these aspects are surely going to be used in your next endeavours, even if they are not related to game design.

For the anxiety scenario, acknowledging the lack of knowledge or task complexity can lead to many possible outcomes. You could stop the task to dedicate time to studying it and learn better ways to approach it. You could also reach out to peers for help. Many of these decisions and steps are discussed in more detail in Chapter 4, Planning, in which these points can be considered to improve your planning and experience.

Returning to game design, these last two aspects of the anxiety scenario, lack of skills (inaptitude) and lack of knowledge (ignorance) are commonly found in the players' experience. The following section discusses what we can learn and tackle them.

3.2 PLAYER INAPTITUDE AND PLAYER IGNORANCE

A game's difficulty is a major concern while designing games, especially since it encompasses many aspects of development. The idea of "a more difficult game" can be related to multiple factors, but most of them are connected to either knowledge or skill. Either the player perceives the game as difficult due to not knowing enough about it to make good decisions, or the player lacks the appropriate skills to overcome the game's challenges. The latter is especially true for games focused on the `Mechanics` and `Economy` cores since they are more closely related to playful interactions.

There are other factors that may play a role in the perceived difficulty, which are related to the other cores. For example, a dark and sinister `Aesthetics` mood can evoke a feeling of dread, stressing the players and affecting their perceptions. A game focused on a specific culture, which uses slang and expressions, might be perceived as hard to understand by those outside said culture, which is not necessarily related to any in-game knowledge. The same applies to trivia-base games, in which the player needs outside knowledge to proceed or win. Randomness and luck might also affect the perceived difficulty and are considered outside the player's control. Card games, for example, might have vastly different experiences based on the order of cards being drawn.

Notice that I have been using the term "perceived" difficulty instead of just "difficulty" because the plain idea of difficulty is abstract and does not make much sense outside the context of a player's experience. The **perceived difficulty** is how the player perceives the game. It is very subjective. As game designers, we might have an idea of how difficult certain aspects of the game are when we plan and design them (as discussed in Section 3.1), but that is only how we perceive it. Players might have different perceptions.

We can discuss the player's perceived difficulty in terms of inaptitude and ignorance, as follows:

Inaptitude: The player knows what has to be done but lacks agility, skill, dexterity, or reflexes, among others, to perform the task successfully. It is often a mechanical problem and is related to the interaction between the player and the game.

Ignorance: The players do not know what has to be done, even if they are capable of performing it successfully. They lack the understanding or wisdom to act. It is often a knowledge problem and is related to the understanding the player has of the game.

Inaptitude

Inaptitude is hard to tackle and measure, as it is very subjective. Consider, for example, a game in which the player must quickly press a series of buttons in a specific order. The player's ability to quickly press buttons, hand-eye coordination, the capacity to memorise the order, and even familiarity with the game's input system[1] are all very dependent on the player.

A common approach to overcoming Inaptitude is through repetition, allowing the player to repeat the necessary action as much as necessary to build up the skill and perform tasks. Notice, though, that long repetitions can quickly move your player into a boredom state. For that, it is important to consider your game design to ensure that the player will have enough chances to retry in varied ways before getting to more challenging tasks.

Using `Another Starry Sky` as an example, the perceived difficulty during the travel stages is related to the movement speed and the number of obstacles along the way. For the first travel stages, it is better to have a slower movement speed and few obstacles that can be easily avoided, allowing the player to practice

[1] A keyboard player might struggle to perform an action using a joystick, for instance. We discuss this further in Chapter 15.

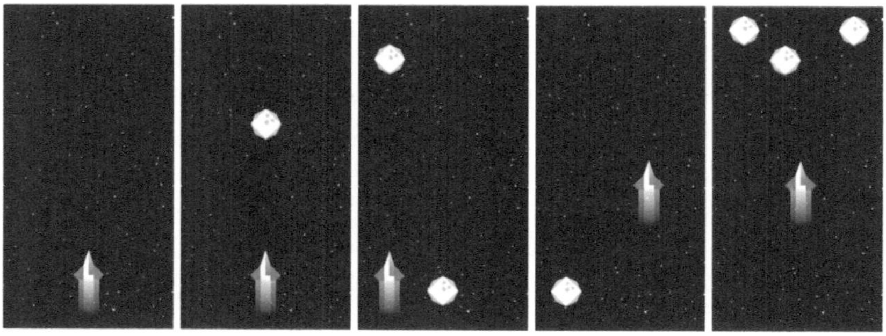

Figure 3.3: Level progression for the `Another Starry Sky` concept game. The sequence of images displays the order of challenges, starting from no challenge on the left image until a bigger challenge on the right image.

the movements to complete a trip. As the player successfully finishes travels, the game can slowly increase the movement speed and amount of obstacles.

Figure 3.3 exemplifies how a first travel level could be played out. From left to right, the challenge is increased and forces the player into moving the spaceship to avoid the obstacles. The first image on the left has just the spaceship flying through the space. There are no challenges, and the player can take the time to experiment with the controls. In the second image, an obstacle comes towards the player in the centre of the screen. The obstacle's position is a conscious one: it is positioned to hit the player, forcing a movement away from the obstacle. The third image shows a second obstacle coming at the player, repeating the previous idea. The fourth image is a moment of relaxation with no obstacles, allowing the player to relax and experiment with the controls again. The last image has a more complex challenge in which the reflexes and placement of the spaceship are important to avoid all obstacles.

Notice that no new mechanics or ideas were introduced in any of the images. The harder challenge (the right-most image) is composed of multiples of the same previous challenge (an obstacle) at once. Thus, it only requires the same action to be used with more control and dexterity.

It is worth discussing what happens if the player fails to complete a level (hitting too many obstacles, for example). We could design that the player has to redo the entire trip from the start, which forces a complete repetition and might help the player grasp the necessary controls. Or, we could also allow a "replay" mechanic that only forces the player to repeat the travel from a few moments before the failure, which forces the player only to repeat the moments in which they had more difficulty surpassing (using a save point system, for example). The choice between these two approaches depends on many aspects, such as the game's purpose and playtesting.

This repetition can also cause the player to get into a boredom state, though. Games with progression mechanics, such as levelling characters or upgrade systems, can tackle this by rewarding the player with small progression iterations, which compensate for the repeated attempts and might yield the player the necessary boost needed to overcome the challenge. These approaches are often in the realm of the `Economy` core, as they are related to the resources in the game, such as the player's level or available upgrades to be used.

Inaptitude is common in games with a strong physical component to them, such as digital games that are played through inputs and non-digital games that require physical movement, such as running, dancing, etc. The concept game **Family Tree** has a physical (verbal) component in the negotiation mechanic: players have to negotiate their goals and needs with each other. As this is a more verbal and mental action, it is harder to deal with inaptitude (the player not knowing how to negotiate with others), but its repetition is part of the game experience. Besides that, teaching the players how to negotiate their needs is part of the game's purpose. Furthermore, the game's event deck and mechanics could start with easier discussions and negotiations to ease the process.

For example, the first event could be deciding which movie the family[2] will watch together. Some players will have a preferred genre, and others might have movie choices that are related to their goals, such as a documentary about an important theme. However, the outcomes of the negotiation can be beneficial to most of the players regardless of the choice. All players might get 2 happiness points, for example, while others that have a significant impact

[2]Again, using a broader idea of family, as stated initially.

from the movie based on their own goals could get 3 happiness points. There could also be one option of a movie that is disliked by all players as an easy option to discard, making the negotiation easier.

Ignorance

Knowing how to perform the negotiation is tackled with strategies for dealing with the player's inaptitude. However, understanding what to do with the outcome of the negotiations deals with the player's ignorance. Player ignorance is when the player does not know how to proceed in the game or with parts of the game. Following on the previous example, what can players do with the happiness points they collected or which deck to draw cards from after a finished negotiation?

Player's ignorance is considerably easier to tackle compared to inaptitude because it is a matter of teaching the player what can be done. But tackling it efficiently is an interesting game design challenge.

Many games use tutorials and manuals to explain the rules and concepts of the game, teaching the player about options, actions, and goals. However, as you might have experienced yourself, partaking in tutorials and reading manuals might not be the most engaging activities. In fact, long tutorials and manuals can lead your player into a boredom state or, in the case of a complex manual, take them into an anxiety state. Balancing the knowledge, content, and didactic of such tools is an important task.

Regardless of the use of tutorials or manuals, there are two main approaches to teaching players:

Active: The player learns the game by playing it.

Passive: The player learns the game through passive means, such as reading and watching.

Notice that, for both cases, tutorials and manuals can be used. You can have an active playable tutorial, like an introduction level or a playable step-by-step guide, or you can have a passive tutorial in which the player watches the game being played with its instructions. You can have a simplified playthrough described in the game's manual, so players can already engage in playing the game while reading the manual, or the manual can describe examples of game moments to familiarise the player. The latter is fairly common in tabletop roleplaying books, in which excepts from characters and game events are described to exemplify how given mechanics or elements are played out, as well as their consequences.

It is also possible, and fairly common in digital games, to have a mix of both approaches. Simpler mechanics are often taught in tutorials at the start of the game, while more complex mechanics and economy mechanisms are presented in text form for players who want to achieve a higher knowledge level of the game's elements. This distinction between basic and complex elements plays a crucial role in the decision-making for which approach to use.

A good rule of thumb is to consider which aspects of the game are mandatory for the player to finish a playthrough and which ones are helpful. This separation can be quite useful in the context of rewards and balancing. More complex knowledge about the game, which is only acquired by studying the game, might yield better rewards to compensate for the effort. This in-depth study of the game can also allow the player into the metagaming aspect of playing [4].

Some games and game genres can even thrive and engage players, especially due to their complexity. Games in the 4X strategy genre (as controversial as they are [37])[3] are known to have highly complex economic systems and engage players due to their intricacies. Even when they have in-game tutorials and manuals, it is not uncommon to access their wiki pages and player guides online to study further and excel in the game. The teaching aspect is a game in itself, and it is where the "fun" (as discussed in Section 2.1) lies for many players and fans alike.

Still somewhat anecdotal evidence, I found through my experience, and the experience of my peers and some of the interviews I conducted, that indie games require more thought into how they deal with player ignorance than other well-established titles. Especially in the context of a game jam or hobby events, players might

[3]The 4X term stands for Exploration, Expansion, Exploitation, and Extermination, which are undoubtedly colonial perspectives into games. Remember when I said that all games are political?

be less inclined to spend time learning how to play smaller games. For that, the easier it is for them to understand, the better and longer they will engage. That might also be the case for prototypes and simpler playtesting sessions, as the players will experience these games (as well as indie and hobby games) as unfinished and might consider any impediments and difficulties as a result of a faulty, incomplete, or amateur game design, rather than on their own lack of understanding.

A good rule of thumb for tackling both inaptitude and ignorance is to have the simplest first-level or first-play moments as easy as possible. I even recommend removing any major obstacles that can lead the player into failing or struggling to advance to the next steps. For games with simple or only one mechanic, the first level can be just the repeated use of it with no space for failure to guarantee that the player will experience it and see its consequences in an obvious form.

I call this approach the **Forced Action Framework**, which is a common technique present in games, especially to achieve a textless tutorial in the case of digital games.

3.3 FORCED ACTION FRAMEWORK

The **Forced Action Framework** is a simple approach to teaching players about the game's concept and mechanics. It is composed of three steps:

1. **Forced Obvious Task:** The player is forced into performing a certain task, which inevitably results in the desired outcome. It is forced because there are either no other allowed actions or none of the possibilities will achieve anything meaningful.

2. **Space for Experimentation:** The player has space to experiment with the learning from the previous step in a safe environment in which mistakes are either not punishing at all or result only in minor inconveniences.

3. **Assessment:** The player is confronted with a proper challenge that validates whether the given knowledge was ac-

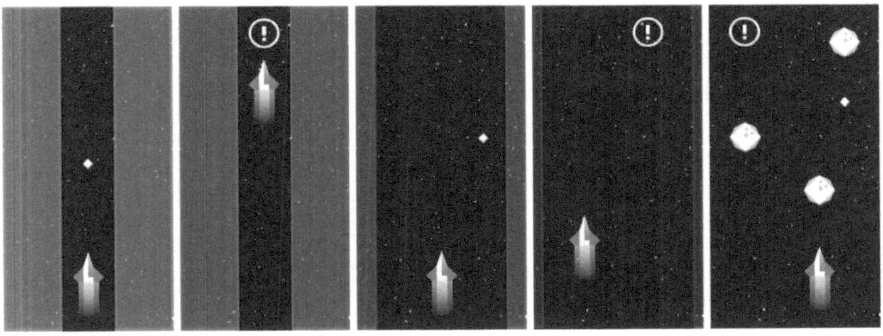

Figure 3.4: Example of the forced action framework applied to the `Another Starry Sky` concept game. The sequence of images displays examples of the forced framework steps to teach the player how to move, where to move (the exclamation mark), what to avoid (the obstacles), and what to collect (the diamond shapes).

quired properly. Failing at the assessment results in moving the player back to one of the previous stages.

Figure 3.4 shows a sequence of these steps in a concept level for `Another Starry Sky`. The leftmost picture shows the player moving in a restricted area in the centre of the screen. As the player proceeds, the goal of the level appears exactly in front of the spaceship (the exclamation mark), which forces the player to interact with it. No other alternative is possible due to the restricted movement area.

The central image has more free space to move, which allows the player to experiment with the controls. The following image shows a wider area and the game's goal in a non-forced placement but without challenges. The player only needs to move towards it to repeat what has been taught during the Forced Obvious Task moment. The rightmost image shows the Assessment stage in which obstacles are placed to force the player into successfully performing a movement sequence to avoid them and arrive at the goal.

Notice that although the three steps are shown consecutively in Figure 3.4, they can be expanded or reduced to allow for more or less exploration time. For example, the rightmost image can come after more steps, including one in which the first obstacles arepresented in a non-threatening or non-challenging setup, which allows the player to get familiar with them before engaging in the Assessment. Alternatively, the experimentation and assessment phase could have been contrived to happen sooner and faster if the mechanics were deemed too simple, and more development effort could be used in other areas of the game.

The first step can also happen multiple times if a given mechanic has multiple consequences or forms of input. Consider, for example, that there are collectables in the levels of `Another Starry Sky`, and, after a successful trip between observation points, the game displays how many collectables were gathered from the total. The collectables example are the diamonds seen in the leftmost, central, and rightmost images of Figure 3.4.

The first collectable is mandatory, as the player has no way of avoiding it. The second collectable is not mandatory. It requires the player to either be conscious or, by chance, move towards it. It is also presented in a safe setting. If the second collectable is not collected, the player then learns its consequence. The third collectable, presented in the Assessment step, is located near an obstacle and requires both intention and skill to be collected. If the player collects it, then it is fair to assume the player has learned about collectables, even if the consequences of not collecting them are not known yet. The latter will be known at some point as soon as the player fails or ignores a collectable, completing all possible outcomes for collectables.

The Forced Action Framework can overlap multiple lessons at the same time and with varying degrees of teaching. If `Another Starry Sky` also has a speed-up mechanic, for example, it could have been shown during these levels, as we just saw, while the player is also exposed to other mechanics. However, as the number of elements being taught at the same time increases, the harder it is to focus on them. For that, I recommend you spread these lessons, allowing players to take their time with each lesson and then combining them into more interesting challenges. This will allow a better approach to handling players' ignorance and inaptitude and also provide many useful tools for level designing, as the level elements can be planned ahead with their given objectives in mind.

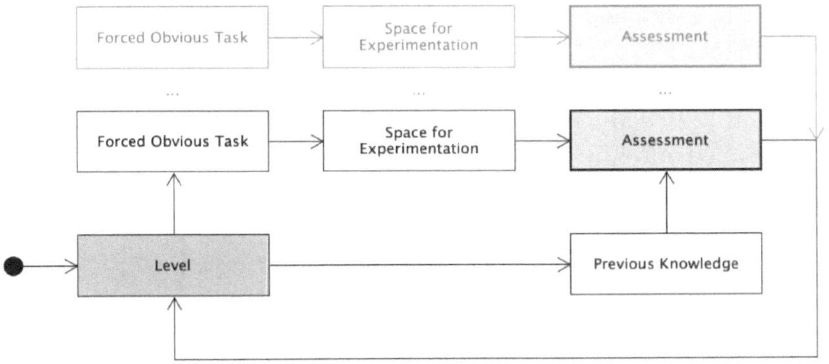

Figure 3.5: General diagram for the Forced Action Framework.

Figure 3.5 shows a general diagram for the Forced Action Framework in which multiple frameworks can happen at the same time, and the assessment is done also considering previous knowledge the player might have from earlier levels and experiences. It is also important to note that instances of the framework do not need to be aligned. A Forced Obvious Task for one mechanic might start during the Space for Experimentation of another, for example. However, as stated previously, balancing the number of multiple instances of this approach at the same time is important.

Moreover, these examples are from a digital game, but this technique also works for non-digital games. For that, we can use the term "level" in a more general way instead of limiting it to a playable level from a digital game. A round in a board game, in which all players take their turns, can also be seen as a level, for example.

Digital games have the advantage of strongly forcing players and restricting their actions due to control of the input and output devices. No matter which buttons you press, if the first level of `Another Starry Sky` only allows you to move straight up, then that is what the game is going to do. With non-digital games, this is not necessarily true. You might have a player enforce certain rules and restrictions, but as she is also a player, nothing prevents her from breaking those rules. A game moderator or storyteller in a tabletop roleplaying (TTRPG) game acts as an enforcer but might bend the rules and create exceptions for the sake of the game's enjoyment.

The example we used for `Family Tree` in the previous section (Section 3.2) demonstrates this. The game's first negotiation can be planned already to be easier to tackle and force the players into reaching a common agreement and understanding the rules and consequences of the game. However, if the deck is not properly built, the players might start the game with a more complex negotiation and get lost in the process. For that, the game's manual and instructions should be clear to avoid these initial mistakes that can undermine the planned teaching. Furthermore, it is always good to consider having one team member present and playing the game during playtests to act as an enforcer of the game rules to guarantee that the Forced Action Framework instances happen as planned.

Finally, the Forced Action Framework might sound linear and limited to only happening once per teaching, but that is not necessarily true. The same mechanic can be present in multiple instances of the framework, as there might be nuances to its use and even variations. Consider, for example, in the `Another Starry Sky`, that the goal (the exclamation mark in Figures 3.3 and 3.4) could have variations in which the player progresses to a different area or that lead to a special area. These could be presented in the same form as the traditional goals used in the examples. Moreover, the Space for Experimentation step can span over multiple iterations, especially in the context of providing repetition to prevent the player from getting stuck due to inaptitude or ignorance.

However, repetition can lead to boredom, which can be helped with the use of another game design technique: the **Goal-Achievement-Reward cycle**.

3.4 GOAL-ACHIEVEMENT-REWARD CYCLES

The **Goal-Achievement-Reward cycle** is a simple construct formed by three parts that can be used to trigger motivation, learning, and interest in the game and its parts. The three parts, given by their names, work as follow:

Goal: is the clear objective of what has to be done.

Achievement: is how the goal can be achieved.

Reward: is how the player is rewarded after completing the goal.

Although simple at first, my experience teaching the Goal-Achievement-Reward cycle, henceforth, the GAR cycle, is one of confusion with its separate parts. Let us use the concept game `Another Starry Sky` again as an example. Looking back at the previous example of travel between two observation points and how we can see it as a GAR cycle:

Goal: reaching the travel's destination.

Achievement: avoiding obstacles and reaching the exclamation mark at the end of the level.

Reward: winning extra resources, which are also dependent on the number of collectables gathered during the level.

One of the main points of confusion in the GAR cycle is the conflation of the goal and the reward. The goal and the reward must be separate elements. The reward is there to give extra motivation to the player, as the goal is going to be achieved anyway. The player already needs to reach the end of the travel to get to a new observation point. There is no point in assuming that "reaching the new location" is a reward.

As a counter-example, consider that you are participating in a noodles contest in which participants must compete to see who eats more noodles. By the end, you win by eating a total of 22 bowls of noodles. Everyone claps, and they tell you won. Your "reward" was eating the 22 bowls of noodles you just ate. There is no extra or true reward.

Particularly, eating 22 bowls of noodles is a pretty good deal, but it does feel underwhelming that there is no trophy or extra reward for winning the contest. One could argue that you might just join the contest without any ambition to win anything but the experience of eating loads of noodles, which is fair, but for others, the extra reward can be an important factor in deciding whether to participate or not. Let's say, for example, that the winner gains one year of free noodles (drinks not included) in the place in which the contest was held. Now, that's a reward!

Let us also break the noodles contest into its GAR parts:

Goal: winning the noodles contest.

Achievement: eating more noodles than the other competitors.

Reward: one year of free noodles (drinks not included) in the contest place.

Another common misconception is swapping the Reward with the Goal. Some could argue that your actual goal in joining the noodles contest is to get the reward. That would mean that your real goal is the reward itself. While that can be true from a personal level, from a game design perspective, the distinction is important because it separates what has to be done (the goal) from what is gained by doing so (the reward). Moreover, rewards can be achieved from different means and different goals, while the contrary is not necessarily true.

From a development point of view, it is easier to work with fixed game goals rather than on rewards, at least while establishing the **complete prototype**.

Moreover, in the context of the game design cycle presented in Section 2.3, the goal for the game's prototype can be the same as the one used for a GAR cycle. In fact, if you are following the procedure to build a **complete prototype**, you can add a reward for achieving the goal, motivating the player, and you have gotten yourself a GAR cycle.

The achievement and reward aspect of the GAR cycle can also repeat while the player is reaching for the goal, *i.e.*, the player can be rewarded while progressing through the goal. This is particularly true for longer GAR cycles with larger goals. In `Another Starry Sky`, the major goal is to return home and to solve the mystery of the rogue vessel. Returning home is done by travelling through observation points and successfully reading the stars to find which observation point to move to next. Each travel through the observation points is a GAR cycle on its own, as shown in the previous examples. But there is a bigger GAR cycle encompassing those,

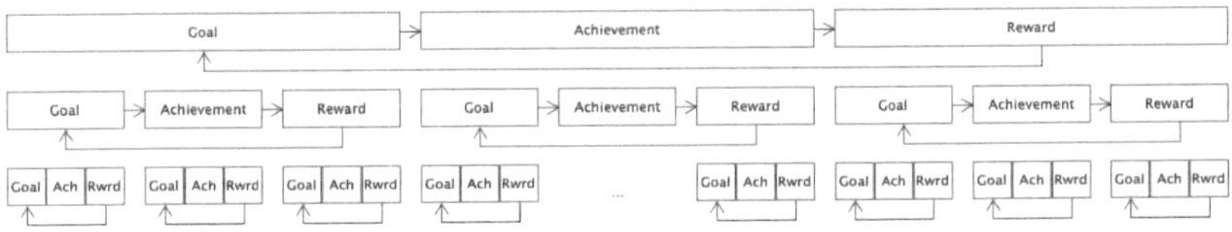

Figure 3.6: Multiple levels of GAR cycles happening simultaneously.

which is the goal of getting back home. Let us break the major cycle into its GAR parts:

Goal: return home.

Achievement: reading the stars to locate the player and travelling through observation points.

Reward: finish the game; unlocks final items; unlocks final/extra side quests.

Notice that the bigger GAR cycle can have more rewards, even elements that, for the moment, are just ideas (final items and extra quests). One could even argue that the final reward for the game's main goal is the game's ending, but that gets back to the previous discussion and conflation of goals and rewards.

I have also used the term "cycle" for the GAR system, but only now can we see how it is cyclical throughout the game. The GAR cycle of space travelling repeats for each space travel. Some cycles, like the bigger one that encompasses finishing the game, might only repeat in a new playthrough (or a new game+ mode, for example). Those could be seen more as arcs or lines, but the overall principle applies the same. Smaller GAR cycles, like the stargazing mechanic or the travelling mechanic, though, repeat more often throughout the playthrough. A general diagram for multiple levels of GAR cycles is shown in Figure 3.6.

GAR cycles are also the backbone of quest systems. Each quest has a specific goal, one or multiple ways of achieving it, followed by a reward. These can bring more variety to the game and create new ways of expanding the elements of the `Narrative` and `Aesthetics` core. These can also be smaller GAR cycles that run repeatedly during the playthrough, parallel to the game's main objective.

GAR Cycles and Surprise Rewards

There is another interesting aspect to explore in the GAR cycles: surprise rewards. Some GAR cycles can be implemented in a way in which the reward is not clear. The player either knows there is going to be a reward but does not know what the reward is, or the player does not even know the existence of a reward. At first, it might sound counter-intuitive to the previous discussion, but it is actually a strong motivational tool. Consider again the noodles' contents: what if the final prize was a mystery? Participants will join and compete, but the final prize for the winner will be unravelled by the end of the competition. The added curiosity element can motivate even non-participants to join the event to find out what the mysterious prize is.

For some mechanics, having a clear reward allows players to plan better. If the player knows exactly how many resources are available in a space travel level in `Another Starry Sky`, then the player can decide how much effort to put into getting them. More stressful or harder sections could be skipped as the player might have gotten enough resources from other sections. This allows players to experience the game on their own accord. We do not need to constantly push our players to challenge themselves. Sometimes, a relaxing experience is all they want.

Other mechanics and mechanisms can instead be empowered by the unclarity of the rewards. If, after successful arrival at an observation point, the player gets a chance to find a new clue to what happened to the rogue vessel, players might be more engaged in exploring and travelling through space to solve the mystery. Already knowing the existence of clues or what the clues are might completely destroy the detective-esque aspect of this part of the game.

Balancing known and unknown rewards is a good way of balancing the experience, especially from an ethical perspective.

Many sources on game design discuss elements of goals and rewards using another famous psychology theory: operant conditioning [38]. Operant conditioning is the association of a (probability) of a given reward, given a certain action [34]. Our previous GAR example for travelling through observation points to find clues is a form of operant conditioning: the player is getting conditioned to perform an action (travelling) to possibly receive a reward (a clue). On its own, this is not necessarily problematic, as it is an approach to teaching by rewarding the "correct" behaviour, but there is a lot to unpack from it.

Commonly, games present killing mechanics: enemies are killed to award players with extra resources [5, 39]. This might be seen as a small GAR cycle. The player defeats the enemy with some sort of weapon or tool and then is awarded resources. These resources can be randomised. For example, a specific enemy might have a 1% drop chance of awarding the player with a powerful item that players crave to have. Then, players might engage in this repeated GAR cycle for hours until getting the wanted reward.

This example combines both the GAR cycle and the surprise reward. It is also a form of operant conditioning, as the player associates killing enemies with getting rewards. As many might dismiss this discussion, this is an ethical consideration of what sort of conditioning our games have.

Notice that this opens the space for more diverse game design. Stealth games might not have any sort of reward for killing enemies, but they reward the players if they can achieve the level's goal by being unnoticed, which reinforces the stealth element and provides other forms of conditioning.

Operant Conditioning and Addiction

Research also shows that operant conditioning can cause video game addiction and other hazards to players. Foddy Bennet, in his article "Addiction: The Pleasures and Perils of Operant Behaviour", discusses how operant conditioning, especially in the case of willful behaviour, can trigger addiction-like experiences. The following statement comes from the Videogame section of his article [40, p. 60]:

> *Videogames are unlike drugs and perhaps even food in one sense: they are specifically designed to be maximally addictive.*

> *They are unlike gambling machines in that their perceived addictiveness is often touted as a selling point, a laudable quality for the best games to have. If this were simply a casual, exaggerated use of the term "addiction", then it would be easy to dismiss these things. However, the evidence suggests that they are genuinely addictive and that the addicted players suffer from an addiction that was intentionally engineered by the designer and joyfully appreciated by the user.*

Another common example of this problem in multiplayer digital games is the use of loot boxes. You might have thought about those when I discussed the idea of surprise rewards. Loot boxes are part of a reward mechanic in which the player gets new resources for the game, often in the form of cosmetic items, *i.e.*, that do not interfere with the gameplay elements. The problem with them is twofold: one is that they are a strong operant conditioning mechanic designed to get players addicted; two is that they are often connected to monetisation strategies. These two aspects combined form a designed addicting mechanism that exploits players for monetary gain, especially minors, younger and immature players that might not make the best judgement of their decisions [34].

That is not to say we should aim at completely removing randomised elements or stay away from GAR cycles due to their connection to operant conditioning, but that we should be aware of their consequences and what we do with them. Having a clear game purpose can help with that. Moreover, it is hard to avoid those approaches entirely since they are connected to teaching the players and motivating them. Let us look at the concept game `Family Tree` and how we can see the negotiation mechanic as a GAR cycle that aims at a more positive operant conditioning process.

In `Family Tree`, the players draw cards for the events that need to be unfolded in the day. Every player has to decide which actions to take on the day, and these actions must either be related to their individual goals or related to the tasks of the day. For example, the daily task requires the family members to clean the house, but only two players are necessary to do so. For that, two players must be moved to the daily task for that day. The other two might do other tasks, such as pursuing their own goals or other objectives they might have. After negotiating which family members will participate in the cleaning, the players are positioned on the board, and the outcomes of the day are drawn out. Each player then gets happiness points according to their action in the day. Breaking this into the GAR elements, we have:

Goal: perform the daily tasks.

Achievement: negotiating which players will do which tasks.

Reward: happiness points according to the players' tasks.

The results of the tasks are given by their outcomes, which ultimately are transformed into happiness points. The main mechanic, negotiation, is part of operant conditioning, as the players must reach a conclusion to separate their tasks and perform their duties. As the game requires a balanced distribution of happiness to progress and make the family tree grow, the negotiation process rewards a balanced and healthy exchange of responsibilities, conceding and discussing how the options better affect the group. The reward, although unbalanced in certain turns, can even out in the following turns, as the previous decision sums up for the coming ones. Then, good social behaviour is rewarded, which is integral to the game's purpose.

3.5 GAME DESIGN CYCLE REVISITED

Combining the elements from this section, we have an expanded overview of the game design cycle that includes methods to tackle player's inaptitude and ignorance while considering engagement and motivation. The diagram shown in Figure 3.7 shows the expanded view of the game design cycle, including these techniques and approaches.

Let us then revise the expanded version of the game design cycle:

1. First, we choose a starting core to develop our ideas.
2. Then, we establish a game mechanic and a goal that is achievable by using the given mechanic. The result is a **complete prototype**.

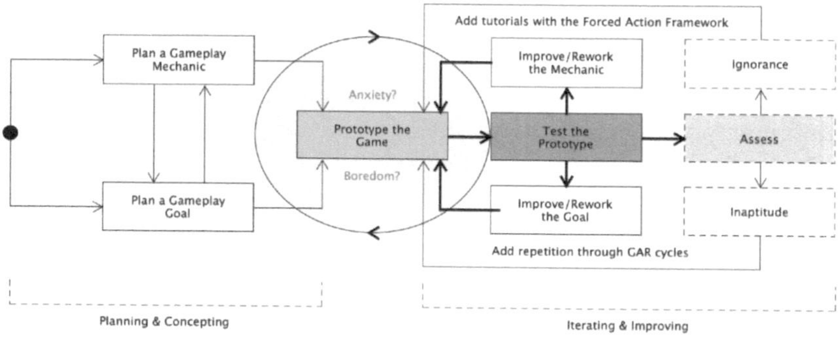

Figure 3.7: Expanded Game Design Cycle, including the elements of Flow, Player Inaptitude, Player Ignorance, and GAR Cycles.

3. The prototype is playtested, be it internally, within the team, or externally, with playtesters.
4. We assess the experience of the game mechanic and the goal.
5. Given their assessment, changes are made to improve them.
6. We assess the player's experience, whether there are signs of ignorance or inaptitude. We also assess the player's flow. Were the players able to stay in the flow, or were they leaning towards an anxiety or boredom state?
7. In the case of a player's ignorance, we can use the Forced Action Framework to better introduce the player to how the game elements work.
8. In the case of a player's inaptitude, the players need more time to develop their skills. We can approach it by introducing/modifying GAR cycles in the game that help to motivate and engage the repetition process.
9. In both cases, it should help to move the player away from the anxiety or boredom states and towards the flow state.
10. New additions to the game, based on the game design cores, are introduced.

11. From here, we repeat all the steps, starting with the 3rd step. If new mechanics were added, then the entire cycle repeats from the 2nd step.

The game design cycle and its steps do not need to happen consecutively. As part of the development team is working on a new game mechanic, another part can be testing the prototype and reworking the existing elements. Elements that belong to the `Aesthetics` and `Narrative` can be produced in parallel to the entire cycle and tested in their own cycles. As much as the steps sound like a mandatory and formal approach, the game design cycle is more of a simplified guide to approaching iterative testing and improvement. Moreover, it is highly user-centric, as most of the steps and decisions are based on feedback from playtesting sessions.

Moreover, as discussed in Chapter 2, although we discuss the start of the cycle by using one game mechanic, many designers do not start with a game mechanic in mind. It is an individual choice which core to start with. Eventually, one mechanic needs to be planned; otherwise, we can never playtest the game. On the other hand, the cores can be tested on their own via other means. A story can be read and assessed on its own without a game mechanic, for example. `Economy` systems can be calculated and tested on paper or spreadsheet software. Moods can be experienced with images and other approaches before being interactive.

Furthermore, having a clear idea of the game's purpose is a good way of achieving cohesive and coherent development. The purpose could be simple, such as making a fun game, or more complex, such as teaching a subject or enabling a feeling. It is also fine to start with a blank canvas and random ideas. Keep in mind, though, that this is similar to preparing dinner without any idea in mind. Sure, you could just check what is available and prepare your meal, but it will be easier if you establish some initial base, such as which cuisine you want or what sort of dish.

Questions to Start Game Designing

Finally, if you prefer to have a more formal approach to how to start the process, there are 5 questions I usually ask my students and peers when starting a game design process. These questions are fairly generic and can help you organise your initial ideas:

1. **How is the game played?** That is, which mechanics do we have, or how do we interact with the game? These methods and mechanics can change later, but it is good to consider them at the start. I also recommend you decide on the most simple and straightforward answer possible. If you are having a hard time answering this question, consider if you are not in one of these situations:

   Lack of technical confidence or knowledge: Consider changing the technology or working on simpler prototype versions for the first iterations.

   Focus on the other cores: Consider which mechanics help to develop the core further or use known mechanics from games that are also based on the same core.

   Fear over making a wrong decision: Consider that none of these answers is set in stone. Any idea that does not work can be changed later. It is better to make decisions and start the process. Bad decisions can be reverted later.

2. **How does anyone win this game?** That is, what is the goal that players must reach? Notice that this question ties back to the Game Design Cycle and to setting up a goal. This is not a question in the realm of the `Narrative` core: how does the story end? It is a question from the `Mechanics` core: how does the player use the mechanics to finish the game? Consider that the goal might be temporary, given what has been implemented so far. You can later revisit how the game is won based on playtesting and feedback. However, deciding on a win condition earlier on allows for better planning and organisation.

3. **How does the game get harder/more complex?** Unless the game is very short or has no progression system, it is important to consider which elements of the game will get more complex over time to increase the player's challenges. This question ties back to the Flow discussion presented in

Section 3.1. Moreover, consider that difficulty can arise from other places outside the in-game elements. Having a less flexible player in `Family Tree` might make the negotiations considerably more complex (and exhausting).

4. **How do the player's options influence the game?** This is a question of balancing random elements and strategy. Random elements are completely outside the player's control, even when they were decided by the player. Strategy is the opposite. Strategy is how the players manifest their control over the game, making decisions that are entirely based on their will. When the game leans too much towards randomness, it can get chaotic and frustrating, as the players lack control over it. On the other hand, if the game leans too much towards strategy, it becomes deterministic and easy to predict the next steps, which can make it boring. Consider in this question how the player can make meaningful decisions to reach the goal using the available mechanics and how these decisions achieve a good balance between chance and strategy.

5. **How does the game achieve its purpose?** This question ties back to the main point of the game: its purpose. If your game is aimed at being fun and entertaining, then how does it achieve it? Do players have fun playing it or with aspects of it? If your game is aimed at teaching a subject, then how does the teaching happen, and to what degree? This is surely an unfair question, to be honest. Most of the time, it will be hard, if not impossible, to determine how and if the purpose is achieved with prototypes, but it is important to consider earlier what the plans are to reach it, as most of the tasks during the development will revolve around it.

CHAPTER 4

Planning

PLANNING, OR IN A MORE GENERAL CONTEXT, PROJECT MANAGEMENT, is an integral part of developing projects, regardless of the team and the project's size. I conflated the terms Project Management and Planning, which might cause some disbelief, but I do so for a simple reason: Planning is the core of any management strategy. There is no managing people and resources without a clear plan. Moreover, Project Management and Project Production are topics that deserve books on their own, as you will see cited often during this chapter.

As this book focuses on smaller and indie/independent developments, where teams are often small or organised in small-scale groups [41], this chapter focuses will be on management for these situations.

In these scenarios, topics such as Production and Management tend to be informal and specific to each case, different from large organisations and companies. Pereira and Bernades, in their article "Aspects of Independent Game Production: An Exploratory Study", nod to that as follows [42, p. 2 and p. 6]:

> *Our findings suggest that indie game firms present characteristics common to other micro-firms, displaying a tendency towards informal managerial practices, especially in projects without external funding or rigid delivery dates.*
> *(...) Small and micro-firms tend to be intrinsically different in their approaches to business and organisational characteristics and, as a result, many theories based on larger*

DOI: 10.1201/9781003351191-4

businesses prove to be inappropriate for use in this context, especially when it comes to management processes.

Moreover, Pereira and Bernades [42] present traits and findings from indie development practices such as, but not limited to, the opposition to rigid and hierarchical top-down management; a sense of playfulness associated with creative freedom; reliance on communities, networking, and sharing; authenticity and; autonomy. These traits align with the interviews I conducted while working on this book.

Alternatively, some of the research on game development project management comes from a more capitalistic, productive point of view, although these sources do not necessarily support or advocate for it.

This capitalistic productive standpoint is illustrated in a paper by Sabine Hotho, "'Some Companies Are Fine One Day and Gone the Next': Sustaining Business in the Digital Games Industry", in which the author conducted qualitative interviews with senior members of game production studios [43, p. 96]:

Culture design efforts seem not to deliver: "You've got to move away from this habit as a games designer that you are making a game for yourself. You're not. You need to know the market you are making the game for and make it for them. [...] I think that is a great challenge to people, and I think the only way around that is to basically force the team into doing what you want them to do".[1]

Different from the point of view presented in the paper by Sabine Hotho, this book focuses on the opposite: making games for yourself.

For that, this chapter focuses more on planning and related subjects that can help you achieve your games rather than on how to control people and "force them into doing what you want them to do". Moreover, the proposed strategies and approaches to planning and management attempt non-hierarchical structures in which

[1]To be clear, these statements are not from Sabine Hotho herself, but from interviewees presented in her article, [43].

no one has more power over others and responsibilities are shared based on experience, knowledge, and trust.

The following sections are organised as follows: Section 4.1 discusses the main pitfalls of overall planning, even outside the context of games. Section 4.2 presents the famous agile methodology, focusing on game development practices. Section 4.3 discusses an important document on game design: The **Game Design Document** (GDD). I called it the "boring document" at first, but the idea in this section is to discuss how to **not** make it boring, according to your needs, and demystify some common concepts and misconceptions around these documents. Finally, Section 4.4 deals with a major discussion on the game development process that is often ignored: game development is not software development.

4.1 THE PROBLEM WITH REGULAR PLANNING

Planning happens all the time.

Planning is not only when you organise tasks for your project. Planning happens every time we make decisions based on our (available) time. We are always planning, even if we do not realise that.

When buying food, for example, you take many points into consideration, such as the food's expiration date and when you plan on eating that food. This is also planning.

With that, for this book, we consider planning as more than "making plans". Plans might be discarded at some point, but the act of planning, *i.e.*, considering the alternatives and important aspects to make opinionated decisions, is never truly wasted.

Planning is often a heated topic due to its many approaches. Moreover, planning itself is hard due to its nature: planning is nothing more than an attempt at predicting the future.

That is not to say that planning is impossible or that we should neglect it, but that plans must be seen as predictions. The further we plan, and for the longer period, the higher the chances of it failing. On the other hand, short-term planning has more potential to come to fruition, as there is less space for uncertainties and surprises.

Consider, though, that the notion of time is quite personal. Busy weeks might seem to pass faster than quieter ones.

Organisations might plan for 5 to 10 years, while teenagers might not plan much further than a few days. Those are all valid forms of thinking ahead.

Moreover, planning is easier when it comes from a place of experience. It is harder to predict how long it takes to prepare a recipe for the first time than to guess how long it takes to make your favourite sandwich. Activities we have been performing repeatedly are easier to assess and plan as we are more aware of their processes and details. Analogies are convenient in these situations, as we might grasp the complexity of a given task by comparing it to other similar ones.

Finally, motivation is an important and often neglected aspect of planning. As planning deals with the future, it is easy to decide on incredible goals that require hard work, disregarding the motivation to perform them. Activities can take longer or shorter, depending on the motivation while executing them. Motivation is quite a subjective point in planning, but it is an important one because it helps to consider the humane side of planning rather than just "objective" aspects such as time and experience.

These three aspects often take the central role in planning discussions, which are also shown in Figure 4.1:

Proximity: How close/further will the plan or planning activity take place?

Experience: How similar (or equal) is the plan or planned activity from previous experiences?

Motivation: How motivating or demotivating is the plan or planned activity to who's responsible for it?

These aspects act as a continuum, as seen in Figure 4.1. The closer all three aspects are from the start of the spectrum (Close, Equal, Motivating), the better the chances of a successful plan. The closer all three aspects are from the end of the spectrum (Further, Completely New, Demovating), the worse the chances. Balancing these points is a healthy way to deal with uncertainties and achieve more realistic plans.

For example, a team must use a 3D Printer to print the blocks from `Family Tree`. However, it is a Completely New experience for

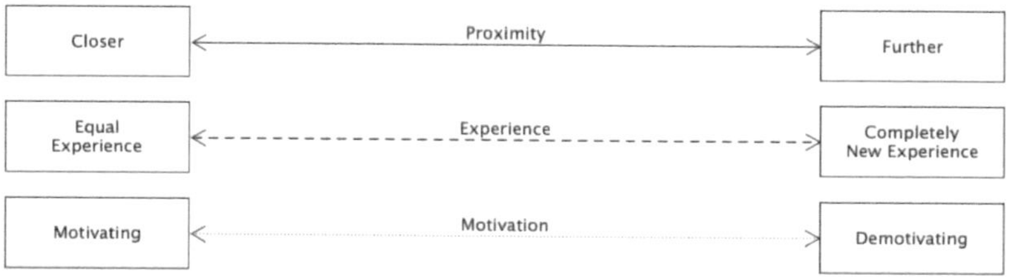

Figure 4.1: Planning aspects: Proximity, Experience, Motivation.

them. The team can start to work on it sooner (Close Proximity). Also, as it is a new activity that can bring some of the game art into a physical form, it can be exceptionally motivating (Motivating).

If an activity is planned only to be executed at a late moment, should you already include it in your plans? It might be wiser to work on it sooner (Close Proximity) or take it out of your plans, keeping it on a to-do list for the future.

Activities in which you lack experience should be converted into experiments. You can plan a moment to learn and experiment with them first to gain experience and expertise before committing to a more serious task. For example, if you have never written a dialogue, you could first study how to approach it and practice with smaller dialogue pieces until you feel more comfortable with the actual task.

The experiment idea applies quite well to more technical-related activities, which might involve important processes and architectural decisions that can impact further steps of game development. Uncertainty and fear of failure are huge demotivating factors. Consider taking the time to reduce them and be open to your team about your questions and insecurities. Also, remember that wrong decisions, no matter the size, can be reverted and changed later. Besides, you simply cannot avoid making mistakes along the way. We cannot predict the future.

Moreover, demotivating activities are quite a problem, and you can look at them again through the lens of the Flow theory (from Section 3.1). Demotivating tasks will take you out of the flow and harm the experience and the planning. Demotivating tasks also tend to move the other aspects to the end of the spectrum.

Demotivating tasks are more likely to be postponed, for example. In any case, it is always good to consider what causes demotivation and what can be done.

From experience, I often see teams treating activities related to documentation, research, and planning as "boring" activities. Any case of a demotivating or "boring" activity needs to be solved on its own, so there are no general guides on tackling them. Honest, open, and transparent communication are the best tools to approach them, especially considering the other two aspects, Proximity and Experience.

Moreover, as the following sections will discuss, some of these problems can be tackled differently with a better and more personalised approach to planning.

4.2 AGILE, VERY QUICK, AND FAST

Many of the "modern"[2] personalised methodologies to planning are based on agile methodologies to some extent [44]. The agile methodology is an umbrella term encompassing many approaches and methodologies that share common traits, specifically incremental, cooperative, adaptative, and straightforward [45, 46]. Although the agile discussion arose from a software engineer perspective, these traits are flexible enough to be applied in many scenarios. The following list explains these traits from a more general perspective:

Incremental: The process is done in incremental small steps that will result in the final goal.

Cooperative: The process is done together with people involved in it, and that might be affected by the final goal.

Adaptative: The process will change to better adapt to new circumstances and findings.

Straightfoward: The process is easy to follow and understand.

[2] I mention "modern" here as the Agile Manifesto was written in 2001, 23 years ago from when this book was written.

This book has vastly discussed the first two, especially considering the game design cycle (Section 2.3). The game design cycle recommends that we work on the game in small iterations that incrementally approach the final result, achieving the game's purpose. We assess the game's purpose by doing different playtests involving the players. The adaptative aspect is also part of the game design cycle, as the iterations are meant to adjust new findings and solve possible problems.

In planning, though, the idea of being adaptative also means that the process can be adapted to better suit the team's and the project's needs (just like the game design cycle should be adapted to better suit your needs). If part of the process does not work or is not suited for your case, change it.

Finally, from these four traits, the game design cycle is meant to be straightforward. This last trait works together with the openness to adaptation: if some part of the process is not easy to follow and understand, it should be changed (or adapted).

In terms of agile methodologies, simplicity is also a protest with other practices that require formal studies and extensive training to be fully comprehended[3].

From the vast array of agile-based methodologies, two are considerably more prevalent than others, especially for general game development and game design: Scrum and Kanban [14, 47, 48]. There is a third one, Extreme Programming (short, XP) [49], that is often cited next to the other two. However, XP will not be discussed for two reasons: first, it is a programming strategy, while game development is not restricted to digital games; second, its task and planning activities are very similar to Scrum [49].

Scrum and Kanban are agile-based methodologies with many similarities but a few important distinctions. However, they are not mutually exclusive. As we discussed previously, being agile also implies being adaptable. Combining methodologies is a valid adaptation. Some authors even use the term Scrumban to refer to the combination of both methodologies [50].

---

[3]Funnily enough, some well-known agile methodologies also have their books, training, and certifications.

One of the main differences between Scrum and Kanban is how each handles time. Scrum manages tasks and planning in time-boxed events called sprints, while Kanban is an ongoing process with continuous planning and improvement. On the other hand, both approaches use the concept of a backlog: an active list of tasks that need to be done to complete the project. The backlog is active because, at any time during development, new tasks might be added/changed/removed from it.

Let us first briefly explain both approaches and discuss their shortcomings. Moreover, the following explanations were written in a game development and design context, not as general management methodologies.

Scrum

Scrum is a time-boxed agile methodology based on sequences of sprints. A **Sprint** is a period in which the development is done [50, 51]. Sprints usually vary from 1 week to 1 month long, but it is common to find cases in which longer and shorter sprints are used for various reasons [51]. Typically, the Sprint's length is fixed during the project, which bounds the planning to its duration. Figure 4.2 shows a simplified Scrum process.

Each Sprint starts with the **Sprint Planning**, in which the team decides which tasks will be performed during the Sprint, taking them off the backlog. The team discusses the tasks' complexities, responsibilities, and conditions during the planning.

During the Sprint, the team works on their tasks and performs daily checkups called **Daily Scrum**[a]. The daily Scrum is meant to be no longer than 15 minutes in which all team members discuss their plans, progress, and any impediments or issues. Thus, any problems can be immediately addressed and solved.

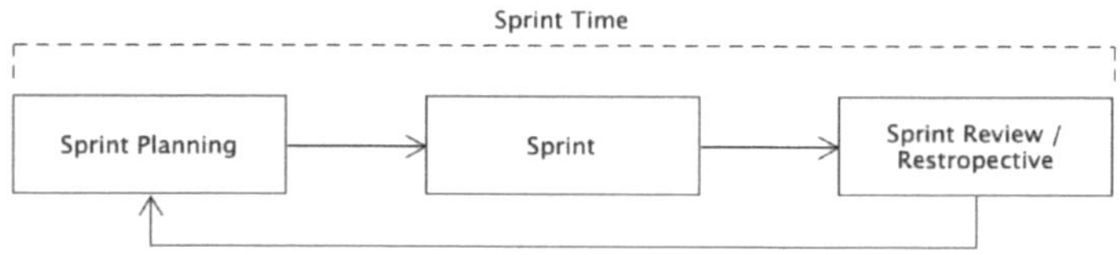

Figure 4.2: Scrum basic elements.

The Sprint ends with the **Sprint Review and Retrospective**. The Sprint Review is a moment for the team to reflect and discuss the results of the Sprint. The review helps support the decisions for the next Sprint's planning on which tasks should be done based on what has been accomplished.

The Sprint Retrospective is a moment for the team to reflect and discuss their performance on the Sprint. Retrospective helps support decisions on how the team, its processes, and relevant elements should be changed to better accommodate the team's needs and experience for the coming Sprints.

The Retrospective is the most vital point for Scrum, as it allows experimentation and improvement to happen freely, and any changes are only bound to the duration of one Sprint. Any issues in the changes made due to one Retrospective can be reverted in the upcoming one without significant compromises.

For example, the team decided to use a new file-sharing service during one Retrospective. However, during the next one, everyone agreed it was not a good experience. As a result, the team can now revert to their previous file-sharing services or try a new one. By the following Retrospective, the decision can be reevaluated.

[a]Other terms commonly used as a synonym to the Daily Scrum are Daily Meeting or Standup Meetings.

Kanban

Although I previously presented Kanban as a methodology, the reality is a bit more complex than that [52]. Kanban is not a formal methodology but a process tool that can be used with other approaches [53]. Kanban is based on three principles: **Visualise the Workflow**, **Measure the Time**, and **Limit the Work in Progress** [47]. All these principles are visited in the **Kanban Board**, which is the primary tool used by Kanban. The Kanban Board is exemplified in Figure 4.3.

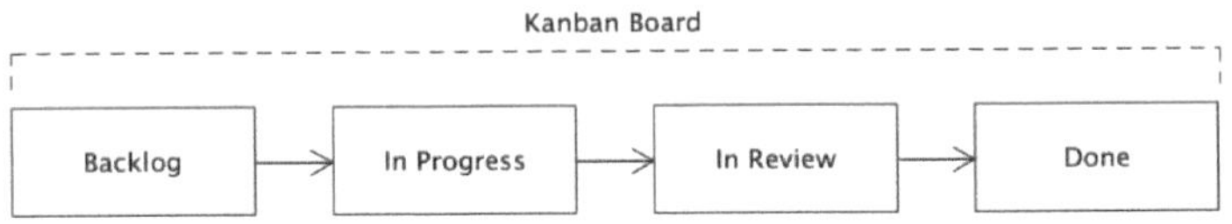

Figure 4.3: Kanban board basic elements.

The Kanban Board is divided into different areas representing the project's workflow. A typical division, especially for game development, is presented in Figure 4.3, which divides it into **Backlog**, **In Progress**, **In Review**, and **Done**. This division is not strict and should reflect your project's workflow. It is just a good starting point. Separating the workflow in the Kanban Board achieves the first principle of Kanban: to visualise the workflow.

The tasks in Kanban are written on cards and placed on the Kanban Board in the respective part of the workflow to which they belong. Planned tasks belong in the Backlog section. Tasks currently being worked on belong in the **In Progress** section. Tasks completed but not approved or integrated remain in the **In Review** section until this process is completed, and then they are moved to the **Done** section.

Tracking the time it takes from each task to move through the Kanban board, *i.e.*, from its start (**In Progress**) until its completion (**Done**), is the principle of measuring time, which helps future decisions. For example, if a given task took a long period to be finished, similar tasks in the **Backlog** could be rediscussed and even split into smaller tasks to improve planning and decision-making.

Finally, the last principle stands that the workload should be limited to a certain amount. In practical terms, this limitation can limit the maximum of tasks being worked on simultaneously or how many tasks one team member can have. For example, we can establish that a team member cannot simultaneously work on more than two tasks (two tasks **In Progress** for that person).

We can also limit the workflow itself. For instance, the team can decide that there cannot be more than four tasks **In Review** at the same time. If that happens, all the efforts should be put into moving at least one of these tasks to **Done** before resuming the work on other activities.

The work-in-progress limitation is an excellent method to balance the workload and ensure tasks are adequately moved through the workflow until the end. It can also show possible bottlenecks. If many art tasks are getting stuck **In Review**, it might be that the artists responsible for checking them are overworked or that the art review process is too complex and lengthy – all of those signal room for improvement.

Both approaches can be used individually or combined. Let us summarise some important aspects that can guide your decision:

Planning On-The-Go x Scheduled Planning: Kanban does not enforce a fixed regularity for planning. The backlog is prioritised and organised as needed. Scrum has planning meetings every Sprint, which helps to create a sense of periodicity and timed windows.

On-Demand Tasks x Fixed Tasks: Due to the on-the-go planning, tasks in Kanban are done as the work is completed, and more tasks are moved to **In Progress**. On the other hand, for Scrum, the tasks to be done were fixed during the planning and will not change until the next Sprint.

Especially for digital games, a common intermediary approach separates the development tasks from bug-fixing tasks, as the latter are unpredictable and usually have a higher priority. Thus, bug-fixing tasks are commonly prioritised and done as soon as possible, regardless of the approach used.

Measuring Work with Points

To achieve a more concrete time estimation, it is common for Scrum and other methodologies to employ a task point system based on complexity. More complex or longer tasks get more points than simpler and shorter ones. The point system helps to estimate the workload and improve the chances of successful planning.

From my experience, working with a point system based on time is usually easier for a couple of reasons: it is more grounded to our real-life experience, it makes it easier to compare tasks, and it simplifies the workload assessment by the end of the planning. The point system I am most familiar with and have seen working well more often than not is the following:

8 points: (up to) a full week of work.

4 points: (up to) half a week of work.

2 points: (up to) a quarter of a week of work.

1 point: (up to) one day of work.

0 points: (up to) one hour.

There are a couple of advantages to using these numbers. First of all, they are (almost) all based on halves. For that, we can sum up a batch of tasks, and the result belongs to or can be easily interpreted inside this same system. For example, if a game designer has two tasks of 2 points and 1 task of 4 points, then this game designer has 8 points in total, which should be roughly one week of work. If a programmer has 3 tasks of 8 points (24 points in total), then we can understand it as 3 weeks of work.

Using this point system, you can distribute the workload and plan activities more easily. If you are working with 1-week sprints, then no team member should have more than 8 points planned. From a Kanban perspective, when the time is measured, an 8-point task takes about one week to be completed; then, upcoming, similar tasks will take roughly the same time.

Another advantage is that these values are still estimations instead of being a strict number of hours or days. If a given task takes a few hours to complete, then it falls under the 1-point category. In cases in which the estimation is in between categories, for instance, a task that takes about 2 to 3 days of work (2 or 4 points), then it is recommended to pick the highest category (4 points). That will reduce stress and prevent a higher workload.

As expected, initial project experiences with time estimation and point systems are bound to fail. Teams are often more optimistic about their own capacities and tend to use lower categories in their initial planning. That is fine. Planning is a hard guessing game, and it will fail often. Consider these approaches for planning as ways in which you can reduce stress and frustration caused by its failures. The most crucial point in planning is not high efficiency but team stability: you want your team to be happy, stress-free, and motivated.

Making games takes time, and a significant part of it is spent on figuring out the game and learning about it. It is a discovery process, and it includes your planning and management strategies. They will adapt and change to suit the experience and journey better, as they can change over time. A project can start in a more Kanban-esque form, in which activities are done on-demand as the game design cycle is iterated, and then proceed to a more Scrum-esque sprint-based strategy as the bulk of the development phase starts.

Another significant part related to these processes is how all the findings and decisions are documented. That is another source of controversy in game design and game development, especially when discussed under the lens of a Game Design Document.

4.3 BORING DOCUMENTS

Although the **Game Design Document** (GDD) is a known name in game design terminology, there is no formal or standard understanding of what it means and how to approach it [20, 54, 55]. That is not necessarily a problem. As discussed many times throughout this book, the game design and development process is very personal and mutable according to many variables, and a search for a uniform or standardised approach is bound to fail. The same happens to other sort of documents and processes connected to it.

During my interviews and research for this book, I had at least two recurring questions about GDDs: if they were used by the interviewee and which form they had (format, pages, etc.). In general, for solo developers and smaller teams, the GDD was usually a very small document that served to organise the main ideas or to introduce new collaborators to the project. For relatively bigger organisations (more than 10 team members), it was common to hear that the GDD was a collection of separate hierarchical documents that organised and compiled decisions and direction for the subteams. For example, the GDD would contain a separate document for the story and another one for the style board.

A contradictory fact I found was that some teams were keen on not writing any documentation prior to the initial development stage (first iterations of the game design cycle) until they were happy with the base for the game. Others stated that they do not start any endeavour before writing the ideas down, as a sort of written brainstorming session. I even had some interviewees stating that they would present and test this initial document with friends and colleagues before committing to any developments.

One common factor that emerged from all interviews, which is also mentioned by most of the literature, was that the GDD is a living, dynamic document. It changes and is updated as the development progresses. It should not be seen as a rulebook that was initially created during the game's "concept phase" and stays as it is for the entirety of the game's development. As obvious as it might sound, it is actually one of the most common myths I see new game designers hold dear. They assume that a game designer's work is mostly based on writing these immutable documents. That is even noted by Jesse Schell's Art of Game Design [20, p. 472]:

> *Many novice game designers and other dreamers have an interesting vision of how the process of game design works. (...), they believe that the process of game design involves a genius game designer sitting down alone at a keyboard and typing out a glorious and perfect game design document.*

Removing the Boredom

GDDs are commonly seen as boring documents because of these misconceptions. To avoid the same stigma, consider the following points for your GDD (if you decide on using one):

Easy to Access: It should be easily accessible by everyone in the team. The easier it is to reach it, the higher the chances of it being actually used. Otherwise, you might have team members constantly asking about its content instead of checking the document themselves, which might be a source of stress, disinformation and demotivation.

Easy to Understand: It should speak the same language as those who are going to use it. I recommend you write it for your team, including terms, memes, slang, and other forms of communication that can facilitate the reading process.

Easy to Navigate: It should be easy to find where the important information is located. Use contrast (bold, italics, font size) and colour (highlights, underlines, colour coding) to achieve a good visual reading of the important bits and facilitate the document's navigation.

Support Alignment: It should help the team to align their views and share a (similar) understanding of the game being made.

Support Decision Making: It should focus on holding the information that will support the game's decision-making.

The latter two are probably the main drives to focus the effort on the GDD. It is fairly easy to find GDD templates online with many fields and information that are not necessary for all projects and will not aid the game's design and development. For example, the game's genre is often cited as a piece of important information, but it really depends on the sort of game and its medium. Depending on the game, the genre might be diffuse and even open for debate as the game is being built.

Another common element is the target audience, which is quite an abstract term. Unless you are working for a very specific and known target audience, such as making a serious game for parents undergoing an adoption process, it is likely that deciding on the target audience will be only an arbitrary, uninformed decision for the sake of having one.

Surely, these two examples, the game's genre and target audience, can be used to make decisions. Both can inform the team on how to proceed, but the main point of the GDD should not be to collect "possible useful decisions". It should be to organise a set of "certainly useful decisions". Furthermore, if it happens that the need for a genre or target audience emerges, the team can work on it with a clear goal as to why it is necessary and how it will help the project.

The information in the GDD should serve the project, not the other way around. You should not dedicate time to the GDD just for the sake of keeping the documentation updated. It is fairly common for developers to abandon the GDD in later stages of the game development, as it was too outdated; the team already knew everything they needed or had moved on to use other specific documents [55].

It is perfectly fine to create other documents next to the GDD, or even those that are part of it, to achieve other, more specific goals. Story-driven games are bound to have more text documents on story, background, and dialogues. Digital games, especially with in-house game engines or systems, will have some sort of code documentation. But those should never reach the status of boring documents: a forced task that interests no one in the team and only exists for its own sake.

The descriptions for the concept games presented in this book are good starting points for a GDD: they are descriptive enough to explain the game, its purpose, and its main elements. Moreover, other specific documents and artefacts that can help the cores, such as a story-focused document (Chapter 11) or a mood board (Chapter 14), will be discussed in more detail in their respective chapters.

4.4 GAME DEVELOPMENT IS NOT SOFTWARE DEVELOPMENT

Many approaches to Planning, Production, and Game Development are based on software development practices [56], which is an odd decision. Reducing games to software is wrong.

Some games have a software component to them, but not all games. Tabletop games, card games, tabletop roleplaying games, sports games, and many other types of games have barely any or no software component to them. In fact, digital games (or, more commonly, video games) are a relatively recent phenomenon, while games already exist for many centuries, independent of the definition used.

This false premise of games being software has bad consequences for the game design and game development processes.

The first issue is assuming that the software component, when present, is the most important aspect of the game. In fact, for digital games, faulty software might lead to an undesirable experience, but it is misleading to assume that other aspects of the game's development, such as the cores of `Aesthetics`, `Narrative`, and `Economy`, are not as relevant. The game's software is as important as its other parts. Moreover, some elements of the `Mechanics` might happen outside the software, such as the players' interactions in local cooperative video games.

As discussed previously, this assumption is often backed up by claims that software, tightly connected to the `Mechanics` core, is the main responsible for a "good game". That is not always true. Some games might have low mechanical and software development and still achieve their purpose. For some digital games, the software aspect can even be quite minimal, such as text-based games made in Twine [57].

The second issue is that software is usually built to solve specific problems for a user. Think about all the software you use and how they are meant to facilitate your life in some aspect. Spreadsheet applications, for example, help to deal with numbers, grids, charts, and even with planning a game's economy, as we will see in the `Economy` section (Chapter 8).

Games are not necessarily developed to solve problems. Some games might have that purpose in mind, such as Serious Games [58] or Exergames [59]. Other games are just meant to relax and entertain their players. Designers can make games for themselves, just for the fun of designing and developing games.

This focus on problem-solving also leads to a third issue, which is using a methodology that is focused on user stories and user journeys, as if the game is built of individual features to help a user achieve something. It is possible to use these strategies, but I often see game designers lose time and motivation trying to phrase the need for a certain mechanic as a user story.

Consider a jump mechanic for a 2D action platformer game, for example. Following good practices for user stories [60], you are likely to create a user story such as: "As a player, I want to be able to jump so I can reach other areas in the level". Nice! How does this phrasing help the development process? Alternatively, if you are doing these practices to name tasks in the backlog, consider just sticking to "Jump Mechanic". Any additional information and detail can be written as part of the task body and are likely not to resemble a user story at all.

A fourth problem that is actually commonly acknowledged in these practices is that it is hard to handle and manage design and art tasks within a software development approach [56]. That is especially the case when these tasks require creative iterations and experimentation before committing to a final "result". One artist can spend days working on the art concept of a character before reaching a version that is embraced by the team. The same applies to writing, composing music, etc.

Software development practices do not embrace this creative space necessary for creative productions. It also does not allow for the flexibility needed during the design and development process to tackle the uncertainties of developing games. Again, games are often "discovered" during their development rather than being simply built from "perfect" ideas.

That does not imply that nothing from software development can be applied to games. On the contrary, many of its practices can be applied to the software component, such as good use of code conventions, software patterns, and code quality metrics. In short, any aspect that can improve the software part is welcome. They just need to be understood as a part of the process and not the lead.

Avoiding the Focus on Software Development

Additionally, even from the software point of view, it is good to consider the effort and focus on game development from a different perspective than regular software development. From my experience, beginner game developers with a background in computer programming tend to focus their development on building engines, tools, and complex systems rather than on the elements that are required to achieve the **complete prototype** stage. All those activities are important and will be done at some point during the video game development, but they should be planned accordingly. A considerable part of the code base might be thrown away after the first playtest iteration.

From my experience, this tendency to focus on developing software rather than games happens often for two reasons:

1. **Fear of leaving the comfort zone:** The developer(s) are used to regular software programming and tend to stick to what they know about, focusing on building systems rather than game systems and mechanics.

2. **Preference on writing code rather than making games:** The developer(s) are actually only engaged in the process because of their enjoyment for writing and working with code, rather than on producing games. For them, the end result is the code itself instead of the playable experience.

The first reason is a common and understandable one. We tend to stick to familiar actions, and it is scary to try new activities and developments, especially when we already have a solid understanding of the techniques involved. I like to compare this with trying out a recipe with new ingredients. Even if you are experienced with cooking, these new additions might be scary and hinder you from trying them out. Here, I am not pushing a self-help moment to tell you you should face the new challenges. The goal is understanding if that is what is happening to you. This will help you to know yourself and your process better. From this point, it is easier to decide which steps to take. The outcome will be fine as long as you are fine with it.

The second reason is, in my experience, very common with beginner game programmers. They tend to fall in love with the possibilities of writing code and spend most of their time testing their skills and knowledge. They will see most of their contributions as valid for the game. Yet most of these contributions are too detached from the rest of the development to be immediately used by the team.

From my experience teaching game design and development, it is very common to have a programmer spend the complete duration of a game development project developing an entire game engine to have it (almost) complete by the end of the deadline. However, at that point, there was no time to make the actual game. You can imagine how frustrating that is for the other team members.

It is important to know the distinction on what drives you to make games, especially if you are in a position that is closely related to the software aspect of it. Communicating that to your peers is important, as knowing this can help with planning and management, as well as with guiding the game's discussions on priorities.

Lastly, a common methodology I see happening when software is seen as the protagonist of game development is that of first building the software and then, in a later stage, combining it with the other elements. This approach is catastrophic.

Combining the game elements, all of them up to and including software, is the actual game development process, and it is the hardest and most laborious task in the entire development. I even kept it in bold here to emphasise this point.

That is why the Game Design Development Cycle proposed in Section 2.3 is focused on iterative and incremental development. All parts of the game are constantly built and combined into a playable version. It helps to bring all components of the game to the foreground, as everything is important to achieve the game's purpose. Besides that, it helps to guide the priorities of the team.

It also improves morale. Having a playable prototype that displays the work of all involved team members is way more motivating and rewarding than looking at fully functional pieces of written code. This, of course, assumes and accepts that, sometimes, software functionality should be deprioritised in favour of implementing the work of others. Moreover, having other team members learn to implement their own work in the game by means of coding or tooling, for example, is of great help and value.

As you work on your own process, especially if you are basing your iterations on the Game Design Cycle and the Cores of Game

Design, consider how the process of integrating the work is done for each core and how it can be improved. If you are working on a digital game, most of the integration will be done in the software, then consider it the glue that holds everything together. The importance of glue is indisputable, but it is nothing without the elements it is meant to glue. As a food analogy, the software works like the mayonnaise on a sandwich: it helps to hold and enhance the other ingredients, and for sure, it is delicious, but the sandwich is the real deal.

II

Mechanics

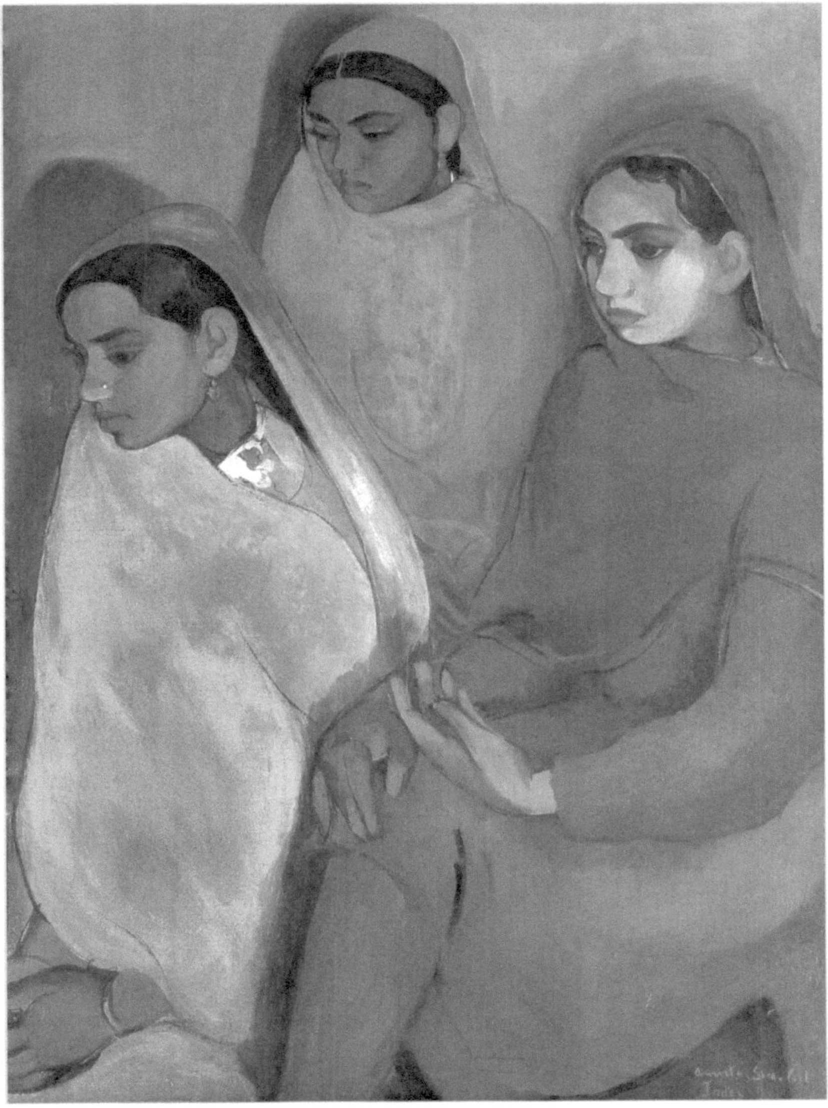

Amrita Sher-Gil – Group of Three Girls (1935).

CHAPTER 5

Starting with Mechanics

MECHANICS ARE PROBABLY THE MOST DISCUSSED ASPECT IN GAME DESIGN. Mechanics are the main activities performed and repeated by the players while gaming. The mechanics are the gateway from which players interact with the game.

Exploring the use of mechanics is a lifetime activity. First, mechanics are endless. Second, for each mechanic, there are a myriad of variations. For each of these variations, there are limitless contexts from which the mechanics can be understood. That is to say that mechanics are **flexible**: depending on the context, they can be understood as different, although mechanically, they work the same.

Let us understand this concept using a very traditional example: jumping. Jumping is a mechanic. Double-jumping is a variation of jumping. Double-jumping in space to avoid asteroids is a variation with context. We can expand this concept to other possibilities and implementations, even in such abstract terms. How far does the first jump go? And the second? Are there means to jump higher? And so it goes on.

Another interesting example is shooting. Shooting is a mechanic. How you shoot is a variation. You could shoot from a 1st person or 3rd person perspective in a digital game, but you could also have a physical shooting element in a board game, for

DOI: 10.1201/9781003351191-5

example[1]. Each one of these has its own characteristics. Moreover, we can explore multiple contexts for what you shoot at. We can have the overused war-type shooting game, in which humanoid players shoot each other to kill themselves [5], but you could also shoot water as a firefighter, saving lives from a fire.

Notice that, although we are discussing the core of `Mechanics`, these variations and contexts can come from the other cores, such as the audiovisual context from the `Aesthetics` or the motivation from the `Narrative`.

Flexibility gives us a wide range of possibilities, but it is also what commonly staggers game designers. How do you choose which one to start with? There are a few points to consider, regardless of the ones discussed in Part I.

5.1 STRONG AND WEAK MECHANICS

Mechanics are often connected to their respective challenges in the game. Every mechanic needs a challenge or task to be paired with, although this is not a forced one-to-one relation. The same challenge can be overcome by multiple mechanics, and the same mechanic can be used to overcome multiple challenges.

When considering mechanics and their respective challenges, I often see them in a range between weak and strong mechanics. A **Strong Mechanic** has more potential for challenges and variations, while a **Weak Mechanic** is simpler and does not offer many possibilities. Notice, though, that those terms are quite subjective, and you can find ways of transforming a weak mechanic into a strong one and vice-versa.

Strong Mechanics

A strong mechanic is often the main mechanic of our **complete prototype**. You should be able to plan and implement multiple types of challenges, including the **complete prototype's** goal, without making significant changes to it.

Consider the jumping mechanic discussed previously. You could achieve multiple types of jumping challenges without modifying

[1]Shooting a rubber band, for example.

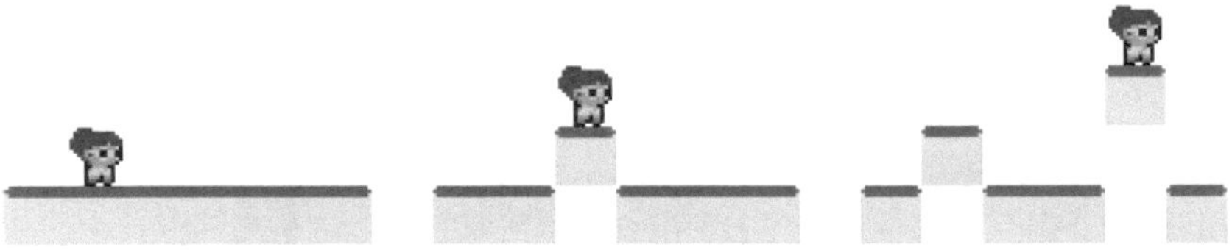

Figure 5.1: Challenges with a Jumping Mechanic in a 2D Platformer.

the jump or adding extra mechanics on top of it. Figure 5.1 shows examples of such variations.

To assess the strength of a given mechanic, ask yourself these three questions:

1. What is the minimal/easiest challenge I can do with it?
2. Which simple variations can I make with the minimal/easiest challenge?
3. What is the hardest challenge I can do with it?

These questions are related to the Forced Action Framework we explored in Section 3.3. The first question helps to establish the Forced Obvious Task. The second one is for the Space for Experimentation, and the latter is a baseline for the Assessment. If you have different answers (different challenges) for all three answers, then your mechanic is likely a strong one. Otherwise, it is either a weak mechanic, or you need more work on conceptualising these challenges.

Figure 5.1 is divided into three parts that exemplify these questions. The first one is trivial and does not even require a jump. The second one is an easy example requiring a simple jump. The third one is slightly more complex, requiring two jumps.

Combining challenges is a good way of exploring opportunities for a mechanic. The example in Figure 5.2 shows an extra step in which another platform is added for a third jump. The new jump requires the previous two jumps to have been made successfully. Failing this last jump has more consequences than the previous two.

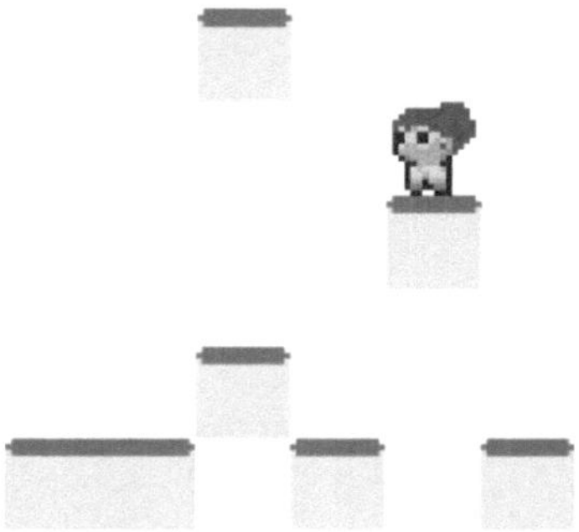

Figure 5.2: Example of a combined Jumping Mechanic Challenge.

Jumping and other more action-oriented mechanics are often strong mechanics because they deal with dexterity, reflexes, and other manual player skills. Adjusting and playing with those factors is an excellent way of creating variations for a strong mechanic. For example, varying the timing for a specific mechanic can already provide many different challenges.

Another good way of experimenting and creating challenges is playing with the **degree of forgiveness** towards mistakes. Looking back at Figure 5.1, the second image is quite forgiving. If the jump fails, the player can immediately try again. That is contrary to the challenges shown in Figure 5.2, as it requires the player to repeat the entire segment all over again.

Weak Mechanics

Contrary to strong mechanics, weak mechanics do not offer a wide range of challenges by themselves. For example, consider a hold/drop item mechanic in the jumping example game we have been using.

If we were to ask ourselves the previous questions on creating challenges with the hold/drop item mechanic, we would not get many diverse answers. Most of them would be variations in carrying objects around. For example, varying the path length. Any other variations would require the use of other mechanics, such as jumping, to make the path's traversal more challenging.

Weak mechanics are not "bad" mechanics, though. Weak mechanics are just not sufficient on their own to sustain the gameplay and provide enough challenge variation. On the other hand, they elevate the strong mechanics and help to integrate elements from the other cores into the game.

Consider the example in Figure 5.3, which shows a common approach to carrying objects: the player must carry the key to open a gate. A trivial example would require the player to move linearly from where the key is towards the gate. A more challenging approach would require other mechanics, such as jumping.

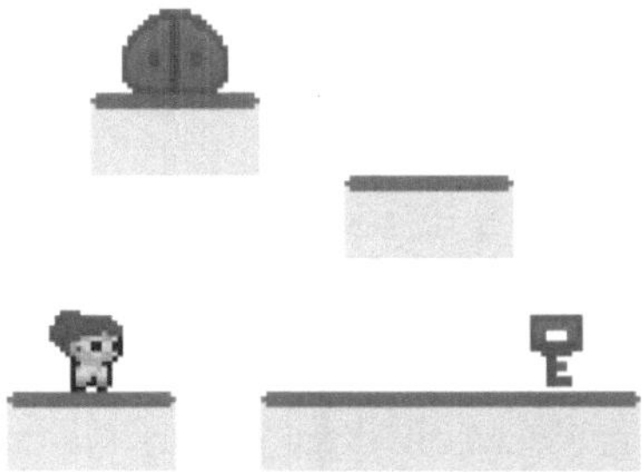

Figure 5.3: Example of the Jumping Mechanic (strong mechanic) with the Hold Mechanic (weak mechanic).

There are ways of strengthening weak mechanics. The hold mechanic, for example, could have a balancing aspect. As the player moves around holding an object, it needs to be balanced. Otherwise, it will fall to the ground. This change might transform the holding mechanic towards a stronger one as more opportunities arise, such as using heavier/lighter items.

On the other hand, not all weak mechanics need to be strengthened. The hold and balancing mechanic might sound fun, but it might increase the overall challenge, making it more anxiety-inducing and stressful to some players.

Some games and genres can also be built mostly on weak mechanics. Visual Novels [17], for example, when played mostly by reading and selecting dialogue options, do not offer specific strong mechanics. Reading and selecting dialogue options do not provide many challenges, but that is not their purpose. The goal and purpose of the game are leaned towards the other cores, such as `Narrative` and `Aesthetics`.

A good strong mechanic is half the criteria for the **complete prototype**. Moreover, the exercise of generating challenges for strong mechanics can easily lead you to a goal for the **complete prototype**.

Using Figure 5.2 as an example, if the challenge is completed when the player reaches the third platform, that could be the prototype's goal. More broadly speaking, the solution to the challenge is the goal.

It might sound obvious at first, but accepting the use of these challenges as the goal is somewhat of a struggle for beginner game designers. As stated in the previous parts of this book (Sections

2.3 and Chapter 3), a common struggle while designing a game is getting away from more abstract game goals, such as telling a story or teaching a subject. Starting from more straightforward and concrete goals for the initial stages is practical and easier, although, for some reason, less intuitive.

Having more abstract goals on the horizon is okay, but they will come later. Focus on your **complete prototype** first. Adjusting and adapting your game once it is playable will be easier.

Mechanics Strength in Non-Digital Games

Consider that some of the discussions between strong and weak mechanics apply just the same to non-digital games. The concept game `Family Tree` has negotiation as a main mechanic. Players must talk to each other and agree on an outcome to proceed. As seen in previous examples for this concept game in Section 3.2, we can plan the initial discussions to be simpler (almost everyone gets a positive outcome), and, as the game progresses, plan more complex discussions that have more elements at stake (in which fewer players can achieve a positive outcome).

On the other hand, empirically, I see that many of the mechanics and interactions in board and card games tend to be more towards the `Economy` core rather than the `Mechanics`, as they do more with strategy and use of resources rather than on how players interact. `Family Tree`, though, has a strong mechanic that is part of the `Mechanics` core.

Moreover, consider that negotiation as a mechanic is trivial when done in a non-digital environment but might be a struggle for digital games. Non-digital games have the mechanical advantage of having access to more humane activities without the concern of how they would be implemented.

Reflecting on these limitations and advantages of different media can also help to design and playtest mechanics in the early prototype stages. Even if you are working on a digital game, prototype and playtest with non-digital assets, such as paper prototypes, can already achieve a similar experience or serve as a good experimentation phase before committing to the final version. The other way around is also valid. I have seen a fair share of student projects working on board games with different dice types and other lucky-based mechanisms. Most of the time, it was more efficient for them to implement their dice and mechanisms in a computer program and play the game to fine-tune it rather than constantly build them physically.

5.2 PLAYER, LEVEL, AND GAME MECHANICS

Besides the distinction between strong and weak mechanics, for planning and development reasons, it is also good to separate mechanics into three categories:

Player Mechanics: Mechanics that the player controls and activates.

Level Mechanics: Mechanics that are part of the level, regardless of the player, even if they can be controlled and activated by the player.

Game Mechanics: Mechanics that are part of the game system as a whole, regardless of the level or the player, even if they can be controlled and activated by the player.

These categories are not extensive nor aim to label every type of mechanical interaction in the game. Still, they help with the initial discussions on strong and weak game mechanics and act as good cornerstones for planning and prototyping. Let us examine how that happens.

The previous section (Section 5.1) aimed entirely at Player Mechanics. Mechanics that the player has control over, like jumping or negotiating with other players. Often, the one mechanic you will plan for your **complete prototype** is a Player Mechanic because you need the players to engage on it to playtest the game. Moreover, the goal for the **complete prototype** is likely related to this Player Mechanic.

Level Mechanics belong to the levels, regardless of whether they appear in only one level of the game or all. I am using the term "level" here, which has a strong digital-game connotation, but you can also understand the turns, phases, and challenges in a non-digital game as levels.

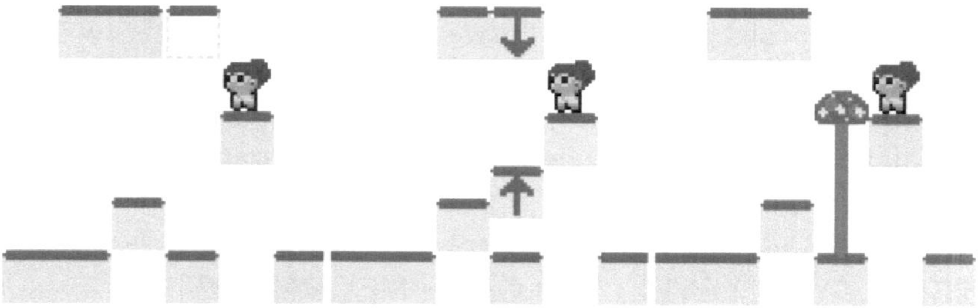

Figure 5.4: Different types of Level Mechanics for the 2D Platformer Game: A disappearing block; Moveable blocks; A Jumpy-Mushroom.

Level Mechanics tend to be simpler and even considered weak mechanics as they do not create many variations for challenges. However, the combination of Level and Player Mechanics will likely produce many possibilities. Consider the examples in Figure 5.4.

The first image in Figure 5.4 has a disappearing block (the block with a dotted outline). It changes, from time to time, between being solid and being transparent. The player can only land and jump from it when it is solid. It is clear how this mechanic requires other, stronger mechanics, such as jumping, to provide more challenges.

The second image in Figure 5.4 has moving blocks that move according to their arrows. The block could move on its own or be activated by the player. Let us explore both possibilities:

Blocks move on their own: With that, the blocks continuously move towards their arrow, and, given some circumstances (such as colliding with other blocks), they change their paths.

Blocks move when interacting with the player: With that, the block moves in the direction they are facing when the player interacts with them (land on them, for example).

Notice that with these options, we can significantly change how the game is played. In the first two approaches (disappearing blocks and moving blocks), the game has a more traditional timing-based gameplay, which players with a good sense of dexterity and reflexes might enjoy. The other approach, interactable moving blocks, shifts away from the timing-based gameplay and transforms the game into a strategy experience in which the player must first think about how to interact with the blocks to progress.

The final image shows yet another approach which changes the experience: the jumpy mushroom. The jumpy-mushroom is a more physics-based mechanic in which the player can bounce and jump further from it based on variables such as mass, speed, gravity, and angle. This third option is not necessarily a strategic gameplay nor entirely timing-based gameplay. It is more of a physics-based gameplay, with room for exploration and experimentation.

Finally, Game Mechanics belong to the game's systems, regardless of the level and the player. Game Mechanics (or Game Systems) are generally more complex than the other types of mechanics as they spam over all others. For example, the mechanics for moving through different levels are part of the game mechanics. Collecting and using pick-ups and collectables in games is often part of the Game Mechanics (remember the example from `Another Starry Sky`, in Section 3.2?).

To better grasp the difference between Player, Level, and Game Mechanics, let us briefly examine the concept games, `Family Tree` and `Another Starry Sky`:

Player, Level, and Game Mechanics: Family Tree

PLAYER MECHANICS

The negotiation mechanic is a strong mechanic in which players have to discuss with each other to decide the outcome of a given objective, goal, or task.

Players also have mechanics regarding drawing cards from the different decks and using them as they want.

LEVEL MECHANICS

The objectives and goals drawn by the cards that trigger negotiations are the game's levels. In a sense, each set-up for negotiation mechanics can be understood as a level.

Simple negotiations, like deciding whether to take a young family member to a party or go alone to the gym, are examples of bare levels with no specific level mechanics.

However, some mechanics can happen only on specific levels. There can be a case in which one player must act as if they are sick (a sore throat, for example) while negotiating with the others. Roleplaying as being sick for that negotiation is an example of a level mechanic, even though the player performs it.

GAME MECHANICS

The tree growth mechanic that depends on the shared happiness points for the entire family is a Game Mechanic. It happens beyond players and levels, even if the players interact and control how it happens.

Player, Level, and Game Mechanics: `Another Starry Sky`

PLAYER MECHANICS

Flying and controlling the spaceship during the travel stages is a strong mechanic performed by the player.

The stargazing mechanic is also a player mechanic, as the player has to compare her own notes with the stars and constellations seen in the current observation point.

LEVEL MECHANICS

The travel stages are levels in `Another Starry Sky`. As already seen in previous sections, the obstacles in the level are a sort of Level Mechanics. The game can offer variations on these obstacles to expand on the Level Mechanics. Some of them can be completely static, while others can move randomly, making them more difficult to avoid.

Each observation point with its own stars and constellations can also be seen as levels. Simpler observation points might have fewer stars, which makes them easier to spot on the player's observation notes. Others might provide unique forms of interaction, such as a more advanced telescope that can see further away or even require some sort of fixing mechanic to be used by the player. These are all examples of Level Mechanics.

GAME MECHANICS

Unlocking new observation points and travel stages is a Game Mechanic in `Another Starry Sky`. As the player reaches new areas and completes tasks, others are unlocked.

Notice that in this example, this Game Mechanic is very much part of the overall game system, *i.e.*, how the game works on a higher level. Besides that, this example is not performed by the player at all; it simply happens when the conditions necessary for it are present.

The collectables present in the travel stages can also be part of Game Mechanics. For example, for every threshold of collectables gotten (every 10, for instance), the game might unlock a clue for what happened to the mysterious space vessel. Even if the collectables are part of the travel stages (levels) and they were collected by the player, the mechanic in which their accumulation triggers a new game event happens regardless of the player and the levels. It is triggered by the game itself, and for that, it can be seen as a Game Mechanic.

Remember: Mechanics are Flexible

Finally, there are two important considerations when using the labelling of Player, Level, and Game Mechanics. The first one is that these labels are not fixed. Mechanics are flexible. We can change them as we like to achieve our goals.

A Level Mechanic can be transformed into a Player Mechanic by assigning it to the player. Getting back to Figure 5.4, the player could be given the ability to move blocks, which would enforce the puzzle-esque aspect of the game. Moreover, we could add Level Mechanics to control how certain blocks react to the moving mechanic, such as blocks that cannot move at all and blocks that can only move for a given amount of steps, as exemplified in Figure 5.5.

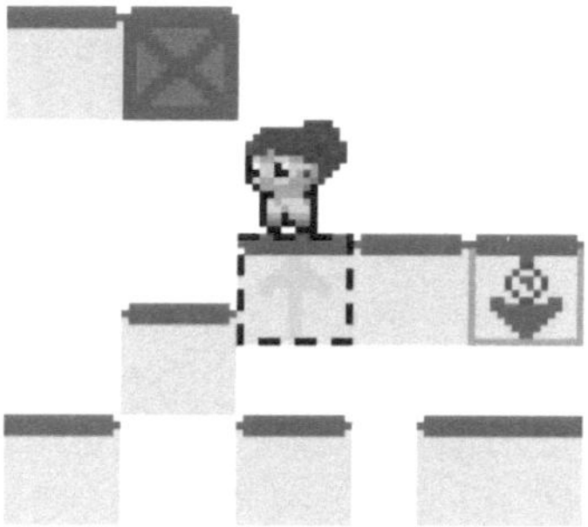

Figure 5.5: Example of a new level layout in which the Movable Block mechanic is a Player Mechanic.

Changing the ownership of Player and Level Mechanics is a good and creative way of generating new experiences. It is good to know this possibility while performing the first playtest sessions with your **complete prototype**. The sooner you realise a Level Mechanic would work better as a Player Mechanic, or vice-versa, the less effort will be required to implement the change.

Although we discussed the interchangeability of Player and Level Mechanics all three types are interchangeable. A Game Mechanic can be transformed into a Player Mechanic by allowing the player to activate it directly of their own will or to happen only in specific moments in a level.

For example, unlocking new clues using collectables in `Another Starry Sky` could be changed from automatic to only available in specific observation points, each one with their conversion rate[2]. That would make this mechanic more of a Level Mechanic than a Game Mechanic.

Nevertheless, this process might not work for all mechanics. The tree growth mechanic from `Family Tree` makes more sense as a Game Mechanic that is activated regardless of the level and the player. Keeping it as a Game Mechanic enforces the game's purpose and message, which is one of community rather than an individual choice (player) or an occasional choice (level).

[2]More on conversion rates in the `Economy` part, in Chapter 8.

Implementation Complexity

The second consideration is more relevant to digital games and games with a significant software development aspect. This labelling has a significant role in the complexity estimation of the mechanics' implementation. Generally, we can see the complexity of these tasks following this rule:

$$\text{Level Mechanics} \leq \text{Player Mechanics} \leq \text{Game Mechanics}$$

Level Mechanics are often self-contained and have smaller/simpler side effects and consequences, which makes them easier to implement, test, and integrate into the game. Player Mechanics, however, are structural to the game and will certainly repeat throughout the game. For that, they require more thought during their testing and integration. Besides that, player mechanics often have more side effects and consequences, which makes them harder to implement.

Finally, Game Mechanics span over the entire game, which makes them more complex due to their difficult integration with other parts of the game and other systems. Testing and integrating Game Mechanics is also complex due to a more extensive set of side effects and consequences they might have, besides being generally harder to trigger as they have more requirements to happen compared to Player and Level Mechanics.

Game Mechanics are also usually related to one or more GAR cycles, which makes them even more coupled with other game elements.

Planning Mechanics

In terms of planning, especially for the early versions of your **complete prototype**, I recommend you to stick to a maximum of 2 Player Mechanics, up to 4 different Level Mechanics, and only 1 Game Mechanic. These numbers are empirical and usually work well for me, as with those, I can generate a good number of levels and challenges for the **complete prototype**.

As a side note on this count, locomotion type of mechanics, such as walking in the 2D Platformer from the images in this chapter or controlling the spaceship in `Another Starry Sky`, should not count towards the limit to 2 Player Mechanics, as they are often too basic for a minimal level of interactivity.

On the other hand, jumping is usually quite a strong mechanic, and I often consider it part of this count. Jumping allows for a wider range of motion and exploration that can undermine other mechanics. If your player can simply jump on top of an obstacle, any other mechanic that deals with that obstacle becomes obsolete. Because of that, it is common to see some games transform the jumping mechanic into a Level Mechanic that is only available in specific portions of the level, reducing its impact.

Consider those aspects when planning your mechanics. If a certain mechanic is too strong to be available all the time, then changing it to a Level or a Game Mechanic can maintain it while keeping its impact under control. Temporary power-ups and limited resources are other possible solutions to handle these cases, which are part of the `Economy` core.

5.3 INSIDE AND OUTSIDE GAME ELEMENTS

Not all interactions in a game happen within the game and its mechanics. Some interactions happen beyond the game but influence it directly. These **Outside Game Elements** are another interesting aspect to consider when working with the `Mechanics` core, as they can be triggered and influenced by the elements that belong directly to the game, the **Inside Game Elements**.

Outside Game Elements are more commonly noted in multiplayer experiences, as the dynamic between players happens outside the game but directly influences it. Some authors refer to this dynamic simply as **Social Interaction**: the purposeful and bilateral communication between people [61].

For example, while playing a game, one player might make funny remarks, increasing everyone's enjoyment, even if the remark has nothing to do with the game. On the other hand, players engaged in idle talk might miss some opportunities in the game and feel the game was unfair. As a game designer, there are not many tools to control these events, but we can explore how good interactions can be facilitated.

Generally, allowing and stimulating player communication is a good way of achieving interesting Outside Game Elements. For example, `Family Tree` is mainly based on players talking to each other because of the negotiation mechanic. The game does not (necessarily) enforce how the negotiations are done. They happen outside the boundaries of the game. It only gets back to the game once the negotiation is concluded and the players proceed with the outcome of it (by sharing Happiness points, for example).

Notice that, although the negotiation might involve only two players, others can interfere as there are no ways of truly forbidding them from doing so. That is a good thing. These spontaneous events might enhance the experience for the players involved, letting the players take more ownership of their gameplay experience.

You should only consider restricting it if that is important for the game's purpose. You could do so, for example, by introducing restrictions, such as using Level Mechanics: maybe a specific stage in `Family Tree` has two family members on a road trip, then they have to make their negotiation in another space (another room, for example) away from the other players. That would enforce the one-to-one negotiation while still providing enough flexibility and context to the players (the latter, clearly done using the `Narrative` core).

Management activities, such as resource management and task division, are often good sources for Outside Game Elements. If the game does not provide any mechanism for it to be done fairly or automatically, the players will likely engage in doing so on their own, even creating rules and systems for it that are completely alien to the game's system.

In the amazing "The Proteus Paradox: How Online Games and Virtual Worlds Change Us - and How They Don't", Nick Yee presents many situations in which these sorts of events unfold in games [62], which include players managing team activities with sign up sheets, schedules, contingency plans, teaching strategies, and given instructions during the game.

Considering Outside Game Elements

While planning and prototyping your mechanics, which are your Inside Game Elements, consider what sort of Outside Game Elements can be triggered and to which extent your game motivates them. Furthermore, assess them during playtest. Consider if any of them are enhancing or harming the experience.

In `Family Tree`, a stubborn and selfish player might ruin the experience by not negotiating with peers and draining the group's energy. We could design a mechanic that punishes such behaviour as a "fatigue" mechanism in which players can vote for bad behaviour and remove and redistribute Happiness points from that player. On the other hand, letting the players solve this situation by talking to each other outside the game might be a more effective solution that emphasises the game's purpose. There are no easy solutions for these situations. It is a matter of playtesting, experimenting, and empathising with the players.

Outside Game Elements in Single Player Games

Although this discussion has been solely in a multiplayer setting, single-player games can also provide Outside Game Elements. Still, those are more likely to be planned by design rather than happen spontaneously. For example, a single-player game might ask players to take real-life pictures or research information online.

Let us use the concept game **`Another Starry Sky`** as an example. The constellations in the observation points might reference real-life painters and their art pieces. The player can figure them out on a lucky base, but the game could give hints so that the player must research outside the game to discover the painters. Some game designers might dislike this approach, as it makes the game less "self-contained", but it can be a rewarding experience for the player.

Metagaming as Outside Game Element

Finally, besides the number of players involved, another aspect that often falls under the lens of Outside Game Elements is metagame strategies [1, 16]. Reiterating the concept, metagame strategies are outside game discussions about the game and how to play it better or more efficiently.

Metagame strategies are a topic of their own and are more closely related to the `Economy` core. Still, the important aspect to consider in terms of mechanics is how they can assess the player's experience. For example, metagame strategies can show you which mechanics are being under or overvalued by players and how more experienced players make these evaluations.

Furthermore, even if it is more common to see metagame strategy discussions on games with a large user base, it also happens on smaller scales, such as during game jams and playtest sessions, as players gather around and hint each other on better ways of advancing through the game.

5.4 OTHER APPROACHES

Using Game Essences

There are other ways of starting your process from the `Mechanics` if you struggle with figuring out which mechanic to start with. One is based on starting with objective categories, also known as **Game Essences**. These essences are well presented in the great "Game Design Workshop: A Playcentric Approach" by Tracy Fullerton [63]. You can see a short list of selected essences below:

Capture: The objective is to take or destroy something from the game or other players.

Race: To achieve an objective faster than the other players or game elements.

Alignment: To arrange elements spatially or conceptually given some rules and constraints.

Forbidden Act: To endure the longest without performing the forbidden act.

Fullerton describes way more essences in the book, but these give a good insight into their use and provide a wide range of ideas.

You can use these essences as a base to establish your game's goal and then explore possible ways of achieving it. These possibilities will be your mechanics. Let us use Capture as an example with the concept game `Memories by the Sea`, in which the objective is to collect all the sea shells. The following proposals could be made for the mechanics:

1. **Finding and interacting with them:** The player must move to their location to collect them.

2. **Digging them from the sand:** The player uses some equipment that collects them.

3. **Using a (un)reliable maps:** The players must use some tool to orient themselves and find the shells.

4. **Listening to their specific sounds:** Seashells emit music, and the player must listen to it to locate them.

Each one of these mechanics has peculiarities. The first one is simpler and has more to do with the level and Level Mechanics to achieve various challenges. The second one is more mechanical, as we can explore multiple ways in which the player controls the equipment. The third one is more puzzle-based and requires some sense of orientation skill from the players. The last one is somewhat more artistic for its use of sound, which pairs well with the `Aesthetics` core.

Notice that although the definition of the Capture essence mentions "take" and "destroy", collect is also a valid and less aggressive interpretation of it.

For that, you should not read the essences as if they are strict rules. They serve as helping tools to explore possibilities. As we discussed Capture, let us look at the other three and how we can interpret them to create ideas and mechanics.

Race

Race is often understood as a literal race to get somewhere physically, like a running competition. However, race is a broader term that embraces achieving something first rather than getting somewhere first. For example, a game in which players must collect a certain number of tokens to win is a race, even if they do not move at all. You can also race against time if you must complete a certain objective before the timer runs out.

Alignment

Alignment is often understood as placing objects in a certain way or a given position, but it is better to understand it as connecting elements. Connecting the stars to form a constellation in `Another Starry Sky` is a form of alignment, even if we are not moving the elements from their original positions. It also does not need to be in the form of a puzzle. An assembly line game in which a continuous sequence of elements is paired with others is also an alignment activity.

Forbidden Act

Finally, the Forbidden Act is about playing by restricting the player from performing a certain action or activity. It has nothing to do with allowing players to commit forbidden or illegal real-life activities in the game. A comedy-based board game in which players cannot laugh or an exergame in which the player cannot stop jumping are examples of the Forbidden Act.

Forbidden Act is also great as an exercise tool to break out from repetitive mechanics. Since many platformer games are based on jumping, a platformer in which jumping is forbidden or highly demotivated can create new and interesting experiences.

As stated previously, there are other essences and combining them is another valid approach. Additionally, some games might have such distinct gameplay that it does not fit in any specific essence. Sometimes, the lack of labels can free your process, creativity and productivity.

Game essences are also beneficial in game jam contexts where you are given a specific theme. You can try the theme against the essences to brainstorm ideas and mechanics. For example, if the theme is "waves", you could come up with the following pairing:

Capture: The objective is to rescue a small boat from the sea. You do so by controlling a bigger ship and avoiding the waves.

Race: Players surf the waves to get points, and the first one to get 1000 points wins. You do so by performing surfing tricks and manoeuvres.

Alignment: The beach areas have different safety levels depending on their waves, which shift with the tide. Depending on their swimming skill level, you must allocate the swimmers to safe areas. You do so by dragging and dropping the swimmers to the correct places.

Forbidden Act: The waves bring plastic and trash from the sea to the shore. You must collect them to clear the beach, but you cannot get wet. You do so by moving back and forth in the sand, avoiding the waves and water.

Learning and Adapting from Other Games

If the essences are not helping you as you wanted or you still feel stuck, another good approach is to analyse the mechanics from other games. Explore what mechanics they provide, assess their strengths, and label them into Player, Level, and Game Mechanics. If you find something you really like, you can use all the methods proposed in this chapter to explore their variations and develop your own mechanics.

Alternatively, returning to the use of the Game Essences, consider which essences are used in these games and how you could swap them. A game based on Capture could be transformed into a Race if the objective is now timed or a competition with other players, for example.

There is no shame in being inspired by other games or starting the process by copying them. As with many creative processes, starting from a blank canvas is terrifying and crippling. The best attitude towards it is starting in any way you see viable, and from there, changes can be made. It does not matter if you started cooking with a burrito in mind and ended up with quesadillas – they are both delicious. Moreover, none of your players will keep track of all the changes and decisions you made while working on your prototype. They will mostly only ever see the final game. The history of how it came to be only matters to you and your team.

The following chapters in the `Mechanics` part are focused on other elements that are closely related to it, such as Player Motivation in Chapter 6 and Level Design in Chapter 7.

If you are still exploring the cores, you can now move to the first chapter of which one of their parts: `Economy` in Chapter 8, `Narrative` in Chapter 11, `Aesthetics` in Chapter 14.

Otherwise, if you want to or prefer a more linear order in reading the book, just continue ahead.

CHAPTER 6

Player Motivation

THERE ARE MANY REASONS TO PLAY GAMES. In fact, the research on players' motivation is quite vast and has its foundations in many psychology theories, including the Flow Theory [33] discussed previously in Section 3.1 [64]. A meta-analysis of these studies, conducted by Hamari and Keronen in 2015, found at least 48 different studies on the subject[1] [64].

From this study, 5 were the factors that seemed to more strongly correlate to each other in motivating people to play games and were also the most investigated aspects in the findings of their analysis. They are listed below with some explanations aimed at the focus of this book.

Perceived Usefulness: How much playing enhances the player in aspects outside the game. As if playing the game is reasoned for more Outside Game Elements.

Perceived Ease of Use: How easy and intuitive is playing the game? That concerns how the game deals with players' Inaptitude and Ignorance.

Playing Intention: The player's interest in playing or continuing to play games. Which can be loosely related to being in the Flow state and keeping the player engaged.

[1] To be precise, 48 were selected studies for their meta-analysis. The actual result they got without any filters was over 900.

DOI: 10.1201/9781003351191-6

Enjoyment: The player's perception of how enjoyable and entertaining the game is. There is a wide range of understandings of what people can enjoy in a game, as discussed in Section 2.1.

Attitude: The player's perception of playing games as a positive or a negative experience, and how much they enjoy it.

Although Player's Intent and Attitudes sound similar, we can easily see their difference using one example. The player's attitude is their overall behaviour towards games. For example, I have an open attitude towards games, and I think they all have their values and deserve attention[2]. On the other hand, the player's intent is their own will to play or continue playing a specific game. Although I am open to games, I am not very interested in games that focus too much on violence. To use a food analogy, you might have an open attitude towards experimenting with different sorts and styles of pizza, but you might not intend to try the ones with fruits.

It is important to consider that the meta-analysis made by Hamari and Keronen also distinguishes between hedonistic and utilitarian games. Hedonitic games are those played for entertainment, while useful as those played for other purposes, such as education. However, they do not distinguish between pre-game motivation and in-game motivation, which is explained by the work of Bostan and Sezen [65]. Pre-game motivation is more akin to marketing, as it motivates someone to pick and play a game, while in-game motivation is that of the player to continue playing it.

As stated in the earlier parts of this book, marketing and other elements related to selling the game, which is part of the pre-game motivation, will not be explored by this book.

Many studies are focused on in-game motivation, and they are often based on theories such as the Self-Determination Theory [66] and Player Typologies [62, 65, 67]. This chapter explores these theories and how they apply to the Cores of Game Design, specifically to the `Mechanics` core.

---

[2]Except, of course, when I personally disagree with their purposes or (lack of) morals.

6.1 EXTRINSIC AND INTRINSIC MOTIVATION

Motivation theorists often discuss two distinct types of motivation: extrinsic and intrinsic motivation [68]. **Extrinsic motivation** is when you are motivated for the outcome. For example, when you perform a given task because of the reward you get from it. Extrinsic motivation is often paired with the perceived usefulness of a task.

Contrarily, **intrinsic motivation** is when you perform tasks for their pleasure and leisure without any meaningful reward or justification beyond the task itself. Intrinsic motivation is often paired with the entertainment of the task.

Some studies suggest that even in similar conditions and expertise, intrinsically motivated people, as opposed to extrinsically motivated, show better performance, persistence and creativity [66]. However, intrinsic motivation is not easily achievable while designing games. The use of extrinsic rewards, threats (obstacles, for example), pressure (difficulty), and imposed goals in games, for example, is known to undermine intrinsic motivation [66].

For example, GAR Cycles, as explained in Section 3.4, are good tools for teaching and guiding the player using extrinsic motivation. The player is given a certain reward for achieving the established goal. One could argue that the option to partake in the GAR cycle could be intrinsic, as the player "intrinsically decides" to do it, but that is not necessarily true, as there are still extrinsic rewards.

On the other hand, we could use a similar perspective as presented by Schell in "The Art of Game Design" [20], that extrinsic and intrinsic motivations work better when seen in a gradient: some activities might be more extrinsically with a bit of intrinsic motivation to them, for example.

Besides that, there are different levels of extrinsic motivation. Ryan and Deci, in their important paper "Self-Determination Theory and the Facilitation of Intrinsic Motivation, Social Development, and Well-Being" [66], label four types of extrinsic motivation, which are:

- **External Regulation:** Motivation comes from external rewards and punishment, much like Operant Conditioning, and, by consequence, GAR Cycles. For example, if you are doing a task in a game to receive a prize.

- **Introjected Regulation:** A small part of the motivation comes from the players, regardless of the external motivation. For example, there is a challenging task in the game that you want to do to test your own skills, regardless of its reward.
- **Identified Regulation:** There is a clear understanding of the task and its reward, which drives motivation. For example, you engage in parts of the game, understanding how they provide you with some value besides their reward.
- **Integrated Regulation:** Almost all or all of the motivation comes internally, as the reasoning and value are clear, but still done due to an external factor. In a game, it happens when your actions are all of your own volition, but you still intend to get a reward, for example. Although you want to perform them, in the end, your main motivation is the reward.

Notice that although GAR Cycles are very evident as part of the external regulation type of motivation, they can still be used in all types of motivation. The same GAR cycle can be subject to all types of regulation. The player's motivation is not necessarily static and might shift as the game progresses.

Let us use the concept game `Another Starry Sky` as an example and the GAR cycle for travelling between observation points[3]. The goal is to reach the new destination. It is achieved by avoiding obstacles and reaching the end of the level. The reward takes the form of extra resources.

- **External Regulation:** The only way to proceed through the game is to travel between observation points. The player is rewarded with new options on the new observation points and extra resources for finishing the task (Reward). The player has to repeat the travel if too many obstacles are collided with (Punishment).

[3]If you don't remember those, read them back at Section 3.4

- **Introjected Regulation:** The player takes the challenge to collect all the collectables during the travel phase, as some are quite difficult. The collectables are still required for the game's resources, but getting them all is not really necessary.
- **Identified Regulation:** The player now collects and tracks the number of collectables and manages the resources to unlock parts of the game. It is possible to complete the game without doing this, but the player wants to find the answers to the game's mystery.
- **Integrated Regulation:** The player is collecting and experiencing (almost) all aspects of the game, with the understanding that every element is connected. The player is no longer doing it for specific rewards or as a challenge but as an approach to playing the game, which ultimately is still aimed at getting the game 100% complete.

Interestingly enough, this range of regulations can be loosely mapped to the previous five motivations discussed at the beginning of the chapter:

External Regulation and Perceived Usefulness: The players undergo activities for how useful they seem to be based on rewards and punishment.

Introjected Regulation, Player Intention and Enjoyment: The players add their own will and enjoyment to the external motivation.

Identified Regulation, Perceived Usefulness and Perceived Ease of Use: The players actively engage mentally to value the activity beyond their external motivational factors.

Integrated Regulation and Attitude: The overall player's attitude towards the game changes with their knowledge, skill, and enjoyment, even if still under the external motivational factors.

From the discussion so far, it seems like most of the decisions we make as game designers are bound to only externally motivate our players, even if we provide means to achieve the integrated regulation type of external motivation, but that is not true. Many factors can trigger intrinsic motivation, some of which are intrinsic to the players. Regardless of the game design decisions, outside game elements influence how players engage in games, and those are often studied under the field of Player Typologies.

6.2 PLAYER TYPOLOGIES

Player typology or player taxonomy is a theory in which players are labelled into groups according to their motivations for playing games or, more specifically, for playing specific games. Many of the studies in the field focus on specific games and genres, especially Massive Multiplayer Online Games (MMOs) [69].

However, one of the initial and more influential studies on this topic, **Bartle's Taxonomy or 4 Player Types**, is based on analyses performed in a sort of precursor to MMO games, the MUD games [67]. MUD, which stands for Multi-User Dungeon, were text-based social online games where players engaged by writing, with barely or no graphics at all [70].

Richard Bartle studied, interviewed, and analysed players' behaviour in one specific MUD game (MUD2). The results were summarised in four main reasons why players enjoyed that game [67]:

Achievement: Enjoyment through achieving game-related goals.

Exploration: Enjoyment through discovering and exploring the game and all of its aspects.

Socialisation : Enjoyment through engaging, talking, and interacting with other players.

Imposition: Enjoyment through imposing themselves and their wills on top of other players, be it through domination (causing distress) or through leadership (commanding and leading).

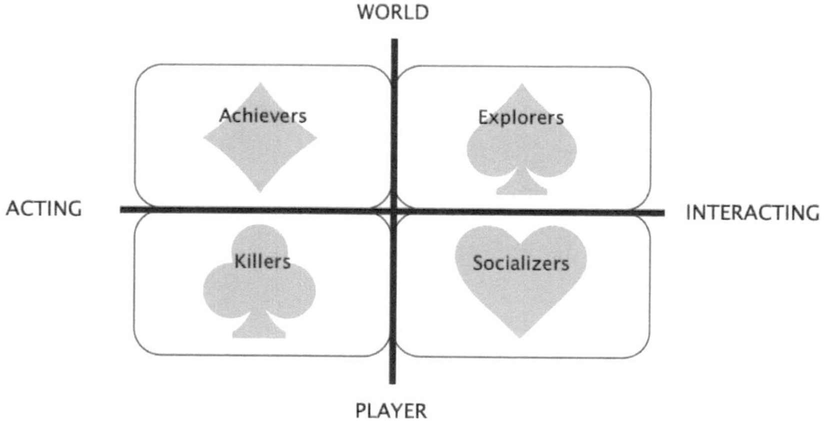

Figure 6.1: Symbols and dimensions used by Bartle's Player Types.

These four reasons were then mapped to what we know as **Bartle's 4 Player Types: Achievers, Explorers, Socialisers, and Killers.** These player types are also mapped into two dimensions: action versus interaction and world-oriented versus player-oriented. Figure 6.1 displays the types and dimensions used.

Achievers and Explorers are more interested in the game itself (World). However, Achievers want to play with the world (Act), while Explorers want to interact and explore it (Interact). On the other hand, Socialisers and Killers are more interested in interacting with other players (Player). However, Socialisers want to interact with the players (Interact). In contrast, Killers want to impose themselves upon them (Act)[4].

We can also use traditional French-suited playing cards as an easy mnemonic to remember the player types. Achievers are the Diamonds, as those are trophies to show off for the goals they achieved. Explorers are the Spades, who are "digging" the game space for new findings. Socialisers are the Hearts, as they are interested in the human interactions provided by the game. Finally, Killers are the Clubs, using them to impose themselves on others.

Bartle discovered that MUD players could be labelled within these four categories and that the interactions between them were

[4]A longer discussion on the Killer player type is presented at the end of this section, at the block **Leaders and Killers**.

important to keep the game interesting and alive. His original article mentions fascinating ways they complement and emphasise each other. The following quote is a good example of these [67, p .5]:

> *A sharp reduction in the number of explorers for whatever reason could mean a gradual reduction in achievers, who get bored if they're not occasionally told of different hoops they can jump through for points; this could affect the number of socialisers (the fewer players there are, the less there is to talk about), and it would certainly lower the killer population (due to a general lack of suitable victims).*

Bartle's taxonomy is often questioned due to its limited experimentation on other genres and statistical validation [69]. However, those points are addressed by Bartle himself in many of his publications and talks. Moreover, in his book, "Designing Virtual Worlds" [71], a more in-depth analysis of the types is presented, which includes the addition of a 3rd dimension (Intrinsic versus Extrinsic Motivation), generating a total of 8 player types (Griefer, Networker, Politician, Friend, Opportunist, Scientist, Planner, and Hacker).

Regardless of the dimensionality, Bartle's taxonomy is meant for multiplayer games. We can study and attempt to use them in single-player games, but that is not what they were meant for. That is the same for other studies and taxonomies, such as the one presented by Yee [72] and Squire and Steinkuehler [73]. Besides that, as Bartle's player types are based on MUD games, they were not tested or validated in other games, such as traditional tabletop games and MMOs.

Still, Bartle's Taxonomy provides a good introduction to player types, their concepts and consequences for the overall game design and development process. Other authors often cite and use them, even in contexts outside game design, such as the popular Octalisys Gamification Framework by Yu-Kai Chou [74].

We can also loosely align how each of the Cores of Game Design can allow the four-player types to follow a simple framework: How can a given core provide means for the player to achieve goals, explore possibilities, interact with other players, and impose themselves on others?

As we are in the `Mechanics` part of the book, we could answer this framework as follows:

Achievers: Which mechanics are used to complete the game's goal?

Explorers: How much freedom for exploration do the mechanics provide?

Socialisers: Which forms of social interaction arise from the mechanics?

Killers: How much does the game allow dominance and player management using its mechanics?

As stated by Bartle himself, these types are not static. They depend on the game being played [71]. You might have an achiever's motivation while playing **`Another Starry Sky`** but enjoy **`Family Tree`** for its social aspect. Moreover, your motivation may change as you play the same game, be it during a play session or multiple sessions. You might have started **`Memories by the Sea`** to complete its goals as an achiever. Still, as you have figured out all the nice views and places to go on the beach, your motivation might move towards exploration and experimentation.

A similar approach and conclusions could be reached using other player typologies, such as the Quantic Foundry 9 Player Types, by Nick Yee [75] (Acrobat, Gardener, Slayer, Skirmisher, Gladiator, Ninja, Bounty Hunter, Architect, Bard); the 7 BrainHex Archetypes (Seeker, Survivor, Daredevil, Mastermind, Conqueror, Socialiser, Achiever), by Nacke, Bateman and Mandryk [76]; the seven-player types based on Game Dynamics Preferences (Mercenary, Adventurer, Commander, Daredevil, Companion, Patterner, Explorer), by Vahlo et al., [77]; and the list goes on and on.

It is important to understand that players' typologies and motivation models are all based on qualitative studies and statistical data. Therefore, they are all forms of generalisation. No model will be perfect and will fit every type of game or every type of player. The best approach towards those models is to look for how they can be translated into your game design and development process.

We could propose, for example, there are three types of players in `Family Tree`: **Arborists**, who want to complete the game and make the tree grow; **Conciliators**, who like to participate in the negotiations, even interfering on the negotiation of other team members; and **Butterflies**, which are there more for the social interaction the game provides and just want to have some time together with others.

In this sense, we could see these player types also as personas, which are fictional representations of users who share common motivations and behaviours [78]. We could use these personas when making decisions in our game design and development process, especially in the `Mechanics` context in which we design how they will interact with the game.

Moreover, we could have thought about other player types for `Family Tree`, such as the **Parasite**, which are players that only care for their own Happiness points and will take on selfish behaviour in all negotiations they are involved. It is part of the design process to decide whether to allow these other player types. One could argue that you cannot prevent someone from joining and acting as a parasite in the game, but we can design the game so as not to fulfil their motivations. Some mechanics and even balancing techniques from the `Economy` core could help with that.

Finally, Bartle's player types are meant for multiplayer games, so there is little to gain from it in single-player games (such as `Another Starry Sky`). Therefore, discussing it in those contexts is not really relevant or helpful. Also, Bartle's theory does not directly support the cores of `Aesthetics` and `Narrative`, but could still be used sparingly to help the creative process.

Leaders and Killers

The term Killer, for the 4th player type, is a bit of an unfortunate one. It has an emotional load that makes it read as someone who enjoys "killing" and "distressing" others, which is not necessarily true.[a]

Killers, as stated before, are motivated by imposition, which can manifest in two extremes: distressing and managing.

In both senses, the killer player wants to control other players, either by being annoying and dominating or by commanding and managing them [67].

The proposed **Conciliator** player type for `Family Tree`, for example, is a sort of "killer-manager type", as it is engaged in "commanding" and "guiding" the negotiation—notice also that this motivation is not necessarily a selfish one. The actions performed by the conciliator can be beneficial to the group.

This nuance is better explained in Bartle's 8 Player Type model [71], in which the new axis (Intrinsic and Extrinsic) separates the killer type into Politicians and Griefers. Politicians impose their control explicitly by taking leadership positions or intentionally causing trouble. Griefers implicitly irritate and dominate other players, which usually makes them associated with a form of self-expression or showing off due to a lack of experience in the game.

With that, when contemplating the Killer type, consider its multiple interpretations. Do not limit your views of Killers to selfish players but also to possible positive and selfless leaders.

[a] This block is inspired by a separate and extended piece on the subject published in my online blog. You can read it at http://tinyurl.com/killer-cgd.

CHAPTER 7

Level Design

FOR THIS BOOK, WE USE THE TERM LEVEL as a planned sequence of one or more game challenges and activities with a given goal.

This definition does limit levels to space or organisation, even though game levels are often associated with environments and physical (virtual) spaces. This is so that this definition can be used in non-digital games. As discussed in Section 5.2, we can understand the stages and phases of a board game, for example, as levels.

Therefore, for this book, we understand **Level Design** as the design and layout of levels through creating and organising sequential challenges for specific goals. The term goal here is used not necessarily as the game's goal (how to win the game) but also as specific **design goals** (such as teaching a game mechanic or telling a piece of the story).

This definition is not aligned with other books, especially those written explicitly about Level Design, such as "Beginning Game Level Design" by Feil and Scattergood [79], or Totten's "Architectural Approach to Level Design" [80]. Both are excellent books on the topic, but their focus is primarily on environments, spaces, and the layout of elements rather than on a general notion of challenges and goals. Still, many of their concepts and ideas are used as a base for this chapter.

This chapter is placed within the `Mechanics` part as it is easier to approach Level Design from a mechanical perspective. Besides that, it goes well with our previous discussion on Player, Level, and Game Mechanics of Section 5.2. Moreover, it is hard to tackle levels

DOI: 10.1201/9781003351191-7

and level design without a **complete prototype**, which needs an established game mechanic (and goal), as you need them to assess your levels.

Surely, this process would be different if you started your process from the other cores. For example the `Economy` core would unlock feedback loops to progress through levels (Chapter 8); the `Narrative` core would use plot points to advance through levels (Chapter 11); and, the `Aesthetics` core would play with mood changes to signify levels (Chapter 14).

The rest of this chapter is organised as follows. First, we discuss the Force-Action Framework again, but now with a focus on pacing, teaching, and conceptual challenge organisation in Section 7.1. After that, we discuss the multiple forms in which we can organise challenges in levels in Section 7.2. From that, we discuss a more specific strategy for allowing player's agency through the use of Risk and Reward techniques in Section 7.3. Finally, in the vein of other level design books, some of these theories are applied in a space-based level design approach that is common in digital games in Section 7.4.

7.1 PACING AND CHALLENGES

The game's pace is the rate or speed at which events happen. This concept is compelling yet very flexible (just like mechanics). In a digital game, the rate at which new obstacles appear is part of the pace, for example. Pace involves more than harmful events, though. The rate at which the player gains new resources is also part of the game's pace.

In a card game, both the rate at which players draw and play cards, as well as the speed at which these players progress through victory, are all parts of the pace.

As you can see, almost every aspect related to how the game is "moving" and "progressing" is pace. Pacing also plays a crucial role in the Flow of the game (Section 3.1). A good pace, whatever it means for your game, will naturally allow for a good sense of flow, as it will help to keep the players focused and engaged.

However, as we know, Flow is very much related to a sense of anxiety versus boredom, which is associated with the game

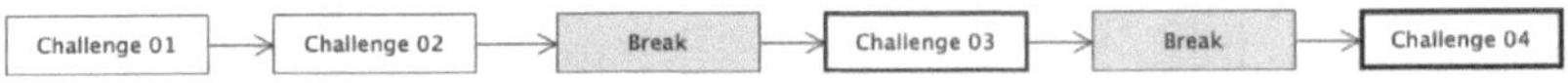

Figure 7.1: Simple example of a linear pace: challenges and breaks. The thicker the outline, the harder the challenge.

challenges. That's where pace and challenges meet. Moreover, the lack of challenges, such as breaks or relaxation, also plays an important role in this discussion. Figure 7.1 shows a conceptual and abstract view of a game's pace with 5 challenges and 2 breaks.

A **challenge** can be any event in the game that requires players to use the mechanics to progress. In `Another Starry Sky`, travelling between observation points can be a challenge. At the same time, segments in the travel that are populated by asteroids can also be labelled and organised as their own challenges. Notice that, by using a more generic understanding of challenge, we break from the idea of a challenge being necessarily a level, although a level will be, ultimately, a (combined) challenge.

For the board game `Family Tree`, each negotiation is a challenge. It requires players to engage in using the mechanics to progress and acquire Happiness points. If a negotiation involves multiple parts and agreements, we could see each one of them as its own challenge that, grouped, forms a bigger one. In this case, we could also understand that each negotiation is a level in `Family Tree`.

A **break** is the opposite. It is a moment in which the player is not confronted with objectives and can relax. It does not mean that players cannot engage in objectives or trigger mechanics during a break, but that those will be at the player's will instead of by design.

Breaks also happen when players solidify their new knowledge of the game. Using Figure 7.1 as an example, if Challenges 01 and 02 teach and reinforce a mechanic, then the following break could allow the player to experiment and learn more about it without interference.

I like to see this dynamic as an analogy to learning a new recipe. Let us use pickled vegetables as an example. You want to learn how to pickle cucumbers and find a good recipe for it. You followed it to the heart and managed to prepare your own pickled cucumbers. Congratulations! That was the challenge. Now that you have done

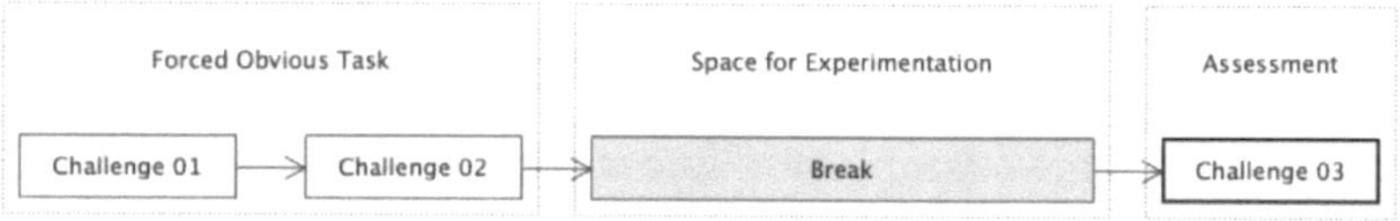

Figure 7.2: Challenges and Breaks seen as part of the Forced Action Framework.

it, you can try the same recipe again to reinforce your learning and possibly fix small mistakes you made on the first try. This second time is the equivalent of our Challenge 02 in Figure 7.1. Now that you have learned how to pickle, why not try onions or carrots now? This experimentation is the break. You are not following a set challenge anymore; you are just experimenting and learning.

This layout of challenges and breaks can also be used to set up the Forced Action Framework, as we saw in Section 3.3. Figure 7.2 shows how the first 3 challenges and breaks we just discussed can be organised under the three phases of the Forced Action Framework.

Notice how the Forced Obvious Task actually encompasses two challenges instead of one. That could be the case if we need to showcase two different outcomes or teach more perspectives from the same mechanic using multiple examples, which are all still obvious and straightforward.

The Space for Experimentation is the entire period of the break between challenges (01 & 02 and 03). Notice that experimentation does not necessarily mean "without any difficulties" but more as no intended lesson or control over the player.

Finally, the Assessment happens in Challenge 03, which is not even the last one in our initial concept in Figure 7.1. Still, it is planned to validate the lessons taught through Challenges 01 and 02.

Another important remark is that, as a common approach to Flow, each step in this organisation results in raising the difficulty and tension in the game. Figure 7.3 shows an example of how the tension (sense of difficulty and pressure) could be perceived while playing through this sequence.

Breaks are used to lower the tension and reduce the player's anxiety, which helps to keep them away from an anxious state. However, as the overall tension rises, given the increase in the

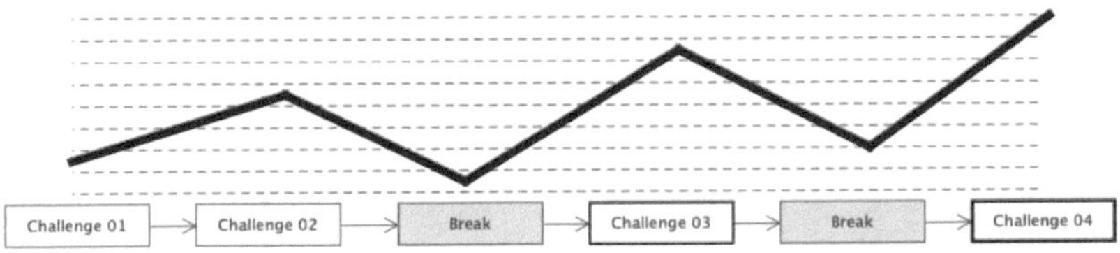

Figure 7.3: Difficulty and tension according to the challenges and breaks.

challenges, breaks have a lower potential to reduce it. That is just natural. Imagine that you are doing some sort of series of exams to get your chef's diploma: the break before facing the final exam is never as relaxing as the break before facing the very first one.

However, this order of challenges and breaks is linear, which might not be the case for your game. The following section explores other types of ordering challenges and their outcomes.

7.2 LINEAR, NON-LINEAR, AND RANDOM CHALLENGE ORDER

There are three main types of orders: **Linear**, **Non-Linear**, and **Random**. You can form other orders by mixing those, which, essentially, will be a form of non-linear order.

Linear Order: When challenges follow each other orderly and consecutively, with a planned and steady increase in difficulty and tension.

Non-Linear Order: When challenges or sets of challenges are available for the player to decide the order in which they will be taken. It is still possible to control the increase of difficulty and tension by gating sets of challenges.

Random Order: When challenges available to the player are not planned by design nor entirely part of a player's decision. There can still be some sort of control by gating the options and also some level of agency if the player still has more than one available option at a time.

Linear order is very much what we have discussed previously. One challenge is followed by the other as designed. Players have no control over which one to overcome next, but they can at least control their timing within breaks to when they want to move on to the next challenge. The player agency can be increased in these cases if the player can revisit previous challenges, for example. That way, even though the progress is still linear, the player has some options within the game.

Non-Linear Order is common in open-world games or games where the player has a multitude of possible challenges to take in no particular order. Consider in `Another Starry Sky`, for example, that every observation point can lead to 3 other observation points for the player to choose.

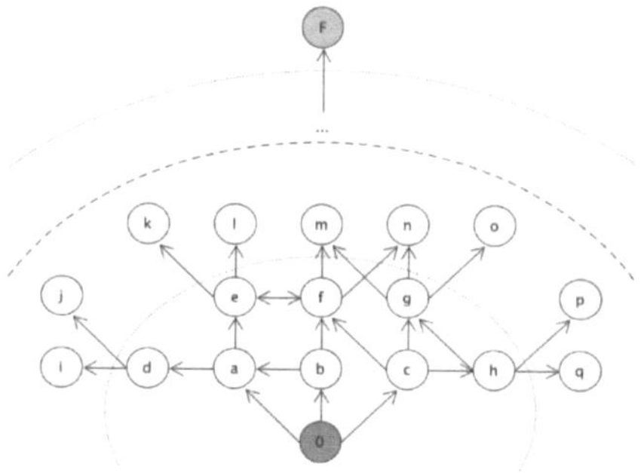

Figure 7.4: Example of possible, non-linear paths and challenges.

Notice that although the player has control over which path to take in Non-Linear Orders, it is still possible to design and plan the increase in difficulty. As stated before, we can use **gates** for that. The idea of a gate is a mechanism that blocks the player's progress until a certain condition of satisfaction is met.

For example, back to `Another Starry Sky`, we could block paths that lead to an outer ring in the observation points until the player has acquired a certain number of clues and collectables. Thus, the player could have up to 3 possible travel points, but from those, some that lead to an outer ring are blocked (gated) until the number of clues and collectables is met. Figure 7.4 illustrates these points.

For these figures, consider that the player starts at the darker sphere, numbered 0, while the observation points are identified with letters that go from a until q. From the start, the player can only move to the observation points a, b, and c. A player could follow the path $0 \rightarrow a$, and then the possible options would be the observation points d and e. If the player follows the path $a \rightarrow e$, then the available options are f, k, and l. However, k and l are in the outer ring, which means they are only available once the player reaches the conditions to open the gate.

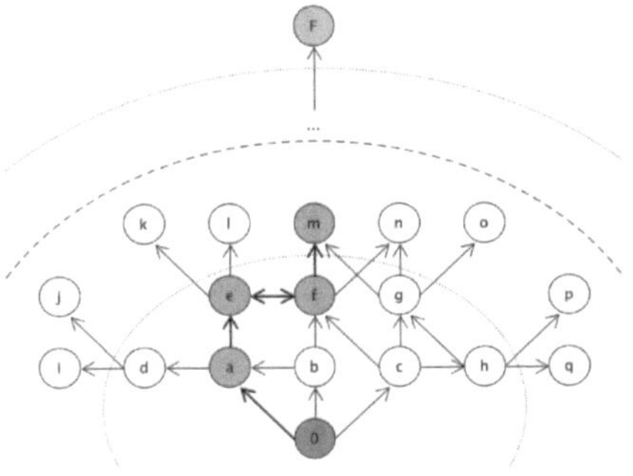

Figure 7.5: Example of a chosen player path given the options available.

Figure 7.5 shows a possible path taken by a player to reach the observation points in the outer ring. The path taken was $a \rightarrow e \rightarrow f \rightarrow m$. For that, we are assuming that the player can get enough collectables and clues from finishing levels a, e and f to unlock m.

Although this is a Non-Linear Order, we can nudge the player towards a Linear order, for instance, by having elements in the game to hint towards the path $a \rightarrow e \rightarrow f \rightarrow m$. For that, we would recur to elements of the `Aesthetics` and `Narrative` cores, for example. The clues you find in a could suggest that the path to e is more likely to get you a better outcome than d. That also adds to the player's agency. Players invested in the `Narrative` might experience the game in a Linear order if they just follow the nudges and hints all the time.

Another important aspect is the difficulty of each challenge. Figure 7.6 shows how we can see the difficulty in this same diagram. The thickness of each circle represents the difficulty. A thicker outline means a harder difficulty.

The balance on difficulty used in Figure 7.6 exemplifies how to design the build-up of tension on challenges using gates. Notice that all of the challenges in the outer ring have a thicker outline compared to the ones on the inside. That guarantees that the player is only challenged with higher difficulties once a certain threshold is met.

Also, notice that this organisation also allows for exploring possibilities for different player types and motivations. A player that seeks a more challenging experience might then take the path $a \rightarrow c \rightarrow g \rightarrow m$ to unlock the outer ring going through the most difficult path.

Random Order

A common misconception is to assume that a player randomly going through all possible paths would experience a sort of Random Order. Random order happens when the next steps are only slightly subject or not subject at all to the players' agencies. This is the case, for example, when drawing a card from a shuffled deck. The order in which the cards are drawn is random. The existence of multiple possible decks to draw cards allows for some level of player agency, but it is still a Random order. Randomly navigating through the levels in `Another Starry Sky` is completely subjective to the player's decision; therefore, it is ultimately a "player-randomised" Non-Linear Order.

Let us use `Family Tree` as an example for Random Order. As the events in the game depend on the cards drawn, each negotiation, as well as their respective difficulty and challenges, happens in a Random Order. To provide a better pace, we could use multiple decks or shuffle the main deck using partitions to organise the difficulty of the challenges in the game. That way, we can allow for some player agency and control the experience to improve the chances of a fair play session.

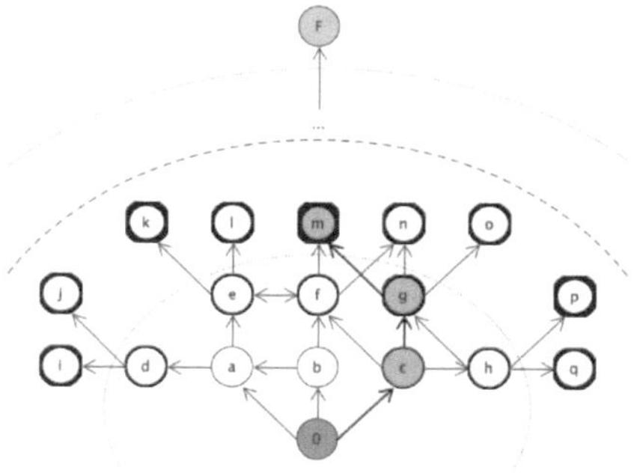

Figure 7.6: Challenges difficulties are represented by the thickness of their borders. Thicker borders mean harder challenges.

Back to digital games, another common example of random difficulty order happens in games that use procedural content generation [81]. Although, even if the challenges are generated programmatically by the game systems, it is still possible to control their outputs with information regarding difficulty, for example, which might help with controlling the pace.

As we discussed player agency many times during this session, we have not discussed what inside game elements could motivate these decisions. A common approach to it is seeing challenges and difficulties as a risk and reward mechanism.

7.3 RISK AND REWARD

Risk and Reward is a simple yet powerful concept. Its main idea is that the bigger the risk, the higher the reward associated with it. With that, we can consider how we plan our challenges and reward players accordingly, given the difficulties imposed.

For a simple example of applying Risk and Reward, let us consider Figure 7.6. Since each level has collectables and clues, the ones with a thicker outline (harder ones) should have a higher amount compared to the thinner outlines (easier ones). Therefore, players taking up a higher risk in a more difficult path will be (potentially) rewarded with more outcomes compared to players taking up fewer challenges.

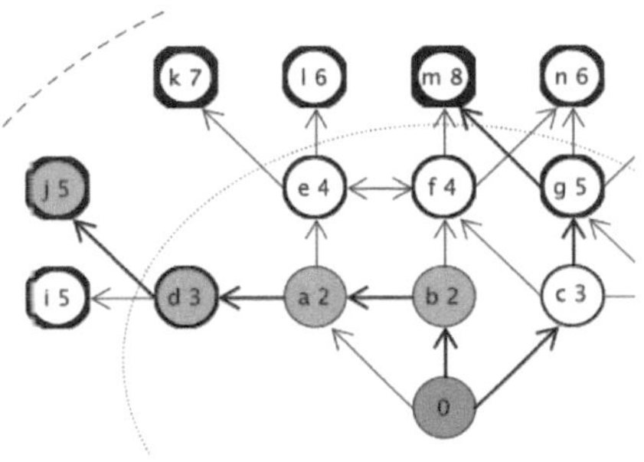

Figure 7.7: Example of possible values and path to reach the outer ring.

Figure 7.7 adds a small number next to each letter to represent the total of collectables and clues per level. Let us assume that a total of 7 collectables and clues must be acquired to reach the outer ring. In this case, the easiest path to achieve it is through $b(2) \rightarrow a(2) \rightarrow d(3) \rightarrow j = 7$. That is not the shortest path, though. That would be $c(3) \rightarrow g(5) \rightarrow m = 8$, which is even higher than the required 7, but it is far more difficult.

By making these choices and distributing the risks and rewards, we can better guide the player and the pace of the game. A beginner or more risk-avert player might travel the $b(2) \rightarrow a(2) \rightarrow d(3) \rightarrow j$, which also ensures 2 levels of the same difficulty (a and b) which will reinforce the mechanics, potentially improving the players' skills and their inaptitude.

Although we have applied this theory to the layout of levels in `Another Starry Sky`, we can also apply it to individual levels. Figure 7.8 shows a conceptual travel level applying this theory.

Figure 7.8 is divided into 5 blocks, numbered from 1 to 5. Each block contains at least one form of challenge. Block 1, for example, has a trivial collectable and a more complex challenge that requires the player to move behind the asteroid.

Block 2 is a sort of break. Although it contains obstacles, they are mostly easy to avoid, especially if the player has ignored the second collectable in block 1.

Block 3 is a repetition of block 1, but its distribution of obstacles forces the player to move around regardless of the choices made in blocks 1 and 2.

Block 4 is a higher-difficulty challenge, as there are more obstacles to avoid, and the collectable is placed in a non-trivial area, which is a good example of a risk and reward setup. For this specific case, we could make it that this collectable is actually a clue and has a higher value compared to the other collectables in the stage, increasing the reward aspect of the challenge.

Finally, block 5 is a form of final break, as it presents an easy solution: the player can pass through it by flying (mostly) straight. On the other hand, it presents some challenges of its own. The first collectable, for example, is an inversion of the previous challenges as it is now placed right in front of the asteroid rather than on its back, which makes it a riskier situation.

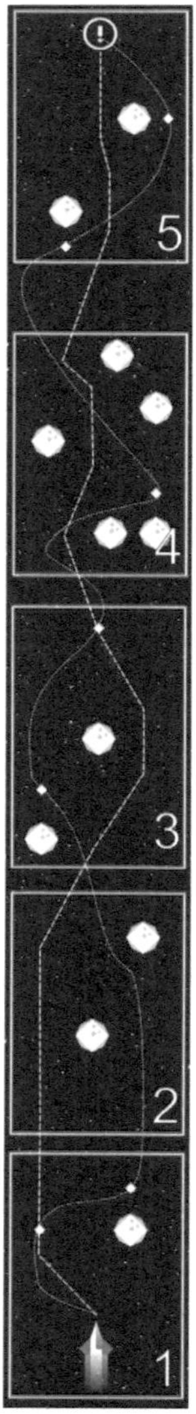

Figure 7.8: Conceptual travel level.

The lines in Figure 7.8 exemplify two different player approaches to this level. The first one, the thicker dotted line, is a risk-avert player that takes the easier and less challenging path to finish the level. It can get up to 2 collectables in this approach. The second one, the thinner pointed line, is an achiever who wants to gather all the collectables in the level and, by doing so, goes through all possible challenges. It can get all 7 collectables by taking this path.

Notice that we have used the same principles of challenges, breaks, risk, and reward and even considered player types in this level. All of these elements reinforce each other, just like the Cores of Game Design.

Also, we can analyse this conceptual level the same as done in Figure 7.7. For that, each block can be seen in an easy approach, $Block(X_{easy})$, and a hard approach, $Block(X_{hard})$. The risk-avert player would take the simple path: $Block(1_{easy}) \rightarrow Block(2_{easy}) \rightarrow Block(3_{easy}) \rightarrow Block(4_{easy}) \rightarrow Block(5_{easy})$, for example.

Any combination of paths is possible and could be diagrammed. Let us assume a more intermediary type of player. This player's path could be $Block(1_{hard}) \rightarrow Block(2_{hard}) \rightarrow Block(3_{easy}) \rightarrow Block(4_{easy}) \rightarrow Block(5_{hard})$.

If you are into mathematics, you could also transform some of these diagrams into equations. For example, let us now consider that the function $Block(X_{easy/hard})$ is the maximum number of collectables that can be collected by taking either the easy or the hard path. For example, $Block(1_{easy}) = 1$ and $Block(1_{hard}) = 2$. With that, if you sum up all the values in a player's path, you can calculate the maximum number of collectables possible. Following the intermediary player type example from the previous paragraph, we would get $2 + 0 + 1 + 0 + 2 = 5$ collectables and clues. Okay, but that is enough math for now!

We can summarise this discussion by saying that the more you ask the players, the more you reward them. We expect rewards that match the effort. If you spend good ingredients and time following a recipe, it better be delicious.

However, the reward does not need to be in the realm of the `Economy`, such as points, collectables, and other forms of resources. Some digital games might reward the player with a nice view or unlock extra story elements. Taking the player's expectations into account when doing so is very important, as an unmatched reward can be frustrating. This is even more important considering the different player motivations.

More achiever-oriented players might be fine with having a star next to their character's name for completing all of the challenges in the game, but more story-oriented players could be frustrated for not getting more information on the characters and mysteries after all the effort they have put into it.

At the heart of applying risk and reward strategy is player agency. If the player has no decision upon taking or not the risk, then you are not properly applying this technique; you are simply imposing a challenge. That is not necessarily a bad approach, as sometimes you might need to use a forced approach (such as the Forced Action Framework) to teach the player or for other reasons.

Yet, giving the option helps to foster the player's individual motivations, which can also help balance the reward expectation. If the player can assess the risk and the reward before making a decision, there is no room for immediate frustration.

7.4 DESIGNING THE SPACE

So far, we have discussed quite an abstract and high-level concept of level design with organising challenges and assessing the risks and rewards associated with them. This section shows a more hands-on approach to (digital) level design. Let us start with the most common and suggested approaches.

Paper Prototypes and Grey-boxes

Many authors on digital level design, as well as many sources, encourage the use of simple tools and methods [25, 63] at the start of level designing, ignoring aspects from the `Aesthetics` core. For that, they often resort to paper prototypes and what we understand as grey-boxing, which is designing a level using only grey boxes[1].

These approaches are good, especially as you might want to focus initially on the structure of your level, such as blocking it or organising its important elements.

If you have some confidence in your drawing skills, I highly recommend you invest your time in a paper prototype rather than a grey-box level, as the paper prototype is cheaper to achieve, requires

[1] You can use different shades of grey in the design, not just black-and-white boxes.

basically no technology and is easier to share. Consider, of course, that you should not aim at making a nicely drawn paper prototype level – skip all matters of perspectives and visuals, and focus on communicating ideas.

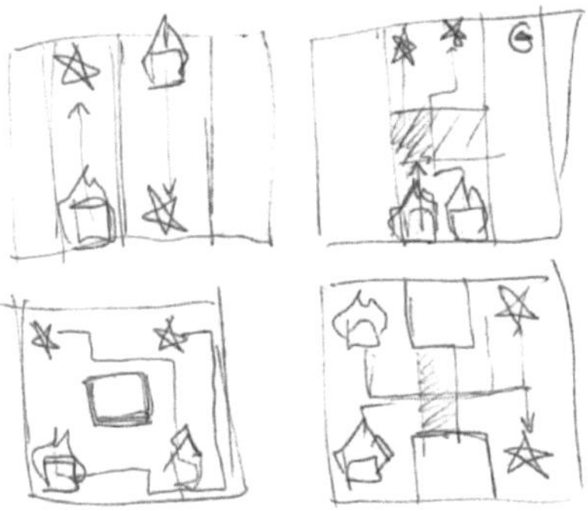

Figure 7.9: Example of paper level design.

A paper prototype is also helpful in the earlier stages of development as you might not have any available tools to start grey-boxing the game. I have seen some designers using 3D modelling tools and similar software to grey-box in the early stages as the game engine of choice was still being set up by the rest of the team, which is also a valid approach (this is also good for starting from the `Aesthetics` core, as seen in Chapter 14). Regardless of your initial choice, the tendency is that, as the project progresses, more game elements will be available to be used for level design, and you might eventually move to level design directly in the engine.

Figure 7.9 shows an example of a **paper level design** I used for a game jam project I worked on[2]. It might be hard to make sense of it as you were not involved in the making of the game, but that is the point of a paper-level design. It should be only concerned with communicating ideas to the development team, nothing and no one else.

Push and Pull

Besides designing the order of the challenges in a level, level design often involves planning and building an environment to guide the player towards the game's goals. Figure 7.10 shows a visual example of what I mean by guiding the player.

[2]You can see more about this game at my website: https://dagongraphics.com/antypoda/

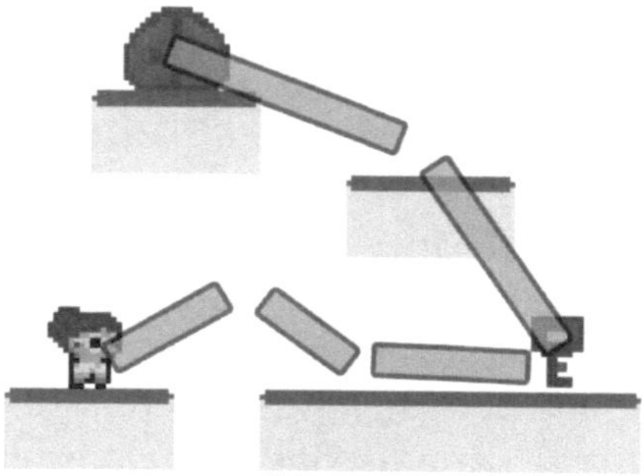

Figure 7.10: Example of a golden path.

Although simple, Figure 7.10 shows how the position of the key and the door might conduct the player into following a specific path. The desired designed path is often referred to as the **critical path** or **golden path** [25, 82, 83].

Considering the size of the level and visible area, guiding the player's movement might be a simple task. However, larger levels might need more tools to properly guide the player. The most common one is using collectables, as we used in previous sections and chapters. Collectables draw players in and make them aware of the area in which the collectable is located. Figure 7.11 shows this process.

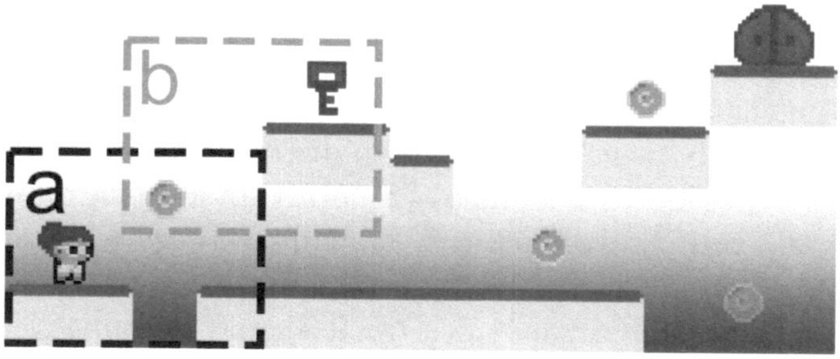

Figure 7.11: Longer level. The dotted black box (a) shows the player's visible area. The dotted grey box (b) is the player's visible area when it moves to collect the coin.

The dotted black box (a) in Figure 7.11 exemplifies the camera view when the player is at the start position. At this moment, the player can only see the coin and the gap, which guides the player to move towards the right side of the screen. When jumping to collect the coin, the player will see the dotted grey box (b) area, which will make the key visible, although unreachable.

From this moment, the player knows where the key is and will try to reach it without the need for any other indication. The same process is applied later to show where the door is located. There are two consecutive coins that, when collected, allow the player to see the door and finish the level.

A common way of referring to this technique is by the term **Push and Pull** [79]. The coin acts as a **pulling element** that pulls the player towards it, leading the player's path. Other elements, such as the gaps and the left unpassable wall at the start of the level, are **pushing elements**, which push the player away from them.

You might have noticed a fourth (transparent) coin at the end of the level, right in the middle of a gap. That is an example of how we can guide the player on uncertain events. Gaps in platformer games are often fatal. In situations in which we want to tell a player that a certain gap is not deadly, we can use coins or other pulling elements to subtly guide the player towards them. Certainly, if there is a coin hovering at that place, there must be a way of getting it. In the case of Figure 7.11, there might be some sort of ground below that gap that the player can step on.

You can also subvert this concept to hide rewards. For example, if you have a clear **golden path** with many pulling elements, you might emphasise some of them to move the player away from a secondary path that is either a shortcut or contains valuable collectables. That rewards players who take the time to explore the game, as that might be the motivation for some of them.

Collectables are often good pulling elements, but you can use other approaches also such as playing with light and dark areas, closed and open spaces, and static versus dynamic elements. Anything that gets the player's attention is a good candidate to be a pulling element. In that sense, exploring elements of the `Aesthetics` is a good way of empowering your level design. That is also why there is a natural tendency to move towards level design in the engine in later stages, as you have more immediate ways of applying more and better pulling elements in your level design.

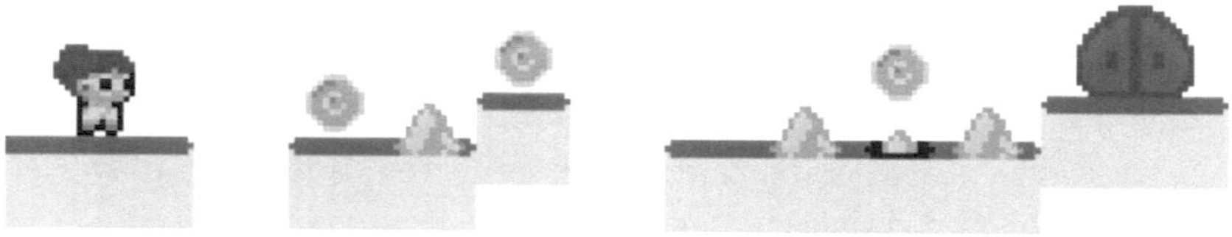

Figure 7.12: Example of an antepiece with spikes.

Antepieces

As far as I know, the concept of an antepiece is not a commonly referred to term in level design lingo, articles, and books. However, I still think it is a useful concept that pairs well with our previously discussed Forced Action Framework. An antepiece is a part of the level that comes before a more important or complex part of the level[3].

The antepiece name comes from an analogy to an antechamber, which is a smaller chamber or room that leads to a bigger room. In level design, we use antepieces as a preparatory event, such as a break before a hard challenge or as an instruction moment in which a challenge is present in a smaller and simplified form.

Figure 7.12 shows an example of a level with timed spikes that appear from the ground. The first segment has two coins and one spike. The spike is easy to avoid, and the coins are there to reward the player for getting this new knowledge. Moreover, the coins help to halt the player, so there is enough time for the time spike mechanic to be seen.

The second segment has three consecutive timed spikes before the door. That is clearly a harder challenge in which the players must time their jumps correctly to avoid being hit. There is a coin placed in the middle of the spikes as a risk and reward element to engage players into an extra level of difficulty for players who choose to collect it.

We can see the antepiece as a common way of achieving the first step of a Forced Action Framework, the Forced Obvious Task.

[3]The only place I could find of a reference to an antepiece was in this TV Tropes article: https://tvtropes.org/pmwiki/pmwiki.php/Main/Antepiece.

However, not all antepieces are necessarily connected to a Forced-Action Framework. Some might just be used as breaks.

Filling the Gaps

As you achieve your **golden path**, the level might still feel bare and unremarkable. It is then the time to increment it with more elements to enforce and support your **golden path**. I call this moment the time to fill the gaps:

Other Paths: Consider if you can add other paths besides the **golden path** to allow multiple ways of traversing the level. For that, consider the player's knowledge and skill. Players who know more or are more skilled are capable of traversing the level in riskier but more rewarding ways.

Hidden Rewards: Consider if the pulling elements leave space for hidden areas and spots that more explorer-like players might investigate. Those might be connected to the other possible paths in the level.

Balance the Challenges: Consider the challenges in the level and how they are helping the player to achieve a good flow. Playtest and compare the players' time and reactions to assess whether some of the challenges in the level should be moved around or even removed.

Ladders and Elevators: Parts of your level might be in hard-to-reach places, and falling from them might cause the player to replay a significant portion of it. To avoid frustration, implement ladders and elevators, *i.e.*, mechanics that help a player return to a previous location they have already conquered. Not doing so might hinder exploration and annoy the players.

Empty Spaces are Good: Not all of the level need to be covered with spikes and coins. Some parts of it can be empty or used for the other cores, such as a story moment (`Narrative`) or a nice view (`Aesthetics`). It also helps to give your players some break.

Reconnect the Dots: When you have paths that lead to different endpoints, consider if any of them can lead back to a previous path. For example, your player has to go a long way to get a key to open the door. Instead of having the player backtrack all the way from the start of the path, have the end of the path lead back to a (good) position towards the door. Alternatively, design the backtrack to be somewhat different so the player does not feel like repeating everything over again.

Figures 7.13 and 7.14 are examples of how all the techniques we discussed in this chapter could be applied to a platformer example game. Figure 7.13 is a paper draft of the level I did using an erasable small whiteboard. It has all the elements of the final level but no concern with measuring sizes or adding the real details. The stars on it, for example, are supposed to be more `Aesthetics` areas, but in the draft, they are shown simply as stars.

Figure 7.14 shows a more finalised version of the level with the appropriate assets and details. The heights and proportions were corrected and adjusted based on the draft. The dotted black path shows the **golden path**, in which the player only needs to overcome a small number of challenges to get the key and open the door. The small dotted grey path shows an achiever path, in which the player has to overcome all of the challenges to acquire all of the collectables in the level.

Notice that, even when taking the achiever route, the player has a minimal amount of backtracking, and when it happens, it is usually fast and with no obstacles.

Finally, note that although there are two breaks in the level, the one on the top right corner is visited by neither of the designed paths. That is not a bad thing, and it does not mean that no player will attempt to go there. It is a break; some players might explore it, and some others might completely ignore it.

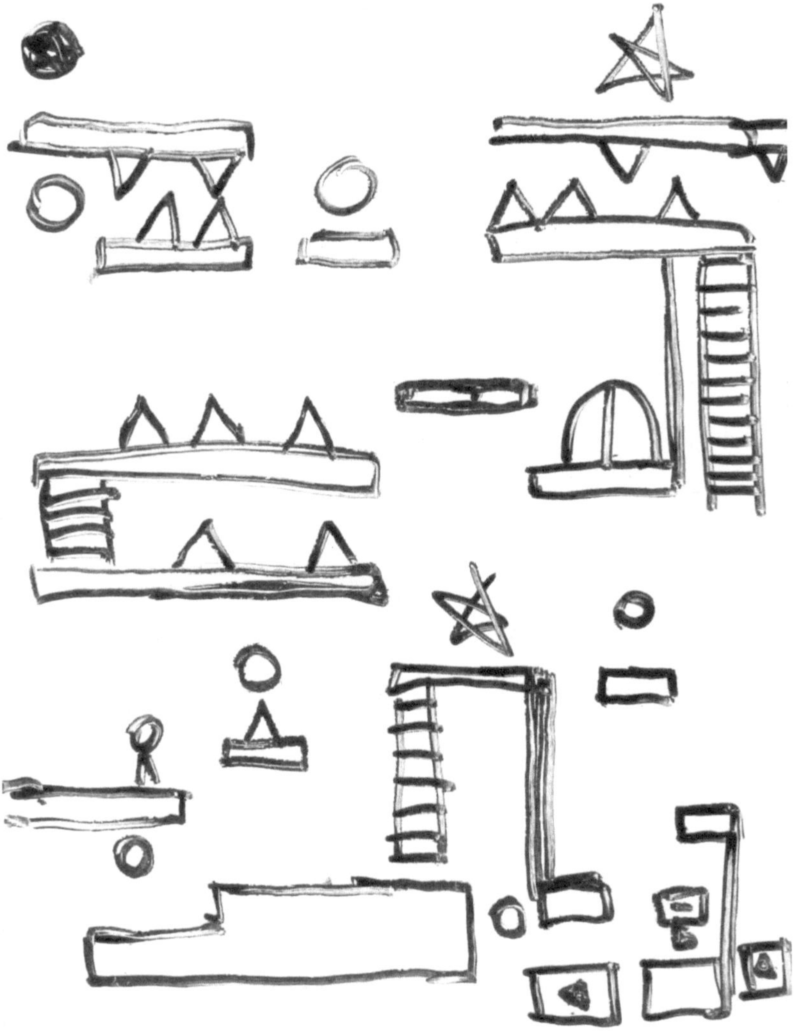

Figure 7.13: Paper draft for the complete level example.

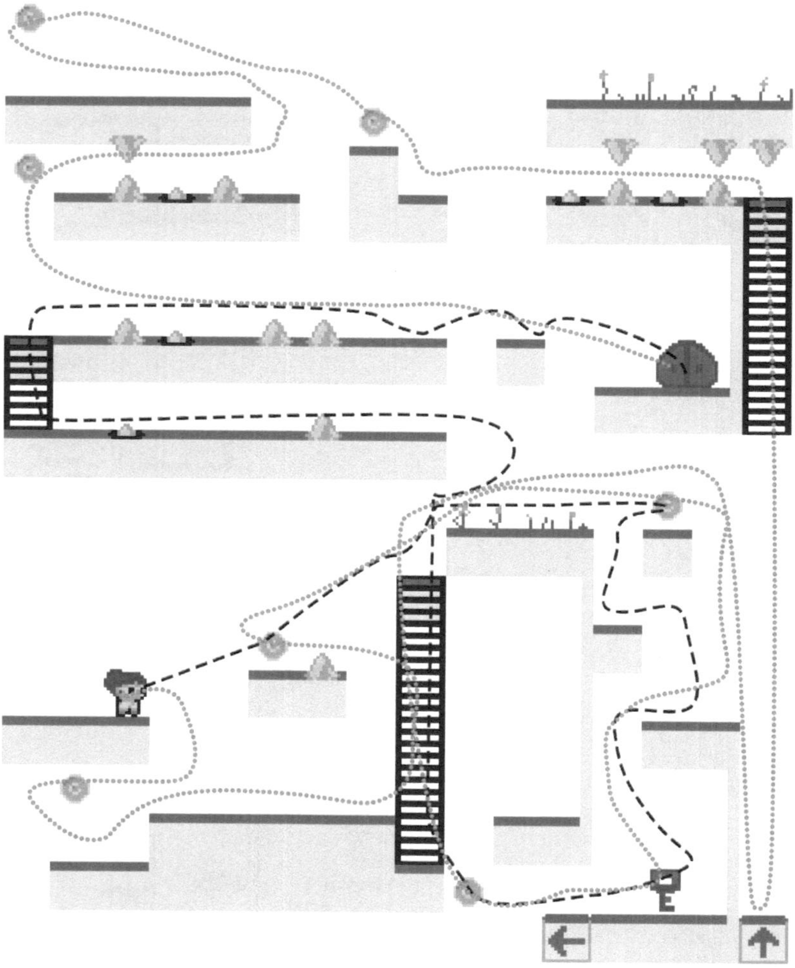

Figure 7.14: Complete level example using all the techniques cited in this chapter.

III

Economy

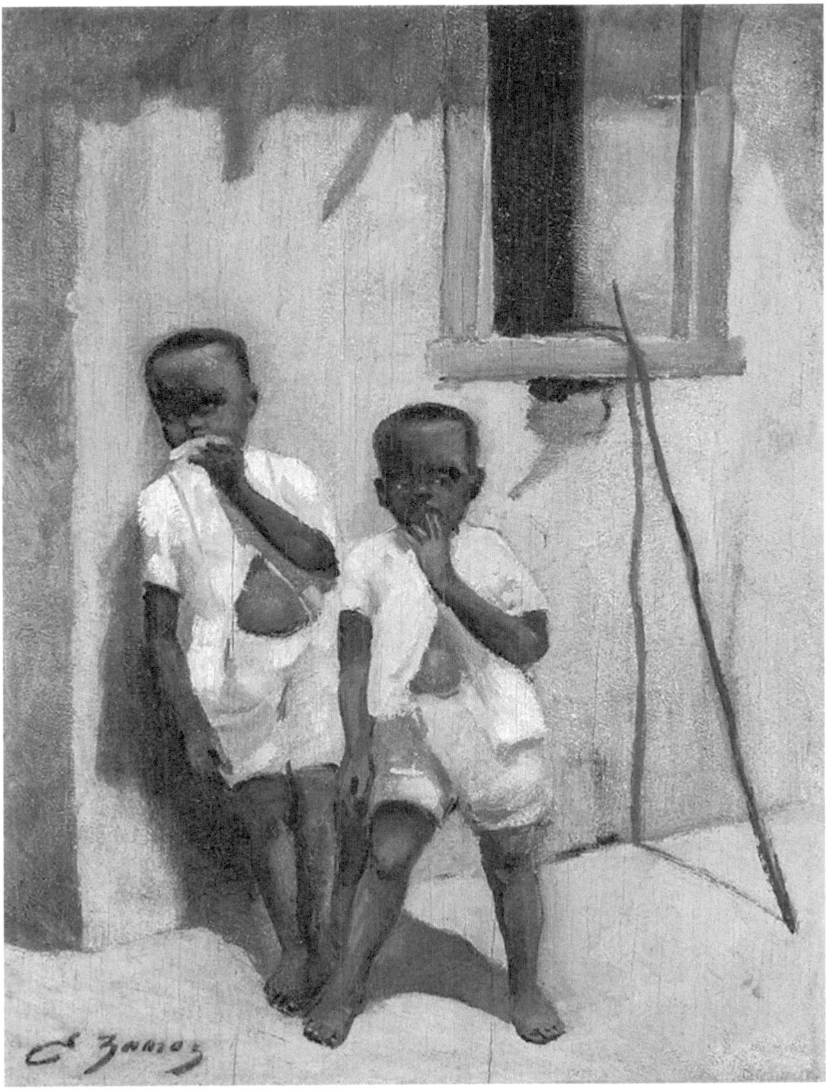

Emmanuel Zamor – Crianças (1860–1919).

CHAPTER 8

Starting with Economy

A GAME'S ECONOMY IS THE SET OF ITS RESOURCES, MECHANISMS, AND THEIR RELATIONSHIPS. Economy is, to my knowledge, not a commonly discussed topic in Game Design literature, at least not as its own topic. However, there are at least two books entirely focused on its discussions, which are the great Game Mechanics: Advanced Game Design, but Ernest Adams and Joris Dormans [9], which serves as the main source for most of this part of the book; and the more recent Game Balance, by Ian Schreiber and Brenda Romero [3], two veterans in the area of game design and its literature.

As discussed in the first chapters of this book, Economy is often conflated with Mechanics, as players often experience aspects of the Economy through the game's systems and mechanics. However, we can study and analyse the Economy aspects of a game separate from the Mechanics as its discipline, and also how it can manifest and integrate with the other cores of Aesthetics and Narrative.

In this section, we discuss the main concepts of the Economy core, as well as important definitions and examples of how we can see it as its separate discipline and design our games and development processes with it at its centre.

DOI: 10.1201/9781003351191-8

8.1 BASIC TYPES OF RESOURCES

Resources are the base of any game's economy, and they are ubiquitous – they are everywhere. So much so, I like to use the definition of resource coined by Adams and Dormans [9, p. 60]:

> *Resources refer to any concept that can be measured numerically. Almost anything in a game can function as a resource: money, energy, time, or units under the player's control are examples of resources, as are items, power-ups, and enemies that oppose the player.*

However, it is not helpful to assume every possible resource is an economic resource. The number of stars in the background of a travelling stage in `Another Starry Sky` can be resources. Still, they are not meaningful to any game design process or the player. On the other hand, the collectables and clues in the stages of the same game are important resources that influence the game's progress.

Resources also do not need to be visible or stated by the game to exist in the game's context. For example, if in a round of negotiations from `Family Tree`, a player might ask to be favoured in a negotiation round, promising to give in in the next. This promise is a resource. It is a type of "you own me one, now" that is not a card or token, but that exists and influences the game. One player might, at one point, have many of these resources and use them in a more strategic moment, even if that is not a written rule in the game.

It is easier to see these distinctions using the resource qualifiers defined by Adams and Dormans [9]. Resources can be:

Tangible: They exist physically in the game world. A coin at a platformer level is a tangible resource.

Intangible: They exist in the game, but they do not exist physically. The number of lives remaining a player has, which is displayed in the user interface, is an intangible resource.

Tangible resources provide opportunities, as they can be moved around and interacted with. For example, a tangible resource can be stolen from a player or affected by other physical elements of the game.

On the other hand, intangible resources are a more conceptual type of resource that mostly exists in user interfaces and other types of head-up displays (more of that in Chapter 16). Intangible resources are not strictly related to digital games, though. Keeping track of resources on a paper or character sheet (in Tabletop Role-playing Games, for instance) are examples of intangible resources in non-digital settings.

The fact that intangible resources are not physically present does not mean they cannot be interacted with. It only means that interacting with them is more likely to happen on a more abstract level. As exemplified before, the remaining lives of a player change as more lives are acquired and when the player dies. But these changes are more abstract than seeing a pile of seashells growing up as the player collects them in `Memories by the Sea`.

Tangible and intangible resources can be converted into each other. When the player collects a coin at a platformer level (a tangible resource), it can be transformed into a +1 in the user interface's coin counter (an intangible resource).

While designing a game's economy, it is important first to understand which resources will be part of the economy and how they relate to other aspects of the game, such as the Game's Purpose.

8.2 PROGRESSION ECONOMY

There is an ongoing debate on the definition of games [9, 16, 35, 63, 84], with contradicting statements. For this book, we do not use any particular definition, as games are a cultural phenomenon that will keep happening, adapting, and changing too many forms, never fully fitting a single definition [85].

At the same time, studying some of those definitions is a good game design exercise. From an Economy perspective, some of these definitions drive interesting discussions. One point of the contest is whether games require a **victory condition** to be games [84]. Instead of discussing it, let us use this premise under the lens of an economy-led game design process and see how it can be helpful to design and develop winnable games.

A **victory condition** is, in itself, a resource (we can count it). With that, any winnable game has at least a minimal economic aspect. We will call it the **victory resource** if it manifests as a single resource that must be acquired (or destroyed) to win the game. Chess is a great example of a game with a **victory resource**: the king. The moment the king is captured, the game is over. Some other games might have more than one **victory resource** when multiple ways of winning are possible.

Alternatively, other games might have an abstract **victory resource** idea acquired through the collection (or destruction) of other resources. These are the **progression resources**. Checkers, for example, does not have a single resource that leads to victory. Instead, the players compete to capture all of the checkers from each other. Each checker is a **progression resource**. Notice that the checker is, at the same time, part of the game mechanics (`Mechanics`), part of the visual of the game (`Aesthetics`), and also part of the economy.

We can extend this concept into more abstract ways of looking at the **victory resource**. For example, let us assume a game in which the players must run from point A to point B, and the first one to reach point B wins. The **distance** between one player and the destination is the **progression resource**, which must be reduced to zero faster than the other players. In this example, each player has their measurement for the **progression resource**, and the **victory resource** is granted to the one that does it faster.

Analysing your game's idea under these lenses helps you focus your development on the elements more likely to impact the player's experience. In the previous race example, we could ask players to clap while running as a joke and count how many claps the winner made. If this number does not influence the game, it was just a waste of time (and of honest claps).

On the other hand, if we feel that the game is just too simple with the running aspect, we could consider other elements to influence the **progression resource**. For example, we could divide the path between points A and B into segments. The winner now is not the one to reach point B the fastest, but the one that was the fastest in most segments. For example, if A and B are split into five segments, Player $P1$ could have been the fastest at segments 1 to 4 and lost at segment 5 to $P2$, but as $P1$ won 4 segments from 5, $P1$ is the final winner. That way, we split the **progression resource** into five discrete values (being the faster at each segment). Surely, running at full speed from start to end and winning all segments is still a valid strategy, but this change opens up other sorts of strategies.

Building upon this example, we could also award different values for each segment. Let us say, for example, that segments 1 to 3 are worth 1 point each, while segment 4 is worth 2 points and segment five is worth 3 points. Now, it is not only a matter of how many segments each player wins but also which segments. If $P1$ won segments 1, 2, and 3, getting a total of 3 points, $P2$ would still win by getting fewer but more valuable segments, with 4 and 5, getting a total of 5 points. These changes also create a sort of balancing mechanism, giving players an extra chance of reverting the odds if they succeed at winning the final segments.

All of these examples were done using the `Economy`, but notice how we could achieve other forms of diversifying this game using the other cores, especially the `Mechanics`. New mechanics could have been added to expand the repertoire of strategies and options available to the players, for example. Assuming this example is a physical game in which players have actually to race from point A to B, some players might save up some energy in the first, less valuable segments and then use all of their efforts to win the later and more valuable segments.

Using **victory resources** and **progression resources** gives us good tools to work the game's economy. They also provide us with means to connect with the other cores easily. Let us apply them to our concept games **`Family Tree`** and **`Another Starry Sky`**.

Victory and Progress: `Family Tree`

In **`Family Tree`**, players win when the tree in the family's backyard is fully grown. The tree's growth is the **progression resource**, and it is actually a tangible resource in the game, as the players get pieces of it and make the tree actually grow while playing.

The tree growth happens in specific moments when the players achieve a specific threshold for their shared Happiness points. For example, let us say that it happens every time all the team members can donate 20 of their Happiness points to grow the tree.

At the same time, as the tree grows, the decks and cards used in the game are changed to reflect the passage of time. The initial negotiations are easier and simpler, based on the first moments of the family living together, but as time progresses, the negotiations become harder and more complex.

With that, as the game progresses, more effort is required to achieve 20 shared Happiness points and grow the tree.

In a sense, you could also see a hierarchy between Happiness points and the three growth resources. Any mechanics and mechanisms that create or remove Happiness points are connected directly to the game's **progression resource**, the tree growth.

Victory and Progress: `Another Starry Sky`

In `Another Starry Sky`, the player must return to her home planet by travelling through observation points and using constellations to guide herself.

Her return home is the **progression resource**, and it is an intangible resource in the game, as it is a matter of distance that is not always clear to the player. As the player moves through observation points, the distance is either increased or reduced, depending on the player's decisions.

With that, the **progression resource** varies during the gameplay, which is not necessarily a problem. Some players might want to explore all the observation points or collect all clues before heading home and finishing the game. We could design that the player could reach her home planet by travelling through 6 observation points, but we could design 26 of them to increase the number of options and experiences.

As the player approaches the home planet, the game ramps

up the challenge and makes the travel stages and constellations harder to overcome. Consecutively, the mood and atmosphere of the game change towards the home planet as the pollution levels increase near it.

Also, returning home is the main objective of the game, but there is a secondary one regarding the mystery of the rogue space vessel that is solved by collecting clues. We could see it as a **secondary progression resource** that, although (partially) disconnected from the main goal, is still subject to the same principles. As the player collects clues and solves the mystery, each new clue and travel also presents a bigger challenge while providing more elements of the `Narrative`.

Notice that, in both games, we have a similar pattern with the **progression resources**:

1. We define the **progression resource** and how it is acquired.
2. We specify values for the acquisition and related mechanisms of the **progression resource**.
3. We explore how the game gets more complex as the **progression resources** are collected.
4. We use the progression as a drive for the other cores, such as adding new mechanics (`Mechanics`), changing the mood (`Aesthetics`), and telling a story (`Narrative`).

I cannot emphasise how the second item is important. **Always specify values for your game's economy.** It does not matter if they are just guesses. They will change later as you play the game and conduct playtesting activities. Not using numbers makes the design process harder as you do not have any solid ground to work on. Specifying 20 Happiness points for `Family Tree` and six observation points for `Another Starry Sky` provides us with a base to work on and make the subsequent decisions easier. Consider it as important as knowing how many people you are making dinner for. Without this knowledge, it is hard even to conceive what you will cook.

8.3 BALANCING AND FAIRNESS

While working with the `Economy` core, we often rework numbers and equations for the game, especially after a playtesting session. For example, consider the threshold we established for **`Family Tree`** of 20 Happiness points to enable the tree growth mechanic. After playtesting, we found that 20 was too much and the game was too long. We can lower it to 10 and playtest again. Luckily, 10 was better, but too fast, especially when the players were lucky with the cards. Then we can try with 15, and so on.

In a sense, we are balancing the game. More specifically, we are trying to balance the game's economy. While doing so, we are reworking the numbers in the economy to reach a specific goal, which is often your game's purpose. If your game's purpose is to be fun and engaging, your changes while balancing the economy are meant to speed up the game and, somehow, trigger a sense of fun.

Balancing is a very hard activity. As your game and its number of resources grow, their interconnections and relations will increase the impact of any change you make. However, balancing is essential. An unbalanced game can ruin the players' experience, even if the game has many other merits.

Perfect Balance is Actually Not a Good Idea

Nevertheless, a perfectly balanced situation where all player options are equally valid can easily reduce their impact. If all roads lead to Rome, it does not matter which one we take. Surely, as a game designer, you can add flavours to each option, making them more of a personal player option rather than a strategic game decision.

For example, consider that in **`Memories by the Sea`**, you can find seashells of different colours for the same goals. However, the colour does not influence the goal. Only the type and other properties of the seashells matter. For that, the colours picked are either a personal preference or are subject to random factors, such as the order in which the players found them. We could balance the colour distribution of the seashells so there are enough seashells of each colour to finish the goal.

We could then make it so that when a goal is completed, a banner coloured with the collected seashells is hung up in the player's user interface. If the player picked seashells randomly, the banner will reflect that, while a more selective player will have banners of specific orders or even with planned textures and patterns. The banner's colour does not influence the rest of the game. It is a cosmetic decision for the player. But design-wise, it is now an economic decision: should we balance the colour distribution?

Besides that, consider that most players do not have complete knowledge of the game. Even if the colour distribution is not perfectly balanced, if there are enough colours and seashells to meet the goals, the players might not even notice that as a possible problem. For that, it is always good to playtest and assess the player's experience regarding balance, especially before balancing.

It is not uncommon for an unbalanced game to be experienced as a balanced one due to the player's limited knowledge. We could have a 1% lower percentage of beige seashells compared to the others, but it is such a slight difference that it goes unnoticed (no one likes beige, anyway). The same applies to other principles, such as required skill level (an option is not balanced but requires a high skill level to perform) or in-game knowledge (an option is not balanced, but the player must know many aspects of the game to use it properly).

Finally, throughout the book, especially the sections for the `Economy` part, I will not focus specifically on "balance" but on what I propose as a more tangible and interesting alternative, **fairness**. Fairness is the subjective feeling that the experience, options, and challenges are appropriate. Even if the numbers do not match precisely or there are overpowered options, other aspects guarantee that the players feel that it is fair. Pursuing a fair experience might even lead to the use of clearly unbalanced features, but that, as a whole, helps the game achieve its purpose.

As a food analogy, consider balancing the same as when we read "salt and pepper to taste". There is no perfect balance that will match everyone's preference. Going a bit lower or higher on the amounts of salt and pepper is usually not enough to completely ruin the dish, and you can always add them to the table. You could even add a hot sauce and other spices if you want to provide even more options for personalisation. In any case, there is no way to please everyone, and that is fine.

8.4 OTHER APPROACHES

The easiest way to start your design process from the `Economy` is certainly picking up resources, especially the **progress resource** or a **victory resource**. From it, you can design possible ways of achieving them, which might soon move your process towards the `Mechanics` core.

Alternatively, you can study the resources used in other games and design how the game would work if they replaced the **progress resource** or **victory resource**. For example, consider a car racing game in which the player wins not by reaching the end goal first but by getting there using the least amount of fuel (different **progress resource**) or by taking the longest possible route (inverting the use of the **victory resource**). On the other hand, I do not recommend starting this process by adding new resources. As we will see in the following chapters, the more resources in the game, the harder it is for the player to learn the game and for the game designer to work with.

Particularly for replacing the **progress resources**, looking for important resources that often serve as keys or gates and change their roles is an excellent exercise. For example, instead of using one literal key to open a door, you might need an X amount of keys to open it, or you can only get some keys after discovering an Y number of closed doors.

Moreover, consider combining different functions in the same resource. For example, in the previous example of a car racing game, you could transform fuel into a general trading resource: you use it to exchange goods with characters/players or to get other resources from the game. Now, it functions as the main mobility resource and unlocks other game features. In this example, races are not just a matter of speed and skill. They also require proper strategy on how the fuel is used as it is linked to other aspects.

If you still feel stuck with starting from the `Economy` core, then consider if you should not explore other cores first. Also, the list below offers some other options that can help you:

Swap Tangible and Intangible Resources: Make a tangible, intangible resource, and vice-versa. The new or lack of physical properties might add new dynamics to the game.

Consider, especially, resources often seen as intangible (such as the player's health) and how it would change if they existed physically in the game's world.

Combine All Resources into One: Consider games with multiple resources and experiment by combining them into a single, all-encompassing resource. How does it change the options in the game? What would you call this resource? Aim at the one resource, but, in the process, consider which combinations thus far improved the game's experience and could be used instead of their old individual versions.

Play with Discreteness: Some resources are often represented with real numbers and fractions, such as a car's speed or a player's height. What would happen if you turn those numbers into discrete and whole increments (they become natural numbers)? For example, if the speed was from 0 m/h to 100 m/h, but always in increments of 10 m/h, without in-between values.

Consider Player-Made Resources: Not all resources must come from the game itself. Some resources, such as tokens and dice from their own collections, could be brought to the game by the players. Consider how using these personalised resources in the game could trigger different dynamics and relations. To avoid a highly unbalanced situation where a player has way more resources than others, evaluate sharing and cooperative mechanics.

Share Resources: In the vein of the last point, consider how you can change the resources to have shared values among different players or that the **progress resource** is somehow shared among multiple players simultaneously. It also does not need to be an entirely cooperative game. Moreover, consider how you can foster that sharing is an important aspect of the game rather than having players selfishly hoard the shared resource.

Furthermore, we have only discussed the main elements of economies in this chapter: **resources**. But economic mechanisms govern resources, and they are a great source (pun intended) of creative approaches to game design. The following chapters in the `Economy` part are focused on how game economies work, including their relations and mechanisms in Chapter 9 and on a more thorough discussion on the value and importance of resources within games in Chapter 10.

If you are still exploring the cores, you can now move to the first chapter of which one of their parts: `Mechanics` in Chapter 5, `Narrative` in Chapter 11, `Aesthetics` in Chapter 14.

Otherwise, if you want to or prefer a more linear order in reading the book, just continue ahead.

CHAPTER 9

Game Economics

WHILE RESOURCES ARE AT THE CENTRE OF A GAME'S ECONOMY, they are governed and controlled through mechanisms and relationships. These mechanisms and relations are the stars of this chapter.

Firstly, we use the term **mechanism** when referring to the economic mechanics, which are not necessarily game mechanics in terms of the `Mechanics` core [9]. They can happen simultaneously and be performed by the same entities, but this is not always the case.

Many of these concepts were coined[1], on Game Mechanics: Advanced Game Design, by Ernest Adams and Joris Dormans [9]. The latter is also responsible for the Machinations Framework [10], a tool that can model, test, and balance game economies. The Machinations Framework will be used to illustrate and simulate the examples and discussions for this chapter. However, this chapter and this book are no tutorials on how to use Machinations. For that, I highly recommend you to check the reference book from Adams and Dormans [9] and its official website [86].

9.1 SOURCES, DRAINS, CONVERTERS, AND TRADERS

Four main mechanisms govern the game's economy. They are:

Sources: which generate resources out of nothing. Sources can be timed or activated upon certain conditions. The number of

[1] To my knowledge.

DOI: 10.1201/9781003351191-9

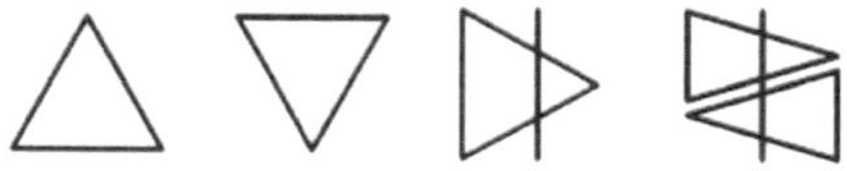

Figure 9.1: Machination symbols for the four mechanisms (in order): Source, Drain, Converter, Trader.

resources a source produces is commonly called its **production rate**.

Drains: which eliminates resources from the game permanently. Drains can be timed or activated given conditions and are subject to some form of **drainage rate**. Drains are not necessarily bad for the player: there are situations in which a resource harms the player's performance.

Converters: which convert resources from one type into another. During this process, the resources converted are permanently transformed into the new ones. In a sense, a converter works simultaneously as a source and a drain: it creates a new resource out of nothing while draining the other one permanently. Converters have a **conversion rate** that determines the number and type of the inputs and outputs.

Traders: which trade resources from different game entities (players, for example). Different from converters, traders do not destroy the resources in the process. Both exchanged resources still exist in the game after the trade but belong to different entities. Trades have a **trading rate** that determines the number and type of the inputs and outputs.

These four mechanisms are illustrated in Machinations by the four symbols of Figure 9.1[86]. In order, they are the source (triangle), drain (upside-down triangle), converter (crossed right-sided triangle), and trader (two crossed-sided triangles). Besides those four mechanisms, **pools** are another important one. **Pools** are resource aggregators. You can understand them as a sort of resource pile. As a source generates a resource, these resources are piled in a pool until another mechanism moves them to another pool or acts on them (draining or converting, for example). Pools are represented with a circle.

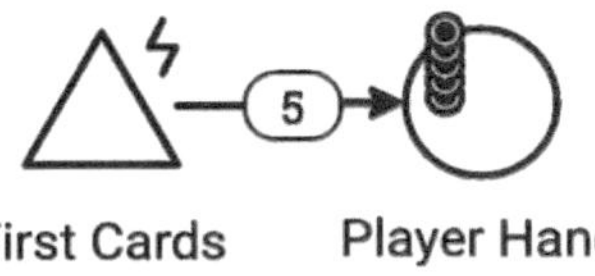

Figure 9.2: Machination example of a diagram (in order): A starting Source generated five resources to the Player Hand pool.

Figure 9.2 shows an example of a simple Machinations diagram. It starts with a source that generates five sources to a pool. The source has a lighting symbol, which means it will only perform this production once, at the game's start. The arrow linking the source and the pool indicates how many resources will be generated (5). The pool shows a stack of 5 resources. The source and pool are named to make the diagram easier to read.

Although there are four mechanisms, they are not always mandatory to achieve a complete game economy. It is common, for example, that single-player games do not offer any sort of trading mechanism.

On that note, a common misconception is to assume merchants in digital games are traders, as the players trade currencies for other resources. That is only the case if the traded resources still exist after the trading is complete. That is the case if players can buy back items they have just sold and if they are precisely those sold, not copies.

This distinction is vital because converters and traders are used to achieve different economic goals. Converters are used to achieve a **global resource equilibrium**: only a limited number of resources of each type exist in the game. Conversion prevents specific resources from being hoarded as they are needed to activate other mechanisms or converted into other types of resources.

For example, players cannot keep many Happiness points in `Family Tree` as they must be converted into tree growth. Thus, during a play session, the total (or global) amount of Happiness resources is often kept in check due to conversion mechanisms.

On the other hand, traders are used to achieving a **players' resource equilibrium**: players hold a similar amount of resources of the same type. Trading guarantees that the amount of resources per type does not change globally but that they belong to different entities. In `Family Tree`, some negotiations allow players to exchange Happiness points, which achieve the collective threshold for tree growth.

Notice that both equilibria do not necessarily translate to balancing the game but help improve the sense of fairness.

On a different note, what defines whether a specific mechanic is either a source, converter, drain, or trader is partially on the game designer.

For instance, consider that in `Another Starry Sky`, the player's spaceship has an amount of health that is decreased every time it hits an obstacle. We could model this process with a drain. Every hit drains health. However, we could also see the lost health as a resource, like a "repair needed point" that needs to be fixed by a spaceship technician. In that sense, the hit mechanic is now a converter: it converts health points into "repair needed points".

These decisions should improve the game's experience and help it reach its purpose. Consider which options tend to simplify the economy and make the most sense from a gameplay perspective. A simpler economy is more accessible and easier to work with. Also, note that the economy is often a complicated topic to teach players as it lies in the realm of player's ignorance. Unless you are working on a highly complex strategy game, consider keeping your mechanisms as simple as possible.

In this context, favour options that require the use and creation of fewer resources. Understanding health damage as a drain uses a single resource (health) that is already part of other areas of the economy. The conversion alternative, on the other hand, requires the creation of a new resource ("repair needed points") and even new game mechanics (the spaceship technician and how the spaceship is repaired). Generally, the fewer resources, the easier it is to learn and work the game economy.

The following blocks show some examples of these mechanisms in the concept games `Another Starry Sky` and `Family Tree`.

Economy Mechanisms: `Family Tree`

Sources

Negotiation Cards generate Happiness points: When the negotiation is concluded, new happiness points are awarded to the involved players.

Some Cards generate Happiness points: Other cards and events might also generate happiness points out of nothing.

Drains

Some Cards take Happiness points: Other cards and events might also reduce happiness points.

Using Cards Destroy Them: Some cards can be used by the players, and once used, they are removed from the game.

Converters

Happiness Points can be used to get other Resources: In certain events, players might convert some of their Happiness points for other cards and tokens.

Collective Happiness Points Grow the Family Tree: The family tree grows when the players collectively convert a certain amount of Happiness points.

Traders

Trading Resources Among Players: Players can exchange some of their resources, such as tokens and cards, with each other at specific moments.

Redraw Cards from the Deck: The player might use Happiness points to return a card from the deck and get another back. Notice that this is a trade rate (Happiness points and a card) for another card. The happiness points are drained, but both cards still exist in the game. They have just changed ownership.

Economy Mechanisms: Another Starry Sky

Sources

Observation Points generate Clues when visited: When the player first enters a new observation point, a new set of clues is given to the player.

Travel Stages generate Collectables: When the player travels between observation points, the travel stages have collectables that were generated by themselves. Once they are collected, the stage does not create them again.

Drains

Hitting an Obstacle drains Health: When the player hits an obstacle, the health is drained. It is refilled when the travel is complete or when the stage is restarted.

Power-ups vanish over Time: Some power-ups in the levels are only there for some time. Once the time runs out and they are not collected by the player, they disappear.

Converters

Collectables converted into Clues: Some mechanics allow the transformation of a given amount of collectables into new clues.

Clues into New Paths: The player can use the clues to unlock or highlight the paths to observation points that have more clues.

Traders

Storing Items in Lockers: The player can store items (collectables, clues, and other resources) in lockers. That frees space in the player inventory and changes the current owner of the items to the locker.

Trading Clues with Characters: Some characters can trade clues with the player. The player can later revert the trade either by giving an original clue back or by offering other resources.

To explore these concepts in a more focused example, the following block presents the concept game `The Quarry`, which could be implemented as a single-player or multiplayer game, both in a digital or physical setting.

Concept Game: The Quarry

`The Quarry` is a concept game in which the player must deplete a stone quarry by mining it. Mining the quarry uses the player's energy and extract stones. **Energy** and **Stones** are resources in the game. Stones can be used to create new tools that improve the mining aspect. Once the player's energy is depleted, the player must sleep to recover it.

The game's quarry has 100 stones, and the player wins once it has no more stones on it.

Mining stones from the quarry is a conversion mechanism that converts energy into stones. The conversion rate depends on the tools available at the player's disposal. At the start of the game, the conversion rate is 1 energy for 1 stone.

The player starts with 3 energies and gains 2 new energies by sleeping. Sleeping increases the number of days that have passed.

The following sections in the chapter will be primarily based on the `The Quarry` game, which will be incremented with new features as we progress.

9.2 OPTIONS THROUGH RESOURCES AND UPGRADES

Resources are connected by more than just the mechanisms that operate over them. Besides being converted or traded, the presence or lack of resources influences the player's perception of other resources and mechanisms. This is particularly important to generate gameplay variations.

The initial description of `The Quarry` reads repetitive and boring. The player can only mine and sleep, collecting stones at the same pace all the time. We need to add more resources and relations to improve this aspect.

For example, let us add that the players can use stones to create new tools that improve the mining conversion rates. For instance, the player can convert 5 stones into 1 pickaxe. The pickaxe is a resource that increases the mining rate by +1 stone. For simplicity's sake, we can assume that the players can have and use all the pickaxes they own at any time (10 pickaxes mean +10 stones per mining).

The pickaxe provides more options as the players decide when to spend their stones on them; however, they are still insufficient to allow for strategy and diverse gameplay dynamics. For that, let us add another option, the chisel.

The chisel is a resource, adding a 20% chance of not using energy while mining. When it happens, one chisel breaks. Chisels can be accumulated, and their chances add up. For example, if a player has 3 chisels, then the player has 60% of not using energy while mining. If the player succeeds in not using energy, then 1 chisel breaks, leaving 2 chisels left (40%). Players can convert 3 stones to make one chisel.

Adding these two new resources allows for multiple strategies and dynamics. One player could invest all stones into pickaxes while another into chisels. A less strict player would play with a combination of both. In contrast, a more analytical player could even design and calculate the odds to find the optimal strategy given these numbers.

In general, it is good to have at least two different options while designing an initial game economy, as it allows for these four general approaches:

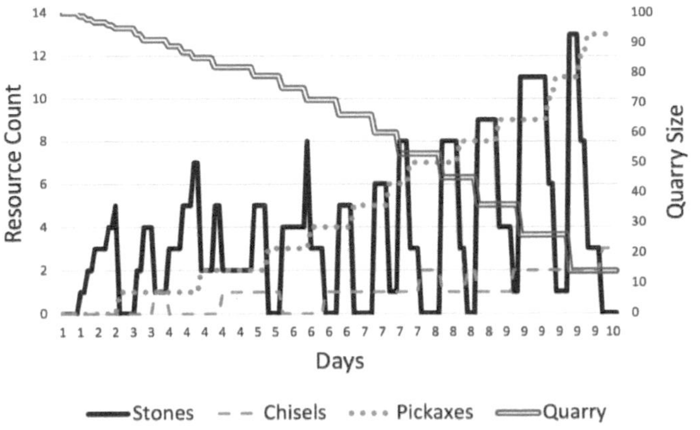

Figure 9.3: The `Quarry` economy chart example.

1. **Only Option 1:** Given two options, the player only goes for one.
2. **Only Option 2:** Given two options, the player only goes for the other.
3. **Hybrid Approach:** Given two options, the player randomly selects either one or the other. They are primarily based on instinct or on the current resource status (which options they can afford at the time).
4. **Optimised Approach:** Given two options, the player calculates a more optimised approach on how to use them to achieve the goal faster and more efficiently.

Although it does not sound much, more often than not, these options are enough to have a good variation of game experiences on your initial playtest sessions.

If we simulate and play `The Quarry` as it is, we would have a similar result as the one charted in Figure 9.3. This simulation was done by implementing `The Quarry`'s economy in Machinations, and it simulates a hybrid approach in which both options are used randomly.

The thicker outline in Figure 9.3 shows the player's stored stones on the given in-game days. Notice how it bounces up and down as the days progress, and they are converted either in chisels or pickaxes. These two are shown as dotted lines. The pickaxes rise over time as they increase the mining rate, while the chisels fluctuate as they are destroyed (drained) when activated. Finally, the quarry is depleted over time, as is seen by the double-dark line in Figure 9.3. Notice how the quarry's depletion rate increases over time as the player produces more pickaxes and chisels. Even with only two options, Figure 9.3 is far from a predictable graph and behaviour.

Stable Bonus and Luck Bonus

Although I have recommended using two options for a basic economy, there is a bit more to it. If you look closely, these two options fundamentally differ in their benefits. The pickaxe is a **stable bonus** that guarantees the same outcome regardless of other aspects of the game. Conversely, the chisel is a **luck bonus** that depends on a chance to influence their outcome. This distinction is important:

Safety versus Risk: Stable bonuses are safe strategies for predictable and steady outcomes. On the other hand, luck bonuses are unpredictable and can turn the tides unexpectability while being riskier than the other approach (Risk and Reward). Both options are fair, but they appeal to different types of players.

Constancy versus Randomness: Stable bonuses tend to make the game pace constant and predictable, which can turn into a dull experience unless the number of stable bonuses is so large that players have difficulty catching up to all their options and outcomes. On the other hand, luck bonuses add randomness to the game, destabilising the pace and forcing players into revising their strategies and options often.

In short, too much predictability makes the game steady and analytical but stale. Also, as the game progresses, a stable game might have a clear winner too soon, undermining the experience for the other players. On the other hand, too little predictability makes the game too chaotic and hard to play. If all options are entirely random, your options and past decisions do not seem to influence the game or matter at all, which undermines the experience for all players.

9.3 FEEDBACK LOOPS

You might have noticed that the pace at which the quarry is depleted in Figure 9.3 is not linear: it does not deplete at the same pace over time. That happens because as the player accumulates pickaxes and chisels, the mining rate increases, which changes the quarry depletion rate.

At the same time, as the quarry depletion rate increases, the amount of mined stones at the player's hand increases, which are then used to create even more pickaxes and chisels. Thus, over time, not only does the depletion rate increase, but the rate itself also does. It gets faster and faster.

Figures 9.4a and 9.4b isolate the curves for pickaxes and the quarry depletion over time. According to it, by the last day, the player has 13 pickaxes, which grants a total of 14 stones per energy. Given 2 energy resources per day, that equals 28 stones or 5 new pickaxes. You can see how, over time, these numbers will ramp up quickly.

In fact, by using spreadsheet software, we can compute an approximate equation for these charts to predict and extrapolate their behaviours beyond our data. For the quarrydepletion,

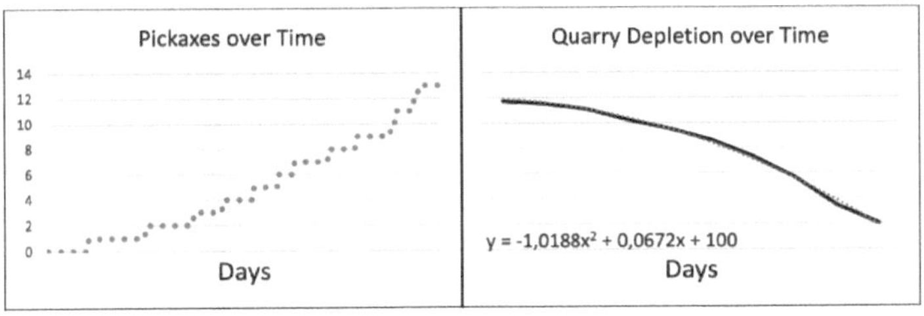

(a) Number of pickaxes owned per day.

(b) Quarry depletion per day.

Figure 9.4: Graphs for the number of pickaxes and quarry depletion.

given the other variables, its equation can be simplified to[2]: $QuarryDepletion(day) = -days^2$.

With that, the quarry depletion behaves as a second-order polynomial (a quadratic curve). This shows how fast the depletion increases as the days pass by. For example, for the 3rd day, the quarry depletion is expected to be −9, which is reasonable. But, for the 30th day, the quarry depletion is expected to be −900, which is way too big of a number for our poor 100 stone-sized quarry.

This behaviour happens because the number of pickaxes and the quarry depletion are part of a **feedback loop** [3]. More specifically, they are a **positive feedback loop**. A positive feedback loop is one in which the very resources used in a sequence of mechanisms influence their own production rates.

Differently from the main mechanisms (sources, drains, converters, and traders), which are subject to the game designer's interpretation and implementation, feedback loops are a mathematical concept and are independent of interpretation. They are a result of the relationship between the mechanisms and resources of an economy.

Positive Feedback Loops destabilise the economy as they produce a **resource escalation**, as we saw with the pickaxes and the quarry depletion. In a multiplayer setting, positive feedback loops can distance players in such a way that, at some point, some players are so ahead in terms of resources that the game does not feel fair or engaging anymore for the other players. On the other hand, players benefiting from a positive feedback loop feel empowered and motivated to proceed.

A common approach to control the effects of a positive feedback loop is to use their counterpart: **negative feedback loops**. Negative feedback loops reduce the production rate of resources to contain their growth. For `The Quarry`, we could implement a negative feedback loop that increases the cost of a pickaxe by +2 for

[2]You might scratch your head for how I just ignored all these numbers for the simplification. In fact, a more precise equation would use all the numbers and elements of the formula, but for the point I am making, only the highest-order element matters. If that is not a good enough explanation for you, I recommend you read about asymptotic analysis then, as it is mainly what I did.

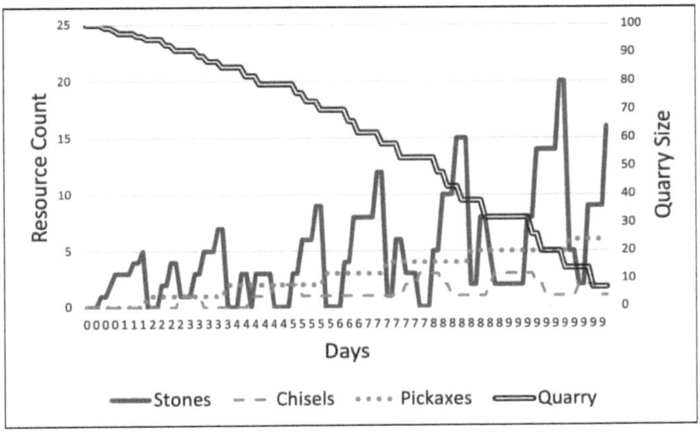

Figure 9.5: `The Quarry` economy chart example with both positive and negative feedback loops for the pickaxes.

every owned pickaxe. If the player has 2 pickaxes, the cost of a 3rd one is increased by +4, for example.

The results of the simulation with both positive and negative loops can be seen in Figure 9.5.

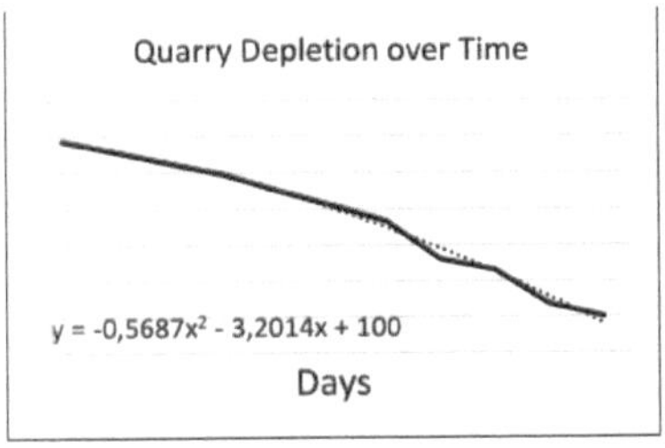

Figure 9.6: Quarry depletion per day with both positive and negative feedback loops.

The addition of a negative feedback loop limits the escalation caused by the positive feedback loop, but it does not stop it. That can be seen in the quarry depletion curve presented in Figure 9.5, which still maintains an increased depletion rate over time as the player owns more pickaxes, but it is less steep than the previous version without the negative feedback loop.

Numerically, as shown in Figure 9.6, the approximate equation for the quarry depletion is now in the order of $-0.5 * days^2$ which is considerably less steep than the previous one, which was $-days^2$. Moreover, the increase in pickaxe costs over time might also make investing stones in chisels a more interesting approach, pushing players towards a hybrid approach.

For that, consider that negative feedback loops not only help to stabilise the game but also promote resource diversification. As the negative effects happen, players might feel inclined to diversify their strategies and recur to other resources that have not been negatively impacted yet. At the same time, the effects of the negative feedback loop in one player can be enough to help other players to catch up.

Additionally, not all resources need to be involved in positive or negative feedback loops. Consider the chisels in `The Quarry`, for example. They are part of the quarry depletion feedback loop as they increase the rate at which it is depleted. But as they are drained automatically when used, the player cannot hoard them the same as pickaxes.

Breaking Optimal Strategies

If you are an analytical player or have tried out "playing" `The Quarry` already, you might have found that there is actually an easy exploit with chisels that allows the player to (almost) infinitely mine from the 6th day onward. With 2 pickaxes and 4 chisels, the player has an 80% chance of getting extra energy while mining, which produces 3 stones. That is enough to make a new chisel and repeat the cycle.

That could be solved with yet another negative feedback loop, but other solutions are as valid and could even be simpler to implement, such as:

Rework the Values: Decrease the chisel chance to a lower value, reducing the chances of the infinite loop chance happening.

Rework the Costs: More expensive chisels require more pickaxes, which might only happen at a later stage in the game where the infinite loop is not necessarily the best or only good strategy.

Rework the Mechanic: Changing the chisel mechanic to break all or more chisels when their effect is activated also prevents the infinite loop chance.

All of these alternatives can also undermine how players perceive the chisel. Increasing its cost or reducing its effects can make them less interesting and even obsolete. Part of a game designer's work is playtesting the new and old values to strike a good balance. Also, changes in how the mechanism works, such as breaking all available chisels when they activate, might completely change how they are perceived by players.

In this specific case, if all chisels break, there is a new risk and reward component. Keeping chisels has a good chance of generating extra energy, but once it happens, all of the investment to collect them is lost. Thus, keeping a small number of chisels makes it less risky to lose them but also a lower chance of benefitting from them.

In general, any change in the game's economy has a big impact on all its parts, which can trigger even more changes. The chisel alternatives to a new negative feedback loop presented might motivate new additions and mechanisms, and that is a good aspect of the process. From a personal experience, working with game economies is easier and more natural when it grows out of simpler versions that are incremented slowly with new components that balance each other.

Applying the Other Cores

This process can also be empowered by the use of the other cores. Collecting and using multiple pickaxes at once might make sense in terms of the `Economy`, but realistically, it does sound like an odd concept. Instead, we could resignify it in the game as each "new pickaxe" is actually an upgrade that makes the current pickaxe better. Giving meaning and justification for these mechanisms is part of the `Narrative` core.

Moreover, the entire game economy can be resignified to other contexts without major issues. **The Quarry** has quite a colonial undertone to it in which the player is exploiting natural resources for some sort of personal gain, while its abstract concept is about a consumption economy in which a pile of resources is being drained by other mechanisms.

With that, we could change **The Quarry** to be about other themes, such as a library: instead of a quarry, the game happens in a library in which the player wants to read all the books (stones). Read books can be converted into knowledge (pickaxes), which increases the rate at which other books are read but is increasingly more difficult to gain. The player could also convert books (stones) into "known cliches" (chisels), which increases the chance of "figuring a book out quickly" without spending energy to read it.

Deadlocks

While not really applicable to `The Quarry`, there is an important concern when planning game economies that we haven't explored: **deadlocks**. A deadlock happens when the players cannot proceed in the game due to a lack of resources. For example, if the player must spend 1 stone to sleep and recover energy. If a player has no stones, then the player cannot act anymore and loses the game.

`The Quarry` already solves this problem as the sleep mechanic has no requirements. In most cases, this is the easier way to break deadlocks: allow important mechanics to be executed for free, even if that means they will reward the player with significantly fewer outcomes than if performed "correctly".

Moreover, you can also consider mechanics that can generate free resources. It might sound odd to give resources out of nothing, but if done in a minimal setting to prevent players from getting stuck without options, it can be an easy solution for deadlocks that, for most of the game, are simply not going to be worth for players to spend time with.

The complete Machinations diagram for `The Quarry` can be seen in Figure 9.7.

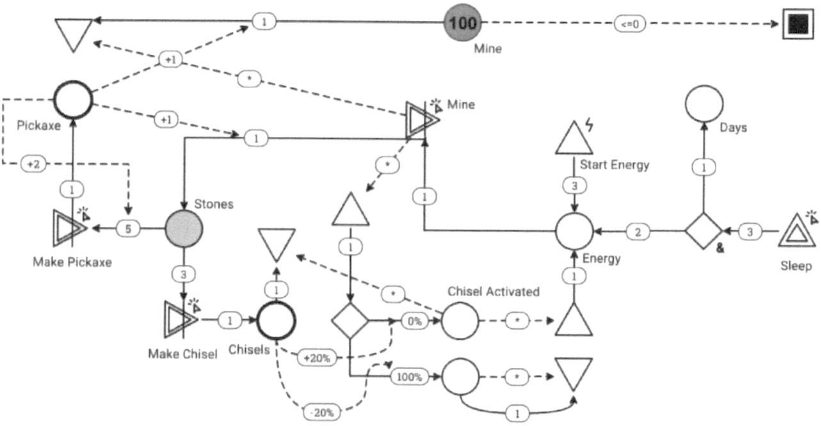

Figure 9.7: `The Quarry` Machinations diagram.

Economy Mechanisms: `The Quarry`

Sources

Sleep: When the player sleeps, it generates energy.

Mining with Chisels: When the player mines, chisels might generate free energy (and be destroyed in the process).

Drains

Quarry Depletion: When the player mines, the quarry is drained.

Activating Chisels: When the chisel effect is activated, it is drained.

Converters

Energy into Stones by Mining: When the player mines, energy is converted into stones.

Stones into Tools: Stones can be converted into tools, such as the pickaxe and the chisel.

In `The Quarry`, there are no trader mechanisms, but we could think about a simple example that does not affect the economy too much.

Traders

Storing Chisels into Chests: The player can store chisels in a chest so they are not used when mining. That allows players to save their chisels for a specific play moment in which they might be more useful.

Other forms of trading, such as trading between players or between other game entities, are likely to recur with the use of either new resources or new mechanisms, which, as seen before, will impact the entire economy.

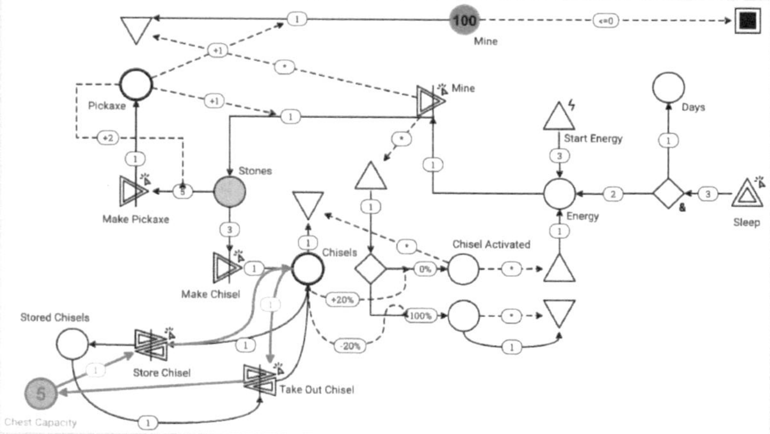

Figure 9.8: `The Quarry` Machinations diagram with the trader mechanic.

Notice that the trading mechanism for putting chisels on the chest could also be implemented differently, such as using conversions or combinations of drains and sources. In fact, the way your economy is going to be modelled depends on your decisions, and there are no strict guidelines on it. As a rule of thumb, aim at having solutions that are easier to explain and to play. As you simulate and play economies in Machinations, also consider which approaches will be easier for your players to learn, as you are not likely going to have other audiovisual tools to help with the teaching process.

This final version of `The Quarry` Machination diagram can be played at: http://tinyurl.com/quarrycgd.

CHAPTER 10

Resource Values

THE RESOURCES OF A GAME ARE THE PROTAGONISTS OF ITS ECONOMY. More resources usually mean a more complex and dynamic economy, making the game harder to learn and excel at. Players also perceive resources differently, assigning personal values to them as they are used. This chapter focuses on this relationship.

10.1 PERCEIVED VALUE

One of the main benefits of exploring a game's economy is amplifying the player's range of options. Resources and mechanisms provide for alternatives and strategies while playing the game. Games with less attention to the economy or an absent economy tend to focus more on player skills, especially physical skills.

Sports, for example, tend to have simple economic mechanisms. In soccer, for instance, the resources (the players, the ball, the number of goals per team, etc.) are mainly not involved in mechanisms. Soccer game designers could even disregard most of the discussion on Economy for their games.

More economy-centred games, such as strategy games, on the other hand, rely on players using strategic thinking to make decisions and progress. For some of these games, the mechanics tend to be significantly simplified and offer almost no room for player skills. Farm simulators [87], for example, are primarily based on handling farm resources and mechanisms rather than on dexterity. This is often independent of whether the game is digital or physical. For digital games, these mechanics will often be implemented

DOI: 10.1201/9781003351191-10

through menu interactions, while for board games, these will be implemented through the use of cards or rolling dice.

The engaging aspect of economy-centred games tends to be on the possibilities its resources provide. The more resource variations and mechanisms, the bigger the room for exploration, experimentation, and player customisation. These are often led by the player's **perceived evaluation** of resources. In other words, the value the players assign arbitrarily to the resources based on their own experience and knowledge of the game and their personal preferences.

A resource's **perceived value** is not a concept that can be easily evaluated as a number, but it is an important aspect to consider while designing games. A player's perception of a resource's value can come from many sources, such as:

Utility: How useful a certain resource (appears) to be.

Rarity: How rare a certain resource is or how hard it is to obtain it.

Experience: How it resembles other highly perceived valued resources from experiences in other games or previous sessions of the same game.

Curiosity: How much the player wants to know more about the resource or its possible effects.

Personal Attachment: How it provides some personal connection to the player beyond the economy and game aspects. Another way of seeing it is as an Outside Game value the player attributes to an Inside Game element.

Personal Preference: In situations where the possible options are perceived as equal, it becomes a matter of personal preference.

It is also common to have a combination of sources of perceived value that lead to the player's perception. In `Another Starry Sky`, given the possible options to which observation point to move next, a player might choose one that seems to have a less complicated path and that is in the direction of a specific constellation the player identifies with, for example.

An **organic perceived value**, *i.e.*, a perceived value that arises from the player's own experience in the game without external influences from metagame analysis and wiki pages, often does not match the economy analytical value of a resource. That is the case because players have an incomplete and often failed understanding of the game's economy and its systems.

In this sense, a perceived value is not a concept that can be generalised or controlled by the game designer directly, as it is highly dependent on the player. Regardless, it is a good source of game design exploration.

Resources with a high utility, for example, resources connected to positive feedback loops or resources that directly empower the player, are resources with a natural tendency to a high perceived value.

Consider the chisel infinite loop in `The Quarry`. As it has a smaller direct impact on the mining capacities, players with a tendency for utility might never find out about the infinite loop as they prioritise making pickaxes. On the other hand, more explorer-type players, who might favour curiosity as their drive for perceived evaluation, might find it very soon through experimentation.

A game designer could alter the percentage rate of the chisel effect and study how players' perceived value of it changes during multiple playtest sessions. That could motivate different player types and reward players who explore multiple options.

Resources with a high rarity are interesting examples to be studied. Even with an absent utility, players tend to assign a high value to resources that are rare to find, especially in social contexts in which they can be exposed to other players. Moreover, rare resources with a high utility might never be used as players might tend to "keep them in case they are needed in the future". For that, it is good to play with rarity (and scarcity) carefully, as its effects are very hard to predict.

Finally, do not underestimate the effects of personal experience and preference in the perceived evaluation of resources. Players have their own backgrounds, history, experiences, and preferences. Even in the face of higher utility or rarity, the players' preferences might dictate the players' behaviour. For that, consider how your game allows players to make decisions that are also based on their preferences, even if those changes are either cosmetics (no effect on the economy) or of low significance (when they have a similar utility within the economy).

Notice that there is a distinction in preferences for playstyle and preference for resources. Preference for playstyle in `The Quarry` is when a player decides whether to go for pickaxes or chisels as they provide different strategies. A preference in the resource is, for example, if `The Quarry` had mattocks and drills instead of only pickaxes, and all three tools act the same. This distinction is important because one is more closely related to the economic mechanisms, while the other is a matter of enabling personal choices.

10.2 CONTEXTUAL VALUE

Another way of understanding and studying perceived value is by separating it into two categories:

Perceived Social Value: The value attributed to a resource that is independent of its relations and economic status, but rather on personal motivations. The use of cosmetic accessories or the preference for a certain character are examples of dynamics driven by perceived social values.

Perceived Economic Value: The value attributed to a resource based on its relations and economic status, such as its utility and attributes. The use of a stronger item or selecting a specific perk in a skill tree are examples of dynamics driven by perceived economic values.

Just as stated before, perceived social and perceived economic values can be mixed and are completely dependent on the player and the game. Even games from a similar genre can spark different sorts of social and economic values and preferences from the same players. But, their distinction matters.

A resource's perceived economic value can be either **context-free** or **context-sensitive**. **Context-free resources** are those which always hold the same inherent value regardless of other events, resources and elements in the game. Progression resources are a good example of context-free resources, as they are always highly valued due to their close connection to the game's goal. **Context-sensitive resources** are those whose values and evaluations depend on other factors, such as other resources and the current status of the game. Situational resources that are only useful in specific situations are a good example of context-sensitive resources.

Considering the last version of `The Quarry` with the trade mechanism to store chisels (see Figure 9.8), we can state that the quarry depletion is an example of a context-free resource, while the chisels are context-sensitive resources.

Context-free resources are important as motivation drivers in the economy, as they are likely to be pursued more directly by players. Consecutively, they tend to naturally devaluate context-sensitive resources. It is especially important to consider if players have direct and easy access to context-free resources, as this might undermine other strategies and lead the game away from its purposes.

In `Family Tree`, the tree's growth is the progression resource and a context-free resource. It is only gained when the players collectively achieve a threshold of Happiness points. If players could individually grow the tree through other mechanisms, the collaborative aspect that is essential to the game's goal would be devalued.

Context-sensitive resources are important as situational and expanding drivers in the economy, as they are likely to be pursued when their perceived value is increased for any reason inside the game. This evaluation and devaluation process, though, often occurs based on context-free resources. This is useful as you can design alternatives and strategies in the game by exploring situations in which context-sensitive resources change their perceived value, especially given their unequal distribution in the game or among players.

In `Family Tree`, Happiness points are context-sensitive resources as their value changes depending on their distribution among other players. If a player has many Happiness points compared to the others, getting more points is not desirable as it prevents all players from growing the tree. On the other hand, Happiness points are necessary for other mechanisms in the economy and negotiations, which trigger game dynamics to be explored.

As the purpose of `Family Tree` is to have players explore how to be happy in a community, exploring the changes in the perceived value of Happiness points allows for designing different experiences that simulate good and bad real-life situations in a community. At moments, players will hold less perceived value for their Happiness points and be more willing to share or lose them in favour of other players or other resources. At other moments, players will hold them closer, making negotiations more difficult but also more meaningful.

Studying the perception of context-sensitive resources is also a good tool for level designing (see Chapter 7), especially for pick-ups and collectable types of resources. In level-based games, levels start with simpler challenges, which make gathering pick-ups and collectables an easier task, increasing their perceived value. However, as the level progresses, the level challenges might take too much of the players' effort, leading them to ignore pick-ups and collectables to finish the level. Thus, the placement of such resources can be designed to achieve different goals, such as:

Help the Player: by being easier to access and giving the player a boost. Thus elevating the perceived value of the context-sensitive resource.

Distract the Player: by being easier to access and moving the player's attention away from other parts of the game, such as other resources or hidden areas.

Reward the Player: by being harder to find, which rewards players who are not focusing solely on progressing through the game.

Challenge the Player: by being harder to get, often in the form of an optional added challenge on top of the mandatory challenges in the level.

Besides all the possibilities and benefits of context-sensitive resources, you should be careful with adding them to the game's economy. As a general rule of thumb, more resources always mean a more complex economy. For that, consider reusing the same resources for multiple situations and scenarios. Besides, this is yet another advantage of context-sensitive resources: their mutability allows them to be reused in vastly different scenarios.

In `Family Tree`, for example, we could consider the addition of new resources such as "Favour Points" or "You Own Me One Card" that act as more specific versions of the dynamics they represent. Favour Points could be given when a player does something for another one, for instance, and could be later exchanged or traded for Happiness points. That could work and expand the repertoire of options in the game, but they also increase the economy's complexity. Instead, we can simply use Happiness points for all of these scenarios.

Surely, at some point, a new resource will be the easiest way to solve an economic problem or to expand the options in the game. That is usually the case when we are dealing with positive and negative feedback loops or when we want to design new strategies towards acquiring a context-free resource, as we did in `The Quarry` by having the pickaxe and the chisel.

Another way of looking at resources is imagining them as different sauces and condiments on a dinner table. It is always good to have some there, and more options will allow people to tailor their dishes towards their own tastes. However, many options will drive them anxious and ruin the experience. For that, you want to, while serving the table, select the sauces and condiments that better complement the dinner and leave the others in the kitchen.

10.3 CALCULATED VALUE

Perceived values are part of the player's experience, but they are elusive to be used for balancing and reaching fairness in a game economy. Instead, it is convenient to look at a more concrete value for the game resources. That is usually done by formulating equations and rules to calculate a resource's value. This **calculated value** is then used as a more concrete and meaningful economy element that can be used to assess and alter the game's economy.

In general, a calculated value of context-sensitive resources is calculated based on context-free resources. In `The Quarry`, we can use the quarry's depletion (context-free resource) to calculate the value of pickaxes and chisels, for example. Due to their meaningful nature, it is usually not fruitful to calculate the value of context-free resources, though, as their value is not normally compared.

To better understand these concepts, let us explore these ideas with the resources in `The Quarry`.

Stone and Pickaxe Values

Each new pickaxe increases the quarry depletion by 2. We could then say that every pickaxe has a value of +2. Also, every pickaxe has a cost defined in terms of owned pickaxes, which is $5 + 2 * OwnedPickaxes$. Thus, a player holding 10 pickaxes holds a +20 value, which was acquired by paying the price of 165. Notice that the cost was not paid on the quarry's depletion resources but on stones. The player had to pay 165 stones.

In `The Quarry`, stones are a context-free resource, as they are directly connected with the progression resource. Stones are a byproduct of the quarry's depletion. Revisiting our pickaxe value, we could state that its value can also be represented as +2 *stones*, rather than just +2 *quarry depletion resources*. Changing the context-free resource used in the calculi helps to ground the discussion on simpler and more meaningful terms. Stones are used to create pickaxes and chisels, making it easier to use when comparing options in the game.

Energy and Chisel Value

Chisels are a bit more complex to calculate as they deal with chance. Each chisel has a 20% chance of recovering one energy resource. Energy resources are context-sensitive resources, as their value changes as our mining rates (pickaxes and chisels) improve. Before calculating the chisel, let us first discuss the energy resource.

At the current version of `The Quarry`, the player can only use energy to mine. For that, each energy resource is valued by the number of stones acquired by spending it on mining. Ignoring the chisel for now, we can calculate the energy value as $1+2*OwnedPickaxes$, *i.e.*, each energy is converted to 1 plus 2 times the number of pickaxes. With 10 pickaxes, each energy is valued at 11 stones.

Getting back to the chisels, we can then establish that a chisel is worth the chisel's probability times the energy, or $ChiselChance *$

$1Energy$. As the energy can be measured in terms of stones, we can rephrase the equations as $ChiselChance{*}1(1{+}2{*}OwnedPickaxes)$. There are different ways of handling the $ChiselChance$ numerically, but for simplicity, let us use percentage as a fraction, even if it removes the randomness from the equation. If a chisel has 20%, then we could use $ChiselChance = 0.2$, which results in the following final formula:

$$ChiselValue = 0.2 * (1 + 2 * OwnedPickaxes) \tag{10.1}$$

This equation shows how the more pickaxes the player owns, the higher and more interesting it is to acquire chisels. Moreover, having 5 chisels sums up their fractions into 1, which means a completely new energy resource. That is coherent with the expected game's behaviour[1].

Working with calculated values provides a more concrete method to make decisions in the game's economy. If we were to diversify the options in `The Quarry`, we can think about them in purely numerical terms as they can be compared to the values we have. Let us consider a new mining tool, the Mattock, that increases the quarry depletion by 3. Its value is +3 stones, which is 1 stone higher than the pickaxe. Immediately, we know that it holds a higher economic value and undermines the pickaxe.

If the mattock works the same as a pickaxe, then in practice, there is no reason for players to get pickaxes at all. Mattocks are better. In `Aesthetics` terms, the mattock is simply another "skin" for a pickaxe with better numbers. Table 10.1 shows the values for the costs and ratio of acquiring pickaxes and mattocks if they keep the same numbers.

The ratio was calculated by dividing the cost of acquiring a new pickaxe or mattock by the amount of increased mining rate (-2 for pickaxes and $+3$ for mattocks). Over time, you see that the ratio decreases; that is, the increment is smaller as the new acquisitions get more expensive. For example, from 0 to 1 pickaxe, each stone spent increases the rate by 0.4 ($5*0.4 = +2$), while from 1 to 2 pickaxes, each stone spent only increases the rate[2] by 0.29 ($7 * 0.29 = +2$).

[1]For a more precise calculation, I recommend you to use Machinations [86].

[2]Rounding the numbers, of course.

Table 10.1: Comparison of increment, cost, and ratio for pickaxes and mattocks in `The Quarry`.

	Pickaxe			Mattock			
Qty.	**Increase**	**Cost**	**Ratio**	**Increase**	**Cost**	**Ratio**	**Difference**
1	+2 (2)	5	0,40	+3 (3)	5	0,60	–0,20
2	+2 (4)	7	0,29	+3 (6)	7	0,25	–0,14
3	+2 (6)	9	0,22	+3 (9)	9	0,14	–0,11
4	+2 (8)	11	0,18	+3 (12)	11	0,09	–0,09
5	+2 (10)	13	0,15	+3 (15)	13	0,07	–0,08

For mattocks, the ratio of stone spent per increment is always lower than for pickaxes. For example, while each stone spent increases the rate by 0.22 from 2 to 3 pickaxes, the increment from 2 to 3 mattocks is only 0.14. For mattocks, the cost of stones is lower than pickaxes, which makes them a cheaper and better alternative.

If we are aiming to balance the options completely, we could use this information to balance the mattock. For instance, if we change the initial cost of the mattock to 8 (instead of 5) and the incremental cost to 3 (instead of 2), then both pickaxes and mattock will have a similar ratio, as seen in Table 10.2.

Table 10.2: Comparison of increment, cost, and ratio for pickaxes and mattocks in `The Quarry`. This time, with an increase in mattock cost in **bold**.

	Pickaxe			Mattock			
Qty.	**Increase**	**Cost**	**Ratio**	**Increase**	**Cost**	**Ratio**	**Difference**
1	+2 (2)	5	0,40	+3 (3)	**8**	0,38	0,02
2	+2 (4)	7	0,29	+3 (6)	**11**	0,27	0,02
3	+2 (6)	9	0,22	+3 (9)	**14**	0,21	0,01
4	+2 (8)	11	0,18	+3 (12)	**17**	0,18	0,00
5	+2 (10)	13	0,15	+3 (15)	**20**	0,15	0,00

Perfect balance, such as in this example, tends to be a boring experience and takes away the meaning of choice. Since both options work economically the same way, they revert to a player preference type of option, which, in this case, does not add anything but extra work. If you find yourself in this position, consider these other approaches:

Explore Other Resources: For `The Quarry` we could explore the energy resource further. For example, the mattock could use more energy than a pickaxe, allowing it to keep the extra mining rate at the cost of another resource.

Expand the Mechanics: Instead of simply mining, the mattock could be part of a new mechanic. For example, in a digital setting, the player must aim the mattock at the correct spot to mine successfully, or in a physical setting, the player must successfully pass a dice test.

Introduce Gates: A stronger resource must be unavailable to players until they reach a certain point in the game. The mattock, for example, might only become available once the player reaches a certain amount of pickaxes or through another means, such as an important story moment from the `Narrative`.

On this last point, it is important to consider that although the `Economy` deals mostly with numbers and equations, its relations and mechanisms drive many aspects of the game and can be used to motivate and demotivate players. If we highly increase the cost of a pickaxe, we demotivate players from using it.

However, `Narrative` can help to justify and expand on these decisions. We could argue that, at some point, pickaxes are harder to improve or that a failed attempt at mining hurt the protagonist's hands; therefore, using them has a higher cost. Technically, it still makes the pickaxes unbalanced (for the worse), but the player has a meaning as to why it happened.

The use of other cores within the `Economy` discussion can also drive other forms of player evaluation, such as social value and the general perceived value. However, it can never be completely controlled. Part of working with the `Economy` and, more specifically, with calculated values is to guide the player's perception, but it is never exact nor complete. Moreover, players make economic decisions in games just as they do in real life, which is, to the dismay of many, uninformed, intuitive and irrational.

Some players will use theory crafting and calculated values to form their perfect strategies, but most of them will simply follow their guts and incomplete perception of the game. This is just fine and not a problem to worry about. It actually makes the concern of perfect balancing and a strong mathematical foundation an effort that rarely pays off. Instead, focus on how your effort is helping your game achieve its purpose. If the game's purpose is to be fun, then work the numbers to help its fun aspects. If the game's purpose is to teach a subject, then work the numbers to reward the knowledge acquisition.

Finally, I had students and colleagues often concerned that their games had economic flaws that could be exploited by players who had in-depth knowledge of their games. However, if you happen to make a game that has sparked that much interest in someone to have them get in-depth knowledge of it, then you just won! It does not matter what and how you did it; you have captivated someone with your work. What else can we strive for as game designers?

IV

Narrative

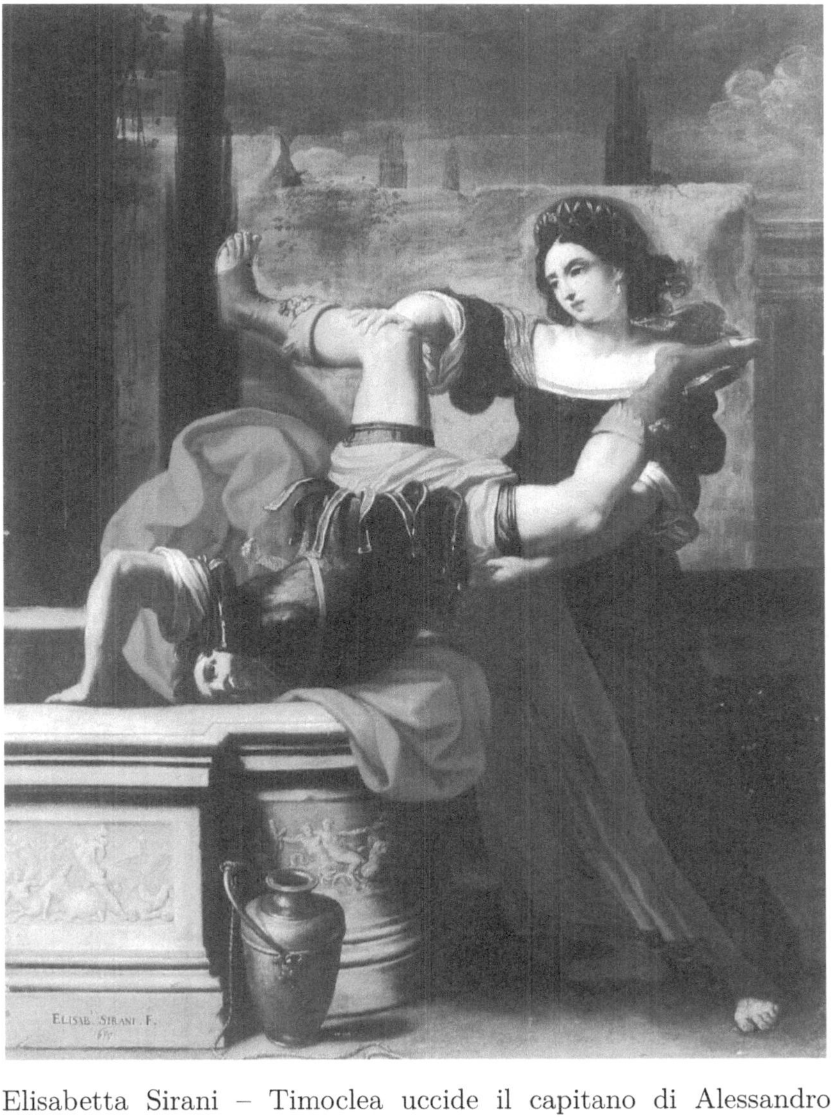

Elisabetta Sirani – Timoclea uccide il capitano di Alessandro Magno (1659).

CHAPTER 11

Starting with Narrative

ALL GAMES HAVE MESSAGES, regardless of how abstract or simple they are. We could even argue that due to that, all games are political. I know it might be a hard pill to swallow, and many gamers and developers are quick to discredit and ignore this claim, but it is true.

Before we get into the discussion on how all games are political through their messages, it is important first to consider how these messages are transmitted to players via the `Narrative` core. The `Narrative` is every aspect of the game responsible for conveying meaning to the player. It is through the `Narrative` that the game and its rules make sense.

For example, the concept of what is the meaning of a Happiness point in **Family Tree** comes from the `Narrative`: it represents how happy a given character is at that game moment. Also, the understanding of the tree's growth as a metaphor for the passage of time is part of the `Narrative`. Moreover, the text written in the cards the player uses contains stories and events that are part of the `Narrative`.

In general, stories and dialogues are the more common manifestation of the `Narrative` core, but it is surely not limited to it. Cinematics in a digital game or the pieces of environmental storytelling at a level are also examples of `Narrative` manifestation. Furthermore, the silence and absence of texts is also a narrative choice. A lot can be said without really saying anything.

DOI: 10.1201/9781003351191-11

As another example, consider the concept game **Another Starry Sky**. It begins with the protagonist crashing into a mysterious rogue space vessel, which damages the player's spaceship. The crash and its outcome can be told entirely through audiovisual means. Still, that would be a form of storytelling.

This chapter elaborates further on these discussions on `Narrative` and its elements, especially focusing on how the game design development cycle can start from it. Many theoretical concepts in this chapter come from the theory work provided by Hannah Nicklin's excellent Writing For Games [88]. In fact, for a more detailed reading on how to write for games, I recommend you use Nicklin's book as a starting point. Other known books on the field address similar topics, but they are either biased towards the North American industry (and culture), such as The Game Narrative Toolbox [89][1], or narrowed to specific genres, such as The Ultimate Guide to Video Game Writing and Design [90][2].

This part of the book is not necessarily on how to write but how we can drive our design and development process through `Narrative` aspects and elements. Writing is an important part of it, but so it is considering what is the game's message.

In this chapter, we will discuss the main drivers of `Narrative` and how they can be used to conduct the game design and development process.

11.1 MESSAGE AND THEME

It is important to differentiate between the **game's message** and the **game's theme**. A **theme** is more of a setting, background, or any particular element that is repeated throughout the game and helps to keep it coherent.

For example, in **Family Tree**, we use a "forest theme" to match the game's name. Alternatively, we could use a more specific theme, such as a "Brazilian Northeastern Caatinga theme"[3]. All of the

[1]Be aware that the authors of The Game Narrative Toolbox use many stereotypes and tropes that readers, like me, might find offensive.

[2]Notably, according to the authors, because that is based on their own limited experience.

[3]Caatinga is a unique biome from Brazil.

game elements would be based on the theme, including elements of the `Aesthetics`, such as their colours, patterns, and shapes.

The **game's message** happens on top of the theme, almost disconnected from it but surely supported by it. The **message** is what the game is telling the player. In `Family Tree`, the game is telling players that living in a community might be difficult and full of complex negotiations for a healthy and happy status, but that it is possible and rewarding. That is why its main progression mechanic is designed to require a balanced happiness threshold; otherwise, the message would be skewed towards rewarding selfish behaviour.

The theme supports the message by lending elements and inspiration. For example, the forest theme inspires narrative aspects, such as providing a background for the game negotiation setups. It also serves as a good motif for other elements, such as having tokens shaped like seeds and game cards shaped like leaves. As you might have noticed, we are again recurring to `Aesthetics` elements, which is just natural. None of the game design cores work alone; they are all supported by each other.

Moreover, starting with the theme might be easier than starting with a message. There might be themes that you are already interested in or that you have never worked on before. From them, it is easier to consider possible stories and game elements to start and, from there, consider the message.

It is also fairly common to not consider the message at all, which does not mean it ceases to exist. The game's message will exist regardless of your conscious choice to have one. It is similar to a political standpoint: if you did not choose one, then someone chose it for you. That will commonly happen through our natural inclination to use cliches, tropes, and other forms of collective consciousness. It is crucial to be aware of this process, not only to control what you are saying with your game but also to manage its creative direction. Some messages also reproduce offensive and problematic values, for example:

The Game about Exploring/Exploiting a New Planet: In this sort of story, the protagonists are newcomers to a new resource-rich environment that needs to be explored/exploited to produce "progress" for the protagonists. The wildlife and inhabitants of the New Planet are enemies, savages, uncivilised, or a combination of these. The message in these games is clearly pro-colonialism and advocates that nature is a means to be used for "progress" by humankind.

The Game about Defeating the Evil Overlord: In this sort of story, the protagonists must face an evil overlord that, usually for no reason, dominates the world and causes all sorts of problems. The protagonists are some sort of chosen ones or different (in a good way) from the other inhabitants of the game's universe, which makes it possible that only they can defeat the overlord. The message of this game is first an oversimplification of world problems as if they manifest and are caused by a single factor; also, it poses the false premise that world change can be driven by the sole work of a small set of special individuals. Moreover, these stories often present a clear bias in which the evil overlord is either of a different race, gender, sexual orientation, or culture [91].

The Game about War/Conflict between Factions: In this sort of story, the protagonists are involved in a conflict between two or more factions that have opposing values. This is a variation of Defeating the Evil Overlord, but where multiple Evil Overlords exist, and the protagonists handle it through the use of violence and participating in the war/conflict efforts. Beyond the previous similarities mentioned, the message of this game is that the use of violence, in many forms, is a valid and effective tool to solve conflicts and that war is a common and necessary form of conflict resolution.

Surely, these examples do not cover all types of games and stories, but if you have played a significant amount of games in your life, you might recognise these patterns in many of them. As much as these messages can be problematic, they can always be reworked and explored. That is only possible, though, once you understand their message. Moreover, this is not meant as a harsh criticism of games of these types and their designers/developers but as an examination of how game messages work even when we do not consciously consider them.

Understanding and managing the message is a challenging task. When I discuss these topics in a classroom, I often hear complaints about how limiting it is not to use some of these examples for game stories. Actually, it is limiting just to using them. There are many other story types to be explored beyond these. What I find an easier way to approach this process, especially in understanding these messages, is to study them and recur to what seems like the complete opposite direction: learning and using **tropes**.

11.2 TROPES

Tropes are storytelling devices or conventions, also known as literary devices, that are generally known and recognised, although not necessarily consciously, by the audience [88, 92, 93]. Tropes are not cliches, but all cliches derive from tropes. For example, the following excerpt comes from the Evil Overlord trope definition [94]. The bold terms denote other tropes.

> *The archetypal* ***High Fantasy*** *villain, often the* ***Big Bad****. He usually lurks in an* ***intimidating fortress*** *in a* ***near-uninhabitable landscape****, plotting to* ***Take Over the World*** *(if he* ***doesn't already rule it*** *or has already taken over parts of it), with hordes upon hordes of beast-like warriors (who may be* ***none too bright****) at his beck and call. (...) This character is often deployed as a* ***Satanic Archetype*** *and associated with* ***eternal darkness****,* ***fire and brimstone****, and* ***Ominous Opera Capes****. For this and other reasons, they are generally male because* ***no woman would be a cruel tyrant who screws up her own realm****. Unless* ***she's a queen****, that is. Appearance-wise, these characters are usually straight expies of* ***Sauron****, clad head to toe in imposing, spiked armour of black iron, or wizened necromancers clad in black robes and deathly pallor. Their origins can vary, but they're most commonly a mortal sorcerer, tyrant or sorcerous tyrant turned terrible and inhuman by their arts, a demon or evil deity of some kind, or* ***a living accumulation of the evil of the world****.*

Learning about the tropes we use is a good way of understanding what might make them problematic. We can learn what to change to move them away from cliches and stereotypes. For the Evil Overlord, its usual portrayal as a satanic male archetype, for example, already suggests possible, more innovative ways in which this character can be construed and used in your story, and also how it affects the game's message. Combined with an interesting theme, this process might lead you to a more interesting villain who is also under your control and helps to push your chosen message instead of the ones it is often associated with.

The workflow I recommend with using tropes is starting the research from the most obvious ones connected to your theme or message. The following blocks explore a few examples of tropes that seem to be connected to the concept games `Another Starry Sky` and `Family Tree`:

Tropes: Another Starry Sky

The easiest starting point for `Another Starry Sky` is the tropes page for Tropes in Space[a]. Some interesting tropes we can find on it are:

Cosmic Motifs[b]: Talks about the use of cosmic elements, such as the Sun, Moon, Stars, and Planets, as symbols and inspiration as they invoke a certain feeling of mystery and infinity.

Inexplicable Cultural Ties[c]: Talks about how, even being from completely different backgrounds, settings, and literally planets, alien civilisations have many inexplicable similarities with our societies, such as the language spoken, the numbering system, and the perception of time. It could be an interesting exercise to attempt subverting this trope in the game by making the non-human species have their own fictional cultures that are as far away from ours as possible.

Space Station[d]: Talks about the common elements in

sci-fi media representation of Space Stations. **Another Starry Sky** has observation points, which are, in essence, space stations, and this trope could help us understand their common use better, as well as inspire us in how they can differ from each other throughout the game.

Moreover, as **Another Starry Sky** deals with using stars and constellations as guiding methods, there are specific trope pages that can help us get inspiration from, such as the Useful Notes page for Constellations[e].

---

[a]https://tvtropes.org/pmwiki/pmwiki.php/Main/TropesInSpace
[b]https://tvtropes.org/pmwiki/pmwiki.php/Main/CosmicMotifs
[c]https://tvtropes.org/pmwiki/pmwiki.php/Main/Inexplicable CulturalTies
[d]https://tvtropes.org/pmwiki/pmwiki.php/Main/SpaceStation
[e]https://tvtropes.org/pmwiki/pmwiki.php/UsefulNotes/Constellations

Tropes: *Family Tree*

Family Tree has two possible and interesting inspirations as good starting points: sitcoms and soap operas. Sitcoms[a], from "Situation Comedy", is a type of media usually focused on the lives of a small group of people, commonly a family or a group of work colleagues. Sitcoms enforce the Status Quo is God[b] trope: every episode is self-contained and has no impact on the others. With that, lessons learned and character development are reset every episode. Soap Operas[c], on the other hand, are a type of media that runs for long periods, telling an ongoing story that continues from episode to episode. Soap Operas constantly use Cliffhangers[d] to hook their audience. Soap Operas are also an interesting cultural phenomenon as they manifest differently in a multitude of cultures, such as Novelas[e] in Latin America and K-Dramas in South Korea, each one of them with their own tropes and references [95].

Some interesting tropes we can find on these pages are:

Slice of Life[f]: Talks about stories that are not centred around conflict but rather on mundane and daily life moments.

Sliding Scale of Idealism Versus Cynicism[g]: Talks about the range of opinions characters and games can have from being hopeful towards a particular ideal (idealism) to accentuates on its negative aspects (cynicism). Inspiration from this trope can help to come up with interesting situations for the negotiation setups in `Family Tree`.

[a] https://tvtropes.org/pmwiki/pmwiki.php/Main/Sitcom
[b] https://tvtropes.org/pmwiki/pmwiki.php/Main/StatusQuoIsGod
[c] https://tvtropes.org/pmwiki/pmwiki.php/Main/SoapOpera
[d] https://tvtropes.org/pmwiki/pmwiki.php/Main/Cliffhanger
[e] https://tvtropes.org/pmwiki/pmwiki.php/Main/Telenovela
[f] https://tvtropes.org/pmwiki/pmwiki.php/Main/SliceOfLife
[g] https://tvtropes.org/pmwiki/pmwiki.php/Main/SlidingScaleOfIdealismVersusCynicism

Using and Avoiding Tropes

It is very unlikely to escape tropes altogether. There are even discussions on the TV Tropes website itself about this vain attempt [96]. I have seen developers try it for the sake of innovation or to avoid cliches entirely, but that comes with two costs:

1. **Tropes are Known Conventions that Viewers are Familiar With:** Avoiding or breaking tropes intentionally and often might be seen as a vain attempt to subvert expectations, which tends towards bad writing and self-mockery. Instead, consider which tropes might help viewers to more easily assimilate parts of your game and which others can be subverted as clear innovation mechanisms to help make your `Narrative` more unique and interesting.

2. **Breaking Tropes requires A Lot of Effort:** To break away from a trope, you must consider forms of avoiding it that negate all of its elements. It might be an easy task for

one or two tropes, but for all of them, it is quite an effort that might not pay off. You are more likely to damage your morale, your health, and your team. Consider how you spend your effort into parts of the `Narrative` to improve your game, its message and its purpose instead of attempting a "tropeless" tale.

Finally, although studying tropes can help you diversify and expand your repertoire of ideas and references, it is not comparable to consuming more and better media. As creatives working on games, we should expand our knowledge and influences as those impact our creative process directly. It is great to use tropes as a source for new and interesting media, but it does not replace your time actually watching movies, reading books and comics, listening to music, visiting art galleries, and so on. Also, do not limit yourself to your own culture or massive pop-culture references. Look for other cultures, other people, other places. The best source for art, especially games, is in real life, not in websites.

11.3 STORY-RELATED TERMS

Another important aspect when considering story-related aspects of your `Narrative` is the terms you use. Nicklin's book presents a good set of definitions that might come in handy throughout the next sections [88]. These terms are often also present in other (video) game writing books, but they are not always defined. The following list presents a simplified list of the terms presented by Nicklin, with a few additions from other books that are relevant to what we will discuss in this part of the book:

Story: Story is all the events that happen chronologically in the game and that are told via narrative means, such as expositions, dialogue, cutscenes, etc. The story exists beyond the game.

Metastory: Metastory is the story that happens outside what is shown explicitly in the game. For example, in **`Another Starry Sky`**, the childhood of the protagonist might never be present in the game's story, but some consequences of it might

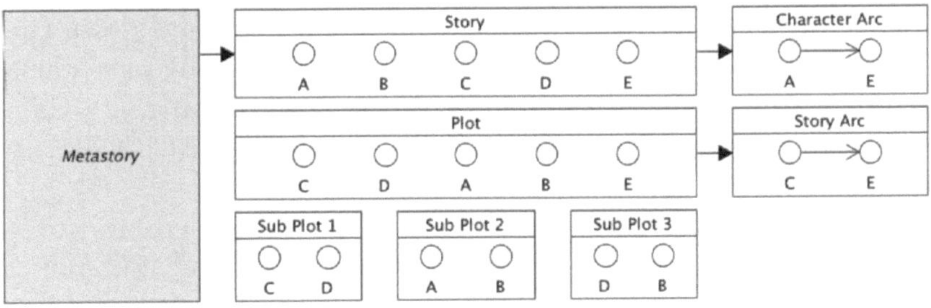

Figure 11.1: Diagram for the story terms presented.

appear, such as childhood friends. The childhood events are part of the metastory, while the childhood friends that appear in the game are part of the story. [90]

Plot: Plot is the order in which the events of the story are told. While the story happens chronologically (that's how time works), the plot is not bound to any chronology or rules[4]. It is easier to design the plot once the story is stable, but from my interviews and experience, there are no strict rules for this process.

Subplot: A subplot is a smaller plot connected to a smaller story that happens within the big story. The meeting with the childhood friend in `Another Starry Sky` could be a subplot: a small story that happens within the game and is concluded in a shorter period.

Arc: Arc is the space in which elements of the story, such as characters, change over time as the plot progresses. Story arcs deal with the changes that happen throughout the entire story and impact the environment in which the story takes place. Character arcs deal with the changes that happen individually within the character as the plot progresses.

Figure 11.1 shows a visual depiction of how these elements are correlated. The metastory happens before the story and the plot, influencing it directly. The story is composed of steps from A to E.

[4]Consider, though, that not all orders will make for a good plot.

A is its start, and E is its end. The plot, however, lays down the story with the order $C \rightarrow D \rightarrow A \rightarrow B \rightarrow E$, *i.e.*, the plot starts by telling the events in the middle of the story (C and D), then returns to the start of the story (A and B), finishing with its last event (E).

Throughout the example story in Figure 11.1, there are three subplots. Subplot 1 spans over the events C and D. Subplot 2 spans over the events A and B. The last one, Subplot 3, spans over the events D and B ($D \rightarrow A \rightarrow B$). The first two subplots are straightforward and happen within the plot's chronology. Subplot 3, on the other hand, mixes two chronologically different events. In a sense, Subplot 3 starts at its conclusion (D) and then we get to see the events of its start (A) and middle (B). If your plot happens in a non-chronological order, it also allows your subplots to explore a more diverse combination of events.

The main **story arc** happens in accordance with the plot, starting at C and finishing at E, as we, the audience, are introduced to the story environment in the events of C. The changes that impact the story environment are complete at the events of E.

Contrary to the story arc, which starts with the first event in the plot and ends at its conclusion, **character arcs** can happen as freely as subplots. However, it feels more natural to have character arcs to follow some sort of natural chronology as we get to experience the change happening gradually.

Story Events

To conclude this section, we have used examples with **story events** in Figure 11.1, but the term "story event" was not defined for a specific reason. There are many terms and opinions as to what constitutes a story event and also as to the granularity within the plot. In this case, I simply used a story event as a significant part of the story that can be reordered at will while designing a plot. Some authors would instead expect a higher granularity and assume a story event is a smaller story unit that moves the plot further. For that, our story would be composed of dozens of story events rather than just five, for example. This last understanding is often discussed with terms such as **story beats**, **plot beats**, or just **beats**.

A **beat** is this story unit that moves the plot, such as a character's action, a specific event, or a dialogue. Thus, for the story event used in this section and the coming ones in this part of the book, we are assuming a **story event** is a collection of chronological story beats that compose a significant part of the story, which can be reordered at will while designing the plot.

This definition is used more for the sake of simplifying the writing and design process for the story rather than for any formal reasoning. It is easier to work with a plot using macro units (story events) rather than micro units (beats). Moreover, as with any other part of the game design development cycle, all of these aspects are bound to be playtested and improved, which are likely to change the micro level rather than the macro level. Focusing on story events helps us to be more flexible towards changes and improvements.

Finally, the examples in this section were kept vague and abstract on purpose. They will be further elaborated with concrete examples in Chapter 12.

11.4 OTHER APPROACHES

There are many ways of starting your `Narrative` process, which is not necessarily through writing a story. However, starting with the story is probably one of the easiest ones. If you are having difficulties coming up with a story or using other elements to start your narrative, consider these two opposing options:

Plan a Story Driver: Many stories have a driver that moves the events forward. The driver is the motivation that sets events in motion to what is going to happen. A new character that arrives in town or a natural event that destabilises the status quo are common sorts of drivers. Instead of thinking immediately about characters and settings, you could start by just considering an interesting situation that makes the story events unfold.

Consider Human Relations: Different from a story driver, which is often a new occurrence that changes the familiar environment in a story, other stories are focused on mundane daily life aspects that create interesting events. The (chosen) family relations or the routine of an office space are often fruitful settings for stories. Instead of thinking immediately about an event that sets the plot forward, you could start by considering the characters and environment and how their relations tell stories.

The two main concept games used throughout this book, `Another Starry Sky` and `Family Tree`, are examples of these two cases. `Another Starry Sky` is a story built on top of a story driver: the crash with the mysterious rogue space vessel. All the events that follow and the main motivation for the player to go an unusual way back home are triggered by the consequences of the story driver. `Family Tree`, on the other hand, does not have a single event that sets its event into motion; it is simply a reflection on the many situations that arise due to the relations within a (chosen) family.

From my experience, game designers usually do not have a hard time coming up with initial setups for their `Narrative` core, with the exception of when they are already focused on a specific game mechanic. On the other hand, it is usually harder to traverse the alternative path: getting to a game mechanic from the `Narrative`. In other words, it is about how to make the story, message, and other narrative aspects into playable elements.

First of all, I always recommend reconsidering if a game is the most suitable medium for your `Narrative`. A book, comic book, or a poem, for example, might be better vessels for your creation. Not everything needs to be a game, and games are not particularly better than any other art forms – they are just different.

If a game is the best or intended outcome, then consider the following recommendations to find suitable mechanics or economy mechanisms to bridge the gap between the `Narrative` core and the others:

Consider the Frequent Verbs: Which verbs are often used in your story? If your story deals with politics and diplomacy, you are likely to have verbs like *talking*, *discussing*, and *negotiating*. From that, consider how they could be transformed into mechanics. If you find yourself with just too many frequent verbs, it might be wise to revise and simplify the story or move the game towards a more economy-based system in which these verbs are economy mechanisms instead.

Consider Visual Novels: Visual novels are a good genre for games that are very focused on `Narrative`, as it abstract the mechanics and intricate systems from the story to happen mostly via text. It is possible to implement other mechanics and economy systems within a visual novel, but that is not an initial and immediate concern to put your story in a playable format.

Consider a Tabletop Roleplaying Game (TTRPG): The most engaging stories often draw their audiences towards the wish to live them. The easiest and cheapest way of achieving it is to use a TTRPG format and let your players roleplay the story. There are plenty of good TTRPG bases you can use already to have your playtesters experiment and play your story before you even need to make up the systems yourself.

Although I often moved from the major concept of `Narrative` towards a story, this core represents more than a story. You can use the other aspects of `Narrative` as starting points for your game design development process. We initially discussed, in Section 11.1, the message and theme of a game. You can start by simply deciding on a message or theme for your game and, from there, develop the `Narrative` and other cores. In that sense, you might even skip a story entirely to focus on the message or theme through diverse means.

The following chapters in the `Narrative` part explore other branches of the core. Chapter 12 Story Structures focuses again on the story aspect of the `Narrative` core and how we can use established methodologies and structures to write stories, as well as how we can break them to achieve other forms of conveying meaning, messages, and theme. Chapter 13 discusses how `Narrative` conveys messages and how those messages are imbued with ethical, moral, and political perspectives, even when often dismissed intentionally by game designers.

If you are still exploring the cores, you can now move to the first chapter of which one of their parts: `Mechanics` in Chapter 5, `Economy` in Chapter 8, `Aesthetics` in Chapter 14.

Otherwise, if you want to or prefer a more linear order in reading the book, just continue ahead.

CHAPTER 12

Story Structures

STORIES ARE DIVERSE. There are many ways of reading, writing, and understanding them. In this chapter, we explore approaches to structuring stories that support the `Narrative` core, as well as the other ones.

12.1 ON CONFLICT

It is a common statement that stories need a (good) **conflict** [89, 97]. That is only partially true, as this view is limited to specific definitions of story. The urge for a conflict often comes from the necessity of a central situation, a **story driver**, that drives the story's progress, as we discussed previously in Section 11.4.

For example, in `Another Starry Sky`, the conflict starts when the protagonist is hit by a rogue space vessel and loses her means to return home. The central situation (being stranded) is the story driver.

However, as seen previously, not all stories need a story driver. A lack of conflict does not mean a lack of story (contrary to what some authors might claim [97]). A focus on the mundane life of our characters might be enough to sustain a story. You probably know a few books, movies, and other stories that mostly describe the daily life of the protagonists. Many video game genres, such as farm sims and management games, are based on the repeated play of mundane events. It does not reduce their story aspect, it just does not follow this particular story format.

DOI: 10.1201/9781003351191-12

Conflicts are tools like tropes. They help to establish story elements and events. Stories can have multiple conflicts and explore them separately, as well as allow players to create and explore their own conflicts. Conflicts can also arise from gameplay elements, such as Inside and Outside Game elements (Section 5.3). In `Family Tree`, for example, the result of a particular negotiation might create a quarrel (a conflict) between players.

Weak and Strong Conflicts

If your story happens to be based on one or more conflicts, it is good to consider its outcomes and its strengths. A **weak conflict** is one in which the solution is either evident or obvious, while a **stronger conflict** might not even present a possible solution at all. The strength of the conflict is not indicative of the story's quality, but it surely influences the creative process. Stronger conflicts provide a more fertile ground for discussions, ramifications, and creativity, while weaker conflicts often require additional elements and (other) conflicts to provide enough material to be worked on. This idea of weak and strong conflicts is similar to the concept of weak and strong mechanics explored in Chapter 5.

A weak conflict is one that can be solved with a few actions and results in a positive outcome for all parties involved. For example, in `Another Starry Sky`, the main conflict can be solved by using technology and skills to return the protagonist to her home planet. These actions might not be easy to perform, but their solution is clear. There are no dilemmas.

`Family Tree`, on the other hand, is built around multiple conflicts with varying strengths. The harder it is to find a solution, if one even exists, the stronger the conflict is. In some negotiations, some players will not be happy with the outcome, which is an important part of the game's purpose.

Arguably, any conflict strength can provide for a good game experience and story. In the case of `Another Starry Sky`, the weak main conflict pushes for extra conflicts and elements, such as the space vessel mystery, to create more narrative elements. In fact, many games, movies, and books are built around weak conflicts but excel in their other aspects, such as character development, sense of humour, adventure, etc. It is a good exercise to analyse story-based media to study their conflicts.

You can also consider a conflict that happens over the course of multiple stories, even if your game only focuses on one of them. A common example is environmental conflicts, such as global warming. Many stories are based on the consequences of global warming and do not include its start or its solution, dealing solely with its consequences and impacts on societies, individuals, ecosystems, etc.

Internal and External Conflicts

Lisa Cron, in her book Story Genius [98], suggests the use of a dual type of conflict for stories, an **internal** and an **external conflict**. An **internal conflict** is one which pertains to the characters individually, such as a psychological issue or a moral dilemma. The **external conflict** is one that happens outside the characters, affecting them and taking them out of their current state. Cron's suggestion is to use both conflicts to reinforce each other and base their solution on each other's resolution. External conflict forces the characters to act, forcing them to solve the internal conflict to resolve the external one.

For example, we could add to `Another Starry Sky` that the protagonist is mourning the death of a close figure who was an avid stargazer. Due to that, the protagonist refuses to use star maps and constellations to avoid grief and relies purely on the technical equipment available in the spaceship. However, due to the crash, these tools are broken and unavailable. To solve the external conflict (being stranded in space), she has to solve her internal conflict (grieving the loss of a close figure) and engage in using star maps and constellations to return home.

The dual conflict is often a helpful approach to handling character arcs, as they push characters into internal changes (internal conflict resolution).

Alternatively, change can also happen passively or as a result of an ongoing process that has no clear start or end. The need for a key factor that causes change is an easy, almost trope-like, approach that makes for simpler storytelling but might lead to a predictable and unrealistic plot.

12.2 THE THREE-ACT STRUCTURE

Many of the resources on writing for games are actually based on other media. Mostly cinema. For some reason, there are quite some authors and game designers who see games as "interactive" movies. I am not a particular fan of this idea, and I believe that it is a narrow perspective on games, especially because this understanding often comes from the idea of video games rather than games. I never heard anyone talking about Chess as a sort of interactive movie about duelling monarchs.

One such understanding is the paradigm of the **Three-Act Structure**, often based on the works of Syd Field in his famous book The Foundations of Screenwriting [97]. Field defines a screenplay paradigm formed of 3 different acts: **Set-Up**, **Confrontation**, and **Resolution**. As follows:

Beginning, Act 1, or Set-Up: The Set-Up is the introduction to the characters, environment, their relationships, and the main conflict.

Middle, Act 2, or Confrontation: The Confrontation are the many obstacles faced by the characters that prevent them from solving the main conflict.

End, Act 3, or Resolution: The Resolution is the conflict solution and outcome of the story to its characters and the world.

These acts are separated by specific **Plot Points**. Plot points are events that move the story in a new direction. The first plot point, between Act 1 and Act 2, is the one which forces the characters to leave their initial state (Act 1) and face the conflict (Act 2). The second plot point, between Act 2 and Act 3, is the one which reveals how the conflict can be solved, leading the characters from their current struggle (Act 2) towards the resolution of the conflict (Act 3). Figure 12.1 shows how the three acts could be mapped to the previous example used in Chapter 11.

Notice that the three acts are mapped towards the plot, not to the story, as the plot is what will be experienced by the players. Moreover, as we see the three acts as representations of the Beginning, Middle, and End, they do not need to be mapped chronologically with the story. Their chronology is related to the player.

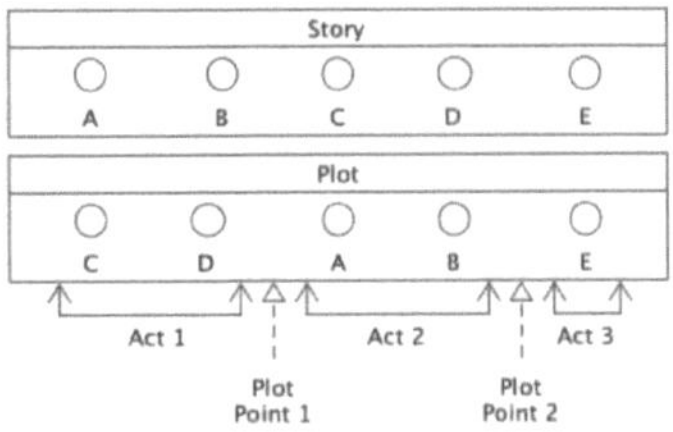

Figure 12.1: Example of the Three-Act Structures applied to the Plot.

As a more concrete example, let us map the events of `Another Starry Sky` into a three-act structure. First, as we have never established the game's story properly, let us consider the following brief outline of its events, mapping them to the events from A to E as in Figure 12.1. To better exemplify the non-chronological plot, for this section, we are assuming the plot order presented in Figure 12.1, which is $C \rightarrow D \rightarrow A \rightarrow B \rightarrow E$.

Starting with the story, we have:

A: The protagonist is undergoing a regular mission in space when her spaceship alarms alert of an imminent collision with another spaceship.

B: After the collision, the protagonist survives and checks what is still working on the spaceship while also investigating the rogue space vessel.

C: The protagonist uses the still-working systems and the stars to guide herself back home, but she struggles with grief while doing so.

D: The protagonist is faced with increasingly hard courses back home, avoiding obstacles during her space travels and solving star maps and constellations to locate her home planet.

E: The protagonist finds herself back home and fixes her spaceship, which also symbolises her healing process by dealing with her grief and loss.

For the plot, we have a different order, in which first, we play the events C and D, which are mostly focused on the mechanical aspect of the game: using the stars for guidance and piloting the spaceship through observation points. Then, we play the chronological beginning of the story, A and B, in which we are introduced to how the protagonist got into the current situation. Finally, the plot ends with the return home, E.

As the plot is laid out, we need to establish the plot points that move the story between the acts. They go as follows:

Plot Point 1 $D \rightarrow A$: The protagonist is faced with a constellation that is highly significant for whom she is mourning as an ultimate challenge towards her healing process.

Plot Point 2 $B \rightarrow E$: The protagonist, by revisiting early moments and memories, finds out how she can solve the last constellation to find her way home.

Notice that, in both cases, the plot points are used to move the events to their chronological time. As C and D happen later in time as A and B, plot point 1 is meant to cause a sort of "flashback", bringing the plot to an early chronological moment. Later on, plot point 2 uses the events from the past, A and B, to move the events back to the current time, E.

From a gameplay perspective, this plot structure allows us to design the mechanical-driven aspect of the game first, which happens in Act 1 (C and D), to then move towards the more story-based part, which happens in Act 2 (A and B). For that, we could even consider having the entire Act 2 happen in a different format, such as a Visual Novel or Point and Click style, as it is mostly meant to explore the `Narrative` core rather than the `Mechanics` or `Economy` core.

Arcs and Plot Points

Returning to arcs and plot points, it is also easy to see that this structure can be extended to more or less acts if you disregard their names. You could work with a 2-act structure and one plot point, for example, understanding that each act contains its relevant events and the plot point is a special event that changes the story to a new state (a new act). With this, you could map board game concepts, for example, that deal with a multi-phase setting, as each phase is an act.

For `Family Tree`, we could use the family tree growth as the plot points. Every time the tree grows in the backyard, new cards and events are introduced to the game, which symbolises the passage of time and the change of acts. The game starts in the first act, which is mostly based on tutorials and early moments of the (chosen) family living together and proceeds to many other acts with increasing levels of difficulty.

You should not see the Three-Act Structure as a strict paradigm to be followed rigidly. First of all, it was not made for game development, but for Hollywood movie scripting: Field's book includes the number of pages each act should have in their script already, considering the budget and production costs based on his experience in Hollywood.

Moreover, Hollywood movies follow a format that caters to a specific, narrow audience, which is far from the whole range of cultures and people around the world. For that, the storytelling format proposed by the Three-Act Structure is severely limiting. It assumes a format of media consumption based on culture and human relations that is not universal. The use of plot points, for example, is an easy storytelling mechanism that keeps audiences engaged and allows for an easy comprehension of the plot. It reduces the character changes and their arcs to single events on time that justify them, while, in reality, change happens over time for a myriad of reasons.

On the other hand, the Three-Act Structure is very easy to use and helps to achieve a basic story structure to work on. From my experience, having a solid start for your story, which includes all its main points (beginning, middle, and end), even without details, makes working with it easier than working on-premises and unfinished ideas. Try to get your first draft of the story laid down as soon as possible and revisit its components and aspects as you work on it. Changes will happen eventually, but it is easier to consider and apply them if you have all the structure laid down already.

Getting back to food analogies, I like to see this process as if you are creating and writing a recipe at the same time. It is better to write the first version of the recipe and follow it, making changes during the preparation and reworking the draft, rather than trying to do both exactly at the same time. You will not write the perfect recipe at first nor cook the perfect dish out of your head. Embrace the change and move on. Eventually, you will reach your nicely written recipe and a full belly.

12.3 QUESTIONING THE HERO'S JOURNEY

Coined by Joseph Campbel as a result of his years of research, the **Hero's Journey** is a template for writing and understanding stories based on a sequence of steps [99]. Campbel also used the term "monomyth" to refer to this template, as his studies, arguably, suggest that many (folk) tales, stories, and (religious) myths were all fundamentally the same at a base level:

> *A hero goes out of his safe place towards an unsafe and magical new location. Magical forces are encountered, and an important victory is obtained. The hero returns to his safe place with the new powers acquired from the unsafe one.*

The original format of Joseph Campbel's Hero Journey is divided into 17 steps, which not all are mandatory and could change according to specific aspects of the story [99]. Other authors have proposed other forms of organising it in fewer steps, such as 7 by Vogler's "The Writer's Journey" [100] and 12 by Hannah Nicklin's "Writing For Games" [88].

The version with 17 steps is presented and briefly explained below:

1. **The Call to Adventure:** When the hero is pushed outside of the safe place.
2. **Refusal of the Call:** The hero initially refuses to leave the safe place.
3. **Supernatural Aid:** The hero is given a new power to help the adventure.
4. **The Crossing of the First Threshold:** The hero ventures forth to the unsafe location and starts mastering it.

5. **Belly of the Whale:** The hero faces the first real challenges that support how unsafe this location is.
6. **The Road of Trials:** The hero is continually faced with challenges to which he might even fail.
7. **The Meeting with the Goddess:** After overcoming challenges, the hero meets with another character who helps him learn about his growth and better prepare for the next steps.
8. **Woman as the Temptress[1]:** The hero is tempted and challenged not to continue his adventure.
9. **Atonement with the Father:** Surpassing the temptation, the hero must overcome his internal struggles, which are holding him back from his true potential.
10. **Apotheosis:** The hero incorporates the changes and overcomes his internal struggles, becoming a new self.
11. **The Ultimate Boon:** The hero achieves his main objectives.
12. **Refusal of the Return:** The hero initially rejects returning to the safe place.
13. **The Magic Flight:** After deciding to return, the hero is faced with potential challenges on the way back.
14. **Rescue from Without:** The hero is helped by the other characters met during the story on his return.
15. **The Crossing of the Return Threshold:** The hero returns to the safe place.
16. **Master of the Two Worlds:** The hero has now conquered both the safe and unsafe places.
17. **Freedom to Live:** The hero, now changed, can rest and enjoy the results of the journey.

---

[1]Not my words. That's how Campbell wrote it.

The hero's journey is also often organised within three segments, just like the Three-Act Structure we saw in Section 12.2: Departure (steps 1 to 5), Initiation (steps 6 to 11), and Return (steps 12 to 17).

Campbell's theory is criticised for many points, such as the emphasis on a triumphant single male (or masculine) protagonist, as well as on the claims for how universal his theory is [101]. Many authors support that, in reality, the hero's journey claims to be a sort of monomyth that comes from a limited and altered perception of myths and stories from various cultures that were read by Campbell with the "lens of a hero's journey" [101].

Besides, the original 17-step list has terms and ideas that might sound outdated and problematic, such as the "Woman as the Temptress", which reinforces the wrong depiction of women in media as either a sexual object or a monster that blocks the path of the "hero" [102, 103].

Using the Hero's Journey

Still, the hero's journey can be used as another tool. There are three methods that I like to employ as creative exercises when developing stories:

Layout the First Draft: It is particularly hard to write stories. It is even harder starting from a clean canvas. For that, I recommend the use of one of the simplified and modernised versions of the hero's journey to lay out a first draft of the story.

Expanding on Individual Steps: Another exercise is to focus on individual steps for an entire story rather than using all of them. For example, you could write a story only on the **Refusal of the Call** or the **Road of Trials**. Each one of these steps offers sufficient tension to be expanded in their own story. In fact, the story of many digital games could be discussed as mostly a **Road of Trials** followed by **The Ultimate Boon**.

Subverting on Individual Steps: Building on the previous exercise, you can subvert the step and explore a story in which the protagonist(s) follows a different outcome from what would be expected in the original hero's journey format. Subverting the steps denies the preconceived idea of what the goal of the hero is in his journey, which might be a powerful tool to present other valuable goals. A hero could refuse the call and have the remaining of the story to follow up on the consequences of it, for example.

The last point, Subverting On Individual Steps, can also be expanded on a broader sense, which is a refusal to accept individual masculine heroes as the only agents of change. Many stories focused on the hero's journey hold this belief that the individual masculine hero is the only one capable of "saving the world" from the singular evil antagonist. Reworking these points can lead to more interesting stories which better reflect the complexities of the world. Singular individuals are not responsible for the change, nor is evil incarnate in a singular entity that can be wiped out, returning the world to a "safe" stage. This is yet another instance of how games are political, as the repetition of this sort of story reinforces the acceptance of their messages.

Again, the hero's journey focuses on a singular hero, which is not a rule you have to abide by. Your story might have multiple or even no protagonists at all. As in its essence, the hero's journey is a structured character arc (as seen in Chapter 11), you can apply it to your characters without the need to use it as the central structure of your story.

CHAPTER 13

Moral and Ethics

THE MESSAGE OF A GAME IS DEEPLY IMBUED IN ITS NARRATIVE in more ways than just on its story. The consequences of the player's action, for example, are an important factor in establishing a message. Actions that contradict the message should be restricted or limited so as not to harm it. At the same time, these limits and restrictions should be rooted in the game's `Narrative`.

In this chapter, we explore and discuss these limits and how they play an important role in working a game's `Narrative`, as well as how we as game designers can strive for more diverse and challenging game designs by exploring the impacts of games and their messages on society.

13.1 SUSPENSION OF DISBELIEF AND MORAL DISENGAGEMENT

Whenever we engage with a piece of media, we naturally and willingly lower our critical thinking and logic, accepting the media as it is, even if it is (loosely) based on real events. For example, when you read the concept of **`Another Starry Sky`**, you probably did not question the existence of spaceships and interstellar travel, as those do not exist in real life yet. You simply accepted it as part of the story. This process is referred to as a **suspension of disbelief**: a momentarily and willingly (even unconsciously) acceptance of unreal and impossible realities for the sake of enjoying them.

However, if I were to present that at the centre of **`Another Starry Sky`** universe, there is a flying tasty marshmallow the size of

DOI: 10.1201/9781003351191-13

galaxies that defies the laws of physics, you could be pushed out of the suspension of disbelief state and activate your critical thinking again. There are boundaries to how much players are willing to let themselves be "fooled" for entertainment.

It sounds odd that players are willing to believe in fantasy only to a certain extent, given that an important aspect of fantasy is that it is not real. Players might easily accept the possibilities of interplanetary travel but are not that excited about physics-defying space food. That is because even fantasy needs to hold to a sort of **internal consistency**. This consistency might come in the form of tropes, which are expectations players have towards a given topic, theme, or setting, or through the media itself with its given rules.

Using `Another Starry Sky` again, if we present it as a game set in a futuristic scenario, players immediately expect common future tropes and ideas. Space travel, highly advanced medicine and intergalactic languages that are weirdly similar to modern English, for example. Anything that goes outside these expectations needs to be laid out by the media. Stargazing to locate and navigate space fits into the possibilities of `Another Starry Sky` universe, even if it might be impractical from a space travel perspective where the position in which we see stars and constellations change depending on where we are.

Elements that defy these expectations can work if carefully presented to players. `Another Starry Sky`'s galaxy-wide marshmallow might be too much without context. However, if the game plays with the idea of space food from the start, such as presenting moons made out of cheese and stars of salt, then the enormous marshmallow becomes easier to swallow (pun intended!).

Consider that the boundaries and expectations from players vary widely, especially considering their background, age, and preferences. Moreover, some of these expectations come from unrealistic tropes and experiences founded on previous experiences. The lack of people of colour in medieval settings, for example, while historically inaccurate, is often taken as realism by gamers and critics alike [104, 105]. Their boundaries are large enough to accept magical creatures and dragons but not non-white characters, especially when they are in relevant positions.

Suspension of disbelief is also an important part of combining the `Narrative` and the other cores, especially the `Mechanics` and `Economy`. Some game mechanics, for example, are abstractions of real-life activities and are accepted by players due to the suspension of disbelief. Farming video games, for example, have fruits and vegetables to grow and mature dozens of times faster than in real life, which is necessary to not bore players with very long and repetitive gameplay[1].

Arguably, this is the same reason players engage in game mechanics that would be unthinkable in real-life settings, such as planting vegetables, eating healthy, doing physical exercises, organising their belongings and, of course, killing enemies.

Jokes aside, suspension of disbelief is often connected to another human behaviour, **moral disengagement** [106]. Moral disengagement, as coined by Bandura [107, 108], is a mechanism in which people disengage their moral reasoning, permitting actions that would otherwise be evaluated as immoral. As stated by Bandura [107, p. 194]:

> *The disengagement may centre on (a) the reconstrual of the conduct itself so it is not viewed as immoral, (b) the operation of the agency of action so that the perpetrators can minimize their role in causing harm, (c) the consequences that flow from actions, or (d) how the victims of maltreatment are regarded by devaluing them as human beings and blaming them for what is being done to them.*

Moral disengagement and suspension of disbelief are responsible for allowing players to enjoy violent games, for example. It does not mean these players would engage in violent actions in real life, though. On the contrary, these actions are only performed **because** they do not happen in real life. At the same time, this also does not imply that violent games are completely harmless (more on that in Section 13.3).

In a game setting, players will disengage their morals and engage in the game morals. If they have to play as an anti-hero or

[1] Bear in mind that that could also be a design decision. Having an activity take a longer time to more closely resemble its real-life counterpart can be an effective mechanism to ensure the game's purpose.

villain character, they will do so to enjoy the game. This process will only stop if either their morals are pushed too far or the suspension of disbelief is broken. Part of working with the `Narrative` core is to consider breaking the suspension of disbelief to achieve some reflection on players.

Games can also have their own moral systems and alignments, as well as their internal characters. These moral systems are interesting tools to be used within the `Narrative` core, which is the topic of the next section.

13.2 THREE AXES OF MORALITY

Alignment, moral alignment or character alignment is a representation of how a certain character views and acts morally and ethically [109]. Defining a character's alignment helps to categorise and generalise character behaviour towards aspects of the game world, such as which (social) class it belongs to or which nationality it has [71]. Moreover, alignment is a good creative tool because it allows designers to work within the boundaries of how a given character is expected to behave.

Probably the most known and used alignment system comes from the famous TTRPG Dungeons and Dragons (D&D) [110]. Characters under the D&D alignment are ruled by two axes: the ethical axis (Lawful versus Chaotic) and the moral axis (Good versus Evil). The ethical axis defines how much a character abides by rules, laws, and honour. A lawful character respects those elements even to their own harm or the detriment of others. On the other hand, a chaotic character disregards those elements and acts according to their own individual will, but not necessarily in a selfish manner. A chaotic character might act unlawfully, for example, to the benefit of self or others.

The ethical axis is disconnected from the moral judgement of good and evil. That's the concern of the moral axis. A good character will care for others in a selfless manner, while an evil character will act selfishly, focusing on itself in disregard to others.

Combining both axes, you can construct characters with a diverse set of possibilities. A chaotic good character, for example, is a sort of rebel who disregards laws for the sake of helping a good cause. A lawful evil character, inversely, is one that serves a system of law so strictly that their actions are constant threats to others.

The D&D moral axes are well-known and work well, especially for characters, but they are somewhat limited when used on a large scale for societies and systems. For that, I propose another system that works differently from the D&D axes but that can be used in combination with it: the **Three-Axes of Morality**.

The idea of the Three-Axes of Morality is based on Gert and Gert [111] definition of morality, which can be summarised as a certain code of conduct defined by an individual, group, or society that determines behaviour. Thus, by this definition, a moral character is one that follows the code. Acting in disregard to the code it is to act immorally. Differently, actions that lie outside the realm of such morality and its code are amoral.

This definition of morality embraces the D&D Moral Alignment system, specifically the ethical axes (Lawful versus Chaotic), but it is more general than that, as the moral code might be disconnected from notions of rules and laws, as well as the concepts of good and evil.

Using this definition, the Three-Axes of Morality are:

Light versus Darkness: The moral agents (light) struggle against opposing immoral agents (dark), usually in the context of good versus evil or lawful versus chaotic. In this axis, characters can be located in any position between Light and Darkness, including the extremes.

Red versus Green: The moral agents belong to one of the extremes of the axis, either Red or Green, as they represent complete opposite sides of a conflict. In this axis, characters can either belong to one or the other extreme or are completely outside of the moral continuum as amoral characters.

Blueberries versus Oranges: The moral code of these characters is completely beyond human comprehension or hardly related to human logic. This axis, different from the others, does not represent a literal continuum; it is just a representation of a moral code for beings that cannot be understood nor have their actions and behaviours explained or compared to others.

All three axes are not mutually exclusive and can manifest simultaneously in a game. However, it is very likely that one of them will be more prominent in the story than the others.

Light versus Darkness

Light versus Darkness is a common moral axis when there is a clear antagonist to be overthrown. These antagonists often belong to one of the extremes of the axis, generally the Darkness one, while the players control the Light characters, *i.e.*, the "good folk".

However, it is not necessary to have characters that belong to both extremes. It is common to find games and media with a focus on characters that lie within the spectrum of Light versus Darkness. On those, characters can be more nuanced and act less predictably, as well as more humane.

Red versus Green

Red versus Green is the common morality in competitive games, in which two or more teams fight for a given objective. In this case, the moral codes of the different agents might even be virtually identical, but their objectives and goals are exclusive of one another.

Chess is a good example of Red versus Green morality. Each player belongs to one of the extremes, even if their pieces "act" exactly the same. Both players want to overthrow each other's kings.

Different from the Light versus Darkness axis, games focused on the Red versus Green morality are more likely to be episodic and short, as each game session is a sort of conflict between teams with barely any overarching story, as that could distract from the moral duality.

Alternatively, there are famous exceptions, such as faction-based MMORPGs, in which players engage in combat based on their factions. In essence, the faction's morals, especially if perceived through an ethical/good versus evil perspective, are identical, and the players' decision to which faction to belong to is based way more on other factors, such as aesthetics, friends' preferences, and any gameplay distinction (as explored in Chapter 6).

Blueberries versus Oranges

Blueberries versus Oranges is not the absence of morality but rather the absence of understanding such moral code, if one even exists. In this axis, moral agents might behave in ways that could be seen as part of Light versus Darkness or Red versus Green, but ultimately, they appear as random and only make sense in terms of their own entities.

This axis is not commonly used as a main morality in games due to its incomprehensive nature, but it is often represented in the form of (alien) gods, eldritch abominations, and supercomputers. These entities might be deemed as chaotic, using the D&D moral alignment system, for example, but their actions should not be labelled simply as "good or evil" as their intent lies beyond such concepts.

While entities operating in a Blueberries versus Oranges morality cannot be understood, other moral agents in the game are likely to follow other axes, and this mismatch can be interesting to explore.

For example, in a fictional setting in which a Blueberries versus Oranges Spaghetti God orbits a planet, its inhabitants might act according to a Light versus Darkness morality in their daily lives. The Spaghetti God interferences in their routines might push them inside the Light versus Darkness continuum in regards to their own interpretations of what those interferences mean. If the Spaghetti God yells "white sauce" all of a sudden, a Light-inclined inhabitant might act in accordance with the Darkness for the sake of guaranteeing "white sauce" for itself and its alien-equivalent of a (chosen) family.

Exploring morality as part of the game's `Narrative` core is a good tool to expand on creative opportunities and assess the game's message. A game's message, such as **`Family Tree`**, which is based on companionship and selflessness, would not pursue a Red versus Green morality in which players would see each other as rivals. Instead, it would dwell on the continuum of Light versus Darkness, assuming all players will act either selfishly (Darkness) or selflessly (Light) depending on the situation and negotiations.

The lack of a specific villain in `Another Starry Sky` is a conscious one, as the events in the story are caused by random consequences. The protagonist's main challenges are of environmental nature (avoiding asteroids, for example) and internal conflict (overcoming grief). In a sense, the universe in `Another Starry Sky` is of Blueberries and Oranges morality. Its internal "reasoning" and "functioning" affect the player directly but cannot be simply explained. But its actions push the player and protagonist into moral dilemmas, such as unravelling the mystery of the rogue space vessel, which might be a result of other moral axes.

13.3 VIOLENCE IN GAMES

As pointed out earlier, I am not a proponent of the idea that games, particularly video games, influence players into becoming more violent or partaking in criminal activities. The usual argument for proponents of this thesis comes from the fact that violent and criminal actions are possible and encouraged in many popular digital games. The first aspect, negatively influencing players, does not seem to be particularly true, although this has been an ongoing research topic for decades [39, 112, 113]. On the other hand, the second aspect, that video games often allow and encourage violent actions, is certainly true, and that's the main point of this section.

In Fundamentals of Game Design, Ernest Adams claims that most games have some level of violence, be it more or less abstract [35]. Take any popular platformer game in which enemies are defeated by being stomped by the player. Is that a violent action? If so, this game has some level of violence. Alternatively, you could disagree, assuming this mechanic is too abstract from real notions of violence.

Wisely, some authors approach the question of violence abstraction by refining the definitions used, specifically the distinction between **violence** and **aggression** [114]. **Aggression** is any action that intends to cause harm, while **violence** is an extreme form of aggression, causing severe physical harm and death. With that, the previous jumping mechanic example is a form of aggression but not necessarily violence. There are also international systems to handle this matter, such as the Entertainment Software Rating Board (ESRB)[115], which presents distinctions such as Cartoon Violence, Fantasy Violence, Intense Violence, and even just plain Violence.

Still, the apparent ubiquity of the presence of violence in games is concerning, especially from a game designer's point of view. It is crucial, as game designers, to ponder over this matter, especially as it often materialises in our own creations. Anecdotally, every year, most of the games I see being developed by colleagues, friends, and students contain some sort of aggression, if not violence.

The two main reasons for that seem to be repetition and simplification. By repetition, I mean that game designers repeat what other games do. Many games, especially digital games, have challenges in the form of enemies, which need to be defeated by some sort of aggressive or violent mechanic. That is particularly true for economy-based games in which enemies or other living elements in the game must be killed to acquire resources, such as living stock or monster drops.

The other reason, simplification, is somewhat deeper than repetition but strongly connected. These games often simplify their conflicts to a trivial, aggressive, or violent solution. The most common examples are games in which a clear antagonist must be defeated to solve all the problems it is causing. It ignores why there is an antagonist in the first place or how any harm caused by it will vanish with its defeat. Moreover, if that antagonist had goons and other entities either under its control or following its cause, why were they doing so? How is the defeat of such an antagonist, especially through aggressive and violent means, enough to resolve all ramifications of the conflict?

The answer is that, most likely, the antagonist is just a symptom of a bigger problem, one that is not manifested in a single entity and that cannot be solved by pulling punches. As anecdotal evidence, consider any long-running franchise based on the never-ending cycle of new antagonists being overthrown. What were the outcomes, if there were, of the last "evil antagonist" defeat?

The simplification caused by reducing conflict resolution to the use of violence is a reflex of accepting violence as a proper and valid tool for solving conflicts, which is simply not the case. No aspect of life can be solved by the use of violence. On the contrary, violence just produces more violence. Surely, this is a complex issue to be tackled in a game, as many will quickly point out, because "games are just entertainment". But are they?

Actually, no. **Games are not just entertainment**. Assuming so, it neglects all of the positive impacts of gaming, game design, and game development. Books are not just books. Movies are not just movies. Cartoons are not just cartoons. Entertainment in itself is more than just a few laughs and good times. It influences us in many aspects, positively and negatively.

If we believe, for instance, that games can help with socialisation [116], with improving visual-spatial cognition skills [117], with education [27], among many others, then we must accept that they can also produce a negative influence, such as addiction [118], short-term aggressive behaviour [112][2], and the endorsement of toxic masculinity traits such as dominance and suppression of emotions [119].

That is not to say that you should immediately stop playing violent games or never make them yourself. But we, as game designers, must be aware of what we consume and what we create. Every game has a message, remember? The `Narrative` will communicate way more than just its plain texts. Achieving the game's goal through killing is a message that enforces the understanding of violence as a conflict solution tool. Consider if that is the message you want to pass, especially to avoid doing so just for the sake of repetition or simplification.

Finally, a common reaction to this discussion is that it is not possible to make interesting and fun games without using violence. That is only the case if that is your own limitations as a game designer. There are plenty of non-violent games that are just as fun as other violent ones. For this book, for example, all the concept games avoid having direct violent mechanics and goals as proof that it is possible to design non-violent games.

[2]Have you ever felt like throwing your joystick on the wall after losing a game? That's short-term aggressive behaviour.

Surely, thinking about different and engaging games without resorting to tools and techniques that have been done many times before, especially from the references we have, is not an easy task, but bear in mind that designing a good and innovative game that pushes its own message is a challenge because designing games is challenging. Being an authentic game designer means accepting this challenge.

V

Aesthetics

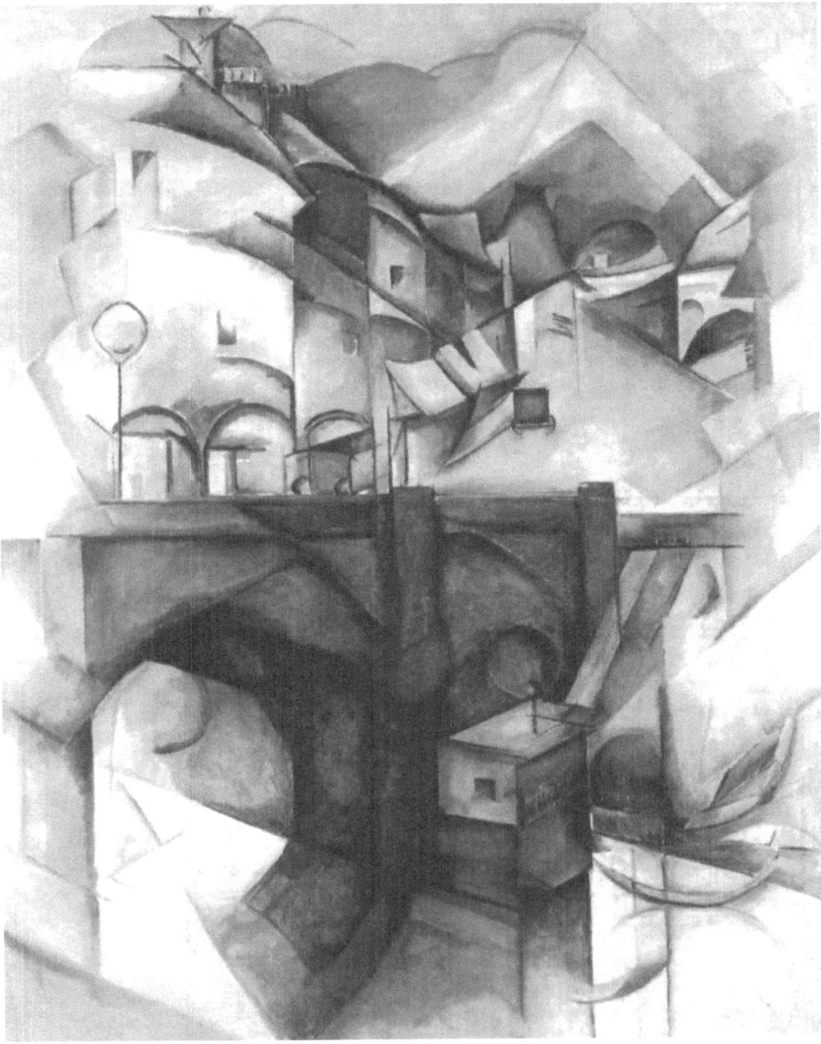

Aleksandra Ekster – Bridge. Sevres (1912).

CHAPTER 14

Starting with Aesthetics

THE GAME AESTHETICS CORE IS RESPONSIBLE FOR THE OVERALL MOOD AND FEEL OF THE GAME. These can manifest in many forms, such as the audiovisual elements or the tactile feeling of the game pieces. These elements empower the cores. A grim story set by the `Narrative` can be emphasised with sombre music and sinister graphics, for example.

Elements of the `Aesthetics` vary greatly depending on the game's medium. Digital games, for example, use digital art assets and music, while physical games may use traditional art means and tactile experiences for their game elements.

This chapter discussed the main approaches for how to start with the `Aesthetics`, as well as how it can be used to assist other parts of the game design development cycle, such as creative alignment and planning.

14.1 MOOD, MOOD BOARDS AND OTHER BOARDS

Mood is a flexible and abstract term in game design. In general, the mood of a game is the emotional feelings conveyed by the game and its elements. Although this definition relies on the emotional aspect, you can see mood as larger and more flexible than emotions. "Happy", for example, is a mood and an emotion, but "Grim" is not really an emotion but is certainly a mood.

DOI: 10.1201/9781003351191-14

The best way to establish a mood is by using tools that communicate it, such as images and sounds that achieve the intended mood. **Mood boards** are good tools for this purpose. A mood board is a general term used to describe a design tool that combines a set of audiovisual media for communication [120]. Unfortunately, this definition overlaps with other similar tools and boards. For that, I prefer to use the following definitions:

Inspirational Board: A collection of audiovisual elements organised in a panel (board) that inspires those who perceive it with ideas and concepts. The inspirational board combines elements to help the creation of new elements. It does not need to follow rules and can be as diverse as necessary to help the creative process.

Mood Board: A collection of audiovisual elements organised in a panel (board) that communicate a mood. When the mood board is perceived by others, they feel its mood in a clear and direct form.

Style Board: An organised collection of audiovisual and textual elements that sets the style guidelines for the production process. The style board establishes the creation rules, such as polycounts[1] for 3D models, the use of fonts, and other steps that must be followed to ensure audiovisual coherence between the art elements and artists.

There are other boards to be considered as tools, such as the **audio board**, which is used to present, usually in an interactive manner, the auditory elements of the game so they can be listened to in context with each other. Another useful board to consider is the **concept board**, in which the main concepts and ideas of the game are organised to support further other boards, such as the style and inspirational boards.

[1]Polycount is a term used to refer to the number of triangles in a 3D model. Other common names for it are tri count and vertex count (for the number of vertices).

Moreover, you are not limited to using only one of each board. If your game has multiple moments and moods, you can establish multiple mood boards. That can help you better organise your documents and your game design document. In fact, during my interviews, it was fairly common to hear from game designers who used a more extensive game design document that a significant part of it was dedicated to organising and compiling a vast collection of mood, inspirational, and style boards.

These boards should also be seen as living elements in your process. Consider having an easy link and access to them so your team is constantly aware of their ideas, especially for mood boards and style boards. In a digital setting, you could have a shared link to your boards on the first pages of your Game Design Document or set them up on a project's wiki page. If possible, and your team works physically in the same location, consider printing the boards and hanging them around your workspace.

However, as the project grows, it is okay to be flexible with updating your boards. For example, style boards with rules for the 3D pipeline might be revisited after performance tests. For physical games, production costs can also force a review of the number of printed colours and material quality in the style board, for instance.

Moreover, although flexible, these boards help with an important challenge in any game design development process: **creative alignment**. By using audiovisual tools that let the entire development team achieve a common understanding, your process is less prone to individual and wrong interpretations of the game elements. That is an important distinction that comes from the `Aesthetics` core compared to the others. It has a stronger influence on the coherence of all game elements, even to the point in which it can drastically change how the game is perceived. The `Aesthetics` glues together the elements designed by the `Narrative`, `Mechanics` and `Economy`.

More precisely, while the `Mechanics` and `Economy` are more abstract cores related to the gameplay, the `Narrative` core adds meaning and context to them, which is only truly perceived and experienced through the `Aesthetics` core.

14.2 CREATIVE ALIGNMENT AND GAMEPLAY

Establishing a clear mood is a good way to align the creative process, as the lack of it might lead to ambiguous and confusing interpretations of the same themes and ideas. For example, consider the concept game `Another Starry Sky`. Its art style could be serious, with a muted colour palette and sombre dialogue. Alternatively, it could also be light-hearted, with bright colours and funny dialogue.

The mood defines which one of those paths will lead the creative process, especially in regard to the audiovisual content. If we decide on a serious tone, then the colours chosen and the art style should enforce it. Besides that, it should also allow for a first impression of how the game will look, even in its earliest conceptual phases.

As their concept starts to take form and the general mood is established, I generally recommend that my students draw a visual concept of how the game, in its final form, would look. As most of the main visual elements have not been developed yet, this drawing should act as a form of abstract sketch to establish a common visual guide.

Figure 14.1 shows an example of such a draft for the `Another Starry Sky` concept game. In this particular case, Figure 14.1 uses pre-made assets, sketched lines and rough symbols to organise and display a few ideas. If you are or have a very talented 2D artist in your team, it usually pays off to work on a more elaborate draft for the following reasons:

1. **Establishes the Player's Perspective:** As the draft pretends to show how the game would look as a final product, we also get to see how the player perceives the game. For digital games, for example, it may help define the type of camera used. The example in Figure 14.1 uses a third-person camera with a top-down view.

2. **Establishes Gameplay Elements:** Working on the draft forces us to consider gameplay elements such as how movement works and the player's placement. Moreover, it can already show how obstacles and collectables would be perceived and their relation to the player in terms of size. On top of that, it can already suggest how parts of the game

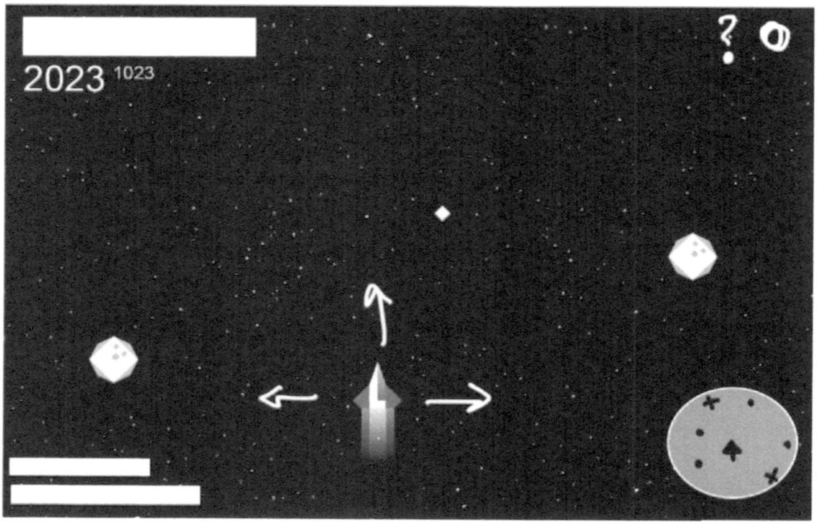

Figure 14.1: Example of draft for the `Another Starry Sky` game screen.

are controlled, such as which axes the player can move (the arrows around the player in Figure 14.1, for example).

3. **Establishes User Interface (UI) Elements:** The draft should also contain the first ideas for the user interface (UI) elements in the game, such as health bar, score counters, settings options, etc. Although many of those aspects might still be up for debate, considering them sooner during the draft-making will help your planning.

Although the example used is from a digital game, the same process can be pursued for other forms of games. The main idea is to sketch how the game would play out, which can also be done from an outside perspective, drawing the players playing the game on a table, for example, or from a specific element, such as drawing a single card from a card game.

For the concept game `Family Tree`, we could approach this process by sketching some cards, for example. Not only would it provide a more tangible understanding of how the game looks and which elements these cards would have, but it would also reveal

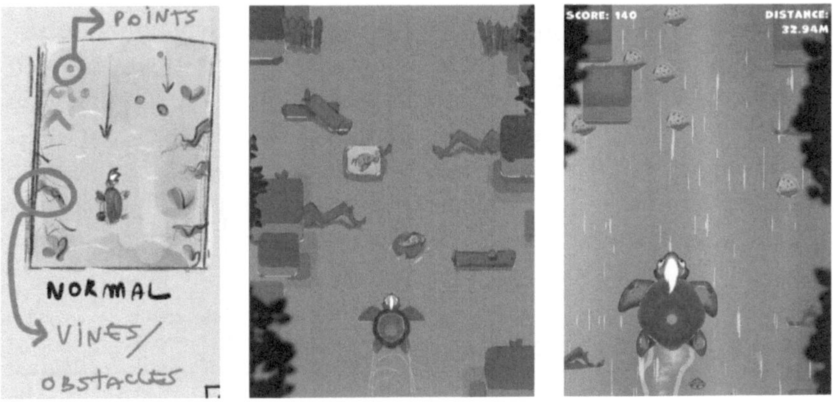

Figure 14.2: Example of two draft stages for a game, followed by a screenshot of the finished game.

possible future concerns, such as how lengthy a card text may be to fit the layout.

Moreover, besides anticipating many discussions on the game elements, this early draft acts as the main creative alignment tool for most of the production process. It connects all the boards and guides conversations as a clear view of the game being developed. It is important to be as close as possible to the actual game, including improving new versions of the draft with updated artwork and other elements.

Figure 14.2 shows multiple stages of this process. In the first image, there is the rough original draft of the game idea. The second image is a better and updated version made by an artist, which already defines abstract elements such as hazards and collectables into visual ideas. The third image is a screenshot of the final playable game as it was submitted for a game jam I participated in while writing this book[2].

Although a more refined and better-drawn draft allows for a better and more concrete shared game vision, the artistry required for this activity is not that relevant. The first draft shown in Figure 14.2 was enough to establish most of the main game elements

[2] You can see more about this game at my website: https://dagongraphics.com/punkturtle

required for the development process. Moreover, depending on the media you are focusing on, there are alternatives that can help you easily achieve a similar result, such as photo bashing, sketching on top of rendered 3D images, and even using UI and wireframe tools. Finally, as the game takes shape, you can use screenshots from the game itself and sketch on top of them, which is especially useful for drafting menus and other user interface elements for digital games.

14.3 AESTHETICS AS GAMEPLAY

Besides being used to assist creative alignment, the `Aesthetics` core is also a rich source of gameplay inspiration, especially considering the multiple senses and feelings invoked by it.

First and most obvious are the visual inspirations and styles that arise from working with mood and inspirational boards. Many game mechanics can derive directly from it as they are likely linked to other games, tropes, and stories (the last two are discussed in Chapter 11). A bucolic and calm mood can invoke mechanics related to farming and contemplation, which are easily connected to economic mechanisms, for example.

Moreover, we can search for mechanics that emphasise the mood. A mysterious and whimsical mood might be emphasised by the use of more exploratory gameplay with puzzles. In more practical terms, we can directly write down actions and activities that either happen or cause that mood, which can be transformed into gameplay mechanics and economy mechanisms.

The concept game **`Another Starry Sky`** has a mystery mood and story which emphasise each other. The stargaze mechanic supports the exploration aspect, while the conversations and dialogues in different space stations lead the player to solve the game's secret. At the same time, the space-travelling mechanics add dynamics and tension to the `Narrative`, as the player is forced into challenges before progressing through the story.

Besides visual aspects, there are other sources of `Aesthetics`. Sound is an interesting one which is often used combined with musical-related gameplay mechanics, but also as an alternative form of input and output for accessibility reasons and experimentation [27, 121, 122].

Physical games can expand this concept further by using other senses as gameplay drivers, such as exploring textures and smells. Different from digital games, physical games are not restricted to their contents and can more easily interact with elements outside the game, such as using daily life objects and activities. A game about colours and smells could have the players navigate their own kitchens to complete objectives.

The concept game **Family Tree**, for example, which emphasises a community-building message, explores the `Aesthetics` core by having players assemble and grow their own family tree with real elements in a collaborative and tangible effort. We could devise that parts of the game involve literal seeds and soil or even have the "family of players" plant a real tree by the end of a meaningful game session.

When building on the idea of using other sensations to create gameplay, I recommend you resort back to the game design cycle proposed in Sections 2.3 and 3.5. Once a game mechanic is established, consider at least one goal to be achieved by it and then prototype it. That will allow you to more quickly assess the game mechanic and how it aligns with your `Aesthetics`. How much do your players actually feel the intended mood?

Creativity-Oriented Game Mechanics and Goals

The `Aesthetics` core suits itself well for more creativity-oriented game mechanics, such as drawing, painting, and composing music. However, these mechanics and the need for creativity often clash with the game's goal. As pointed out by Alex Jaffe, creative-driven gameplay is a cursed game design problem: players will be tempted to use as little creativity as necessary to achieve the game's goal, ignoring the creative aspect [123].

Alternatively, this curse can be handled by reworking the game's goal. As proposed by Greg Lobanov, if the creative mechanic only supports the progression tasks, then players are still incentivised to play creatively, as the goals are not blocked by these mechanics [124]. For example, in a game in which players play a musical instrument, parts of the journey could have the player compose songs creatively for characters, while the game's goal requires the player to play specific songs, in increasing levels of complexity, to unlock new paths and new characters.

14.4 OTHER APPROACHES

The previous sections suggested approaches from how to start with the `Aesthetics` core, which include using different boards, experimenting with mechanics that invoke a certain mood, and exploring creative interactions with senses and feelings. This section pushes these ideas further into practical steps you can take to help you start with this core.

Start from an Inspiration: If you are unsure of which mood to go for, try to navigate through galleries and expositions for inspirations. Use digital museum walks, for example, to explore artworks and art pieces that might engage your creativity. On a more pragmatic note, look at artwork and question which mood it invokes and how that mood could be gamified.

Explore other forms of Art: There are many art forms out there, such as music, dance, theatre, sculpture, architecture, etc. Experiment with some you never had direct contact with. Study it. Consume it. Then, from the experience, gather the feelings and mood it invoked in you and gamify it.

Explore your Senses: As discussed in the previous section, explore other forms of interacting with games and players. Many game designers focus solely on digital games and joysticks, but there are many other forms of input, such as voice, body movements, breathing, etc.

Change your Controller: Alternatively, if you are focused on digital games, consider other forms of handling your joysticks and inputs. Consider non-traditional forms of holding your controller or how parts of it could be used for other purposes. What other feelings could you get from it?

Handling Art

A common criticism I heard while discussing the idea for the cores of game design was that the `Aesthetics` core seems more like a responsibility of the artists rather than of game designers. While the development of `Aesthetics` core elements is indeed part of the artists' work, these elements are important game design drivers.

However, it is very useful for game designers to explore these artistic skills as part of their craft. Some of the ideas for starting with the `Aesthetics` core suggested earlier in this chapter are mostly in the realm of game design but can be explored in more art-oriented tasks.

Your game can start from a drawing, a song, a poem, or any other art form. It can come easier if you are the author of these, as it will more directly speak from your creative process. Explore them. Explore your skills and allow your game design process to embrace more activities. You do not need to be a professional artist to produce art.

The following chapters in the `Aesthetics` part explore other branches of the core. Chapter 15 Audio Visual Language explores more elements of the `Aesthetics` core, which can help organise and shape game ideas. Chapter 16 explores another important game design, User Interfaces (UI) and User Experience (UX), which are more tightly connected to the `Aesthetics` core, even though parts of it as well as its content, are firmly connected to all of the other cores.

If you are still exploring the cores, you can now move to the first chapter of which one of their parts: `Mechanics` in Chapter 5, `Economy` in Chapter 8, `Narrative` in Chapter 11.

Otherwise, if you want to or prefer a more linear order in reading the book, just continue ahead.

CHAPTER 15

Audiovisual Language

AUDIOVISUAL ELEMENTS, SUCH AS IMAGES AND SOUNDS, are important elements to achieve the mood, but they also play an important role in creating a common **Audiovisual Language** for how the game is developed and perceived. This chapter focuses on the processes for achieving this **Audiovisual Language**, and how it ties to the other Cores of Game Design, especially the `Narrative` core.

Some of the concepts explored in the chapter come from general design and drawing theory. You do not need to worry about not being a proficient artist to follow them, but you are surely recommended to explore and expand your skillset into these domains. Being able to draw your ideas, even as simplified and abstract sketches, is an invaluable skill to have as a game designer. It improves your communication and also forces you to consider important aspects of game development.

15.1 SHAPE LANGUAGE

The simplest form of visual language is **shape language**. Shape language is the idea of conveying information based on familiar shapes we are used to. Shape language theories are often based on 3 basic shapes [125], as shown in Figure 15.1:

Square: It is stable and firm.

Circle: It is flexible and welcoming.

Triangle: It is stable and dangerous.

DOI: 10.1201/9781003351191-15

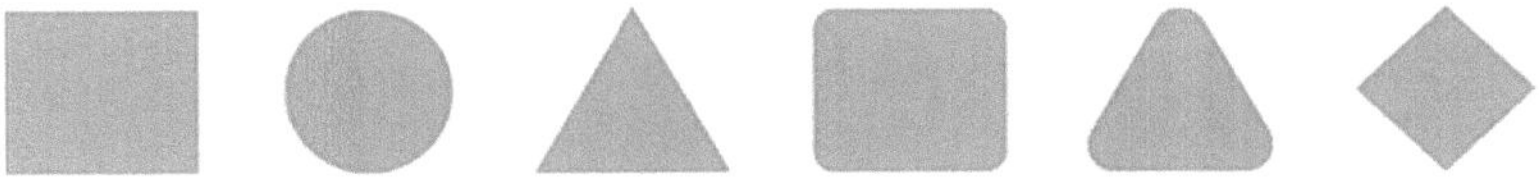

Figure 15.1: Example of basic shapes and some of their variations.

Squares are good as solid shapes that establish order and stability, while circles are the opposite. Triangles are similar to squares but more aggressive due to their pointy ends. These shapes can be changed and combined to achieve other effects, such as rounding squares and triangles, to reduce their sense of stability and aggression, for example. Rotating shapes can also create other meanings, such as the diamond that, while created from a square (or two triangles), is perceived as way less stable.

Using and combining these shapes is an easy way to emphasise the mood of your `Aesthetics`, as well as conveying meaning to your visual elements. Consider, for example, for **`Family Tree`**, the cards will use rounded squares and circles to support the light-hearted mood and community sense. Warnings and dangers in **`Another Starry Sky`**, though, are likely to be presented in triangular shapes to transmit a sense of urgency.

Value and Negative Space

Figure 15.2 expands on shape language further by exploring two important concepts, **value** and **negative space**.

Colour value, or just **value**, is a term used to express how light or dark a visual object is. The higher the value, the lighter the object is. The first square in Figure 15.2 has two very distinct values, a darker one on top and a lighter one below, which makes it be seen as two different shapes or as a sort of flag [126, 127].

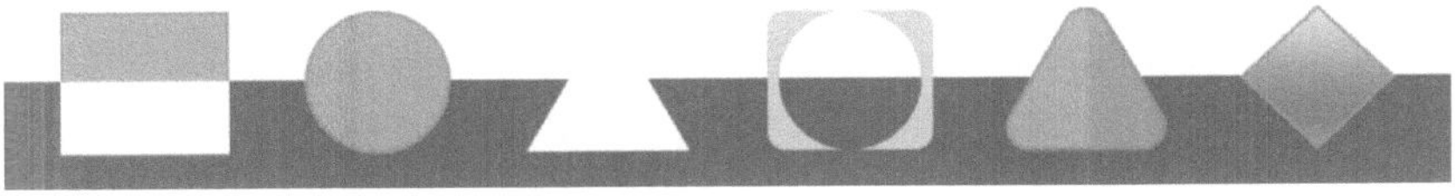

Figure 15.2: Variations on basic shapes and values.

Having a clearly distinct value variation between visual elements can significantly improve their perceptions. On the contrary, objects with different but similar values might be seen as a single object or as a visual mistake or artefact. Compare, for example, the contrast of values from the first square with the second triangle. The second triangle has a less obvious value difference, which makes it harder to perceive and might even appear as a mistake or print failure [128].

Additionally, subtle value differences, such as the gradient presented in the diamond shape, can ease the eyes, which helps make the shape more pleasing.

Negative space refers to the space around and between objects, such as the one in the area above all shapes [129]. Negative space can be used to infer information. There are no triangles in the third shape of Figure 15.2, but the negative space makes us perceive as if one is there. Negative space can also be used in shape creation, as done in the rounded square in which the circle shape (the fourth shape in order) was removed, creating a completely new shape.

Although the negative space is defined as the empty space, it does not need to be completely empty. Negative space also happens with backgrounds, for example, as you can see in the fourth shape (the rounded square shape), in which the removal of the circle creates a negative space that is not fully empty. You can use the composition and organisation of your shapes to create more negative spaces, even when there are technically no empty areas.

15.2 COMPOSITION

In the previous section, we mainly focused on individual elements. However, in most cases, you will deal with multiple elements at once. The arrangement of multiple elements is usually named **composition**.

More generally, composition is the act of arranging elements to convey some meaning or intent. Figure 15.3 shows simple compositions using a combination of square shapes, values, and negative space.

In the first composition, all squares have the same value, which makes them seem like the same shape. The second composition uses

Figure 15.3: Simple compositions using the square shape, values, and negative space.

values to distinguish the shapes better, creating an idea of depth. The third composition inverts the values and the order of shapes, but due to the size of the middle shape, it does not achieve the same idea of depth as the previous one. In this case, the sizes and values make the composition look like three distinct bars rather than a tridimensional relation. Lastly, the fourth composition uses negative space by subtracting these squares to form a new shape and idea.

Figure 15.4 shows a simplified view of composition applied to a painting by Louise Moillon [130], "Plum Basket with Basket of Strawberries" (1632). On the left side, you have a simplified version with circles, establishing the relationship between the main objects in the painting. On the right side, you have the original painting with all its details. Notice how the placement of the major shapes (circles) is sufficient to organise and create a sense of space, depth, and balance, even with abundant elements.

The difference in complexity between Figures 15.3 and 15.4 is quite large, but you should not worry about matching Louise

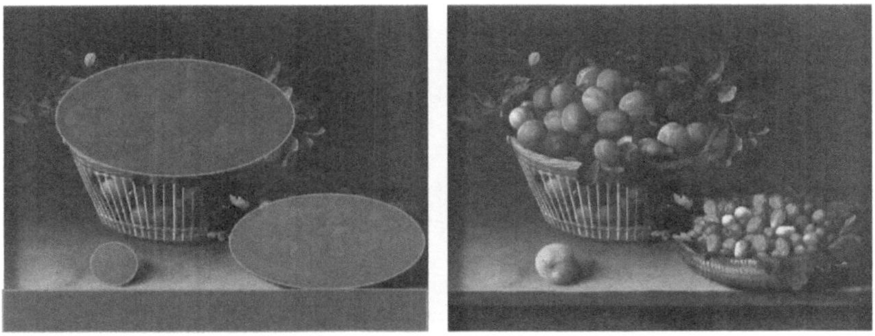

Figure 15.4: Example of composition using the painting Plum Basket with Basket of Strawberries (1632) by Louise Moillon.

Moillon's painting skills to explore composition. There are many techniques and approaches to this process that you can explore. Besides that, before considering composition, it is important to consider **intent**. What do you want your composition to achieve?

For that, it is wise to consider the **Gestalt Theory**, which explains how we perceive the combination of elements as a group rather than the sum of its individual elements [131].

15.3 GESTALT

Gestalt was conceived by German psychologists studying how humans perceive elements [132]. From their studies, gestalt branched to many other fields, including design. For designers (and game designers), gestalt is usually understood under a set of 10 laws[1][131]:

1. **Figure-Ground:** We distinguish what is the foreground (figure) from the background (ground) of an image.
2. **Simplicity:** We perceive elements (and compositions) in their simplest form, regardless of their details.
3. **Proximity:** We perceive closer objects as part of the same group and objects that are apart as separate or independent.
4. **Similarity:** We perceive similar elements as part of the same group and different objects as belonging to other groups.
5. **Symmetry:** We perceive symmetrical objects as part of the same group, even when far apart.
6. **Closure:** We perceive gaps, incomplete elements and enclosed elements even when they are not present.
7. **Common Fate:** We perceive objects that share the same sort of motion (fate) as part of the same group.
8. **Continuity:** We perceive objects in a line or sequence as part of the same group, continuing the line or sequence regardless of other aspects.

[1]We often use 10 laws for design, but Gestalt theorists believe in more laws for other fields [131].

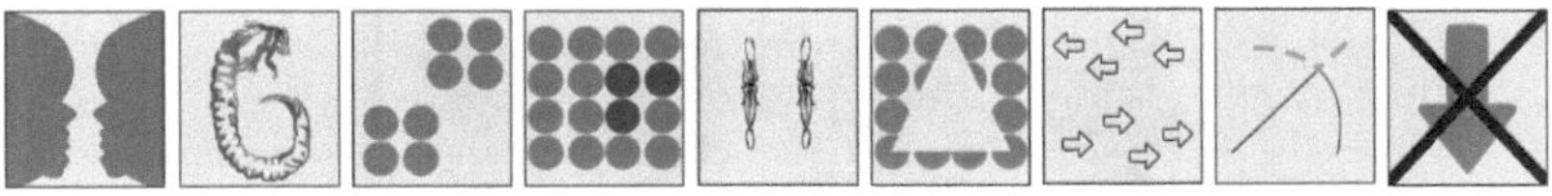

Figure 15.5: Example of composition using the gestalt laws, except Similar Background (or is it really missing?).

9. **Experience:** We perceive objects based on previous experiences with other objects.

10. **Similar Background:** We perceive objects that share a similar background as part of the same group, even when they belong to different compositions.

All Gestalt laws are exemplified in order in Figure 15.5[2]. The entire image itself exemplifies the **Law of Similar Background**. All the examples share the same format, size, and background, making them all perceived as part of the same composition: the Gestalt examples.

Considering the Gestalt laws is an important process for the composition and layout of elements, and it is a simple step. As Gestalt theorists propose, these laws are so ingrained in our minds that we are likely using them frequently and unconsciously. Moreover, these laws have clear overlaps that intensify each other. For instance, the **Laws of Common Fate** and **Similarity** are often seen together as both are related to visual resemblance.

15.4 SKETCHING AND THUMBNAILING

Composition and gestalt are pragmatic approaches to conveying visual information, but they might seem too rigid to express creative ideas. They are often better used when working on established ideas and visual elements. When starting from scratch (from a blank canvas, for example), it is easier and better to directly start **sketching**.

Sketching is not meant to be final artwork or visually pleasing. The sketch is meant to shape your ideas and make them concrete.

[2]The Laws of Simplicity and Symmetry are illustrated by using the letters G and I, respectively, from the public domain Insektofobiya font by Annastasia Samsonova & Jovanny Lemonad.

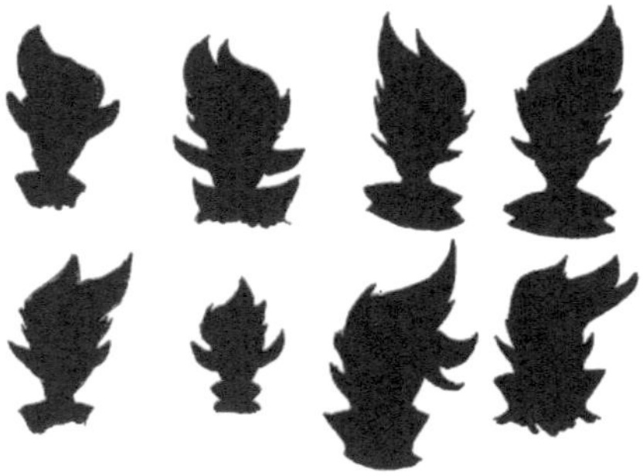

Figure 15.6: Example of thumbnails for the head of a conceptual character.

Do not let your wrong expectations on the drawing quality of your sketches stop you from making them. Your sketches only need to be clear enough to communicate your ideas. You can improve them later by applying shape language, composition, and gestalt theory.

If that is still not encouraging you enough, consider my favourite technique: **thumbnailing** [125, 126, 127, 129]. Thumbnailing is the idea of making a tiny version of your ideas – as big as the nail of a thumb. Given its size, it is not really possible to focus on details, forcing you to work on simpler shapes and forms. Figure 15.6 shows an example of thumbnails for a head of a possible conceptual character for `Another Starry Sky`.

Although I am unaware of specific rules to how you approach thumbnailing, I like to follow a few steps:

1. **Start with lines of a General Shape:** Let your hands loose and make a free shape that matches your base idea.

2. **Outline the Desired Shape:** Given the first step's imperfections, the result will likely have more lines and details than initially intended. Embrace the new additions and outline the desired shape from the base idea with a clear intent.

3. **Fill the Shape:** Use a solid colour tone and fill the shape. If you are working on physical means, I recommend you use some sort of ink or pen for this step.

4. **(Optional) Add/Remove Details from the Shape.**

Thumbnails are usually too small to require artistic skills. You can start with stick figures or basic shapes and move from there. Also, thumbnails improve over time. The more you do them, the more you can take from them and the more effective they are in your creative process. The first ones you make are often very small, timid, and uncreative, but as you progress, the bolder and more creative you get. If you do not believe me, check art books with thumbnails, such as the incredible The Skillful Huntsman by Scott Robertson [129]: in almost all of the pages with thumbnails, the very first ones on the top left are smaller and less interesting than the rest of them.

It is worth repeating that thumbnails are worth done by the dozens. Try to fill entire pages with them for the same concept or idea before you move to something else or before picking one to be further developed and polished. If you feel you are running out of ideas in the process, again, resort to shape language (change the shapes you used), composition (change the arrangement), and gestalt (apply other laws).

Finally, I recommend you work on thumbnails on actual paper with pens. Not being able to erase your lines forces you to incorporate mistakes and flaws you made into the design, leading your creative process away from usual cliches and results. It also teaches you how to handle errors less aggressively: we all make mistakes, and it is better to handle them and incorporate them into our process than to punish ourselves for them.

15.5 SOUNDS

Sound is one of the main elements of a game, regardless of its medium. For digital games, you have the game sounds, music, atmosphere, and effects, for example, while in physical games, you have the sounds produced by interacting with the players and game elements [133].

The presence and use of sound can transform the game's experience significantly. Imagine playing a game with cartoonish visual elements but with a spooky soundtrack. How would that impact your perception of the game? How would it affect the mood?

Working with sound requires the same level of dedication and study as other disciplines in game development, such as drawing, programming, writing, etc. For a game designer, it is very valuable to have some knowledge of working with sound, such as knowing how to pick specific sound effects and basic ideas for composing music, including being able to play musical instruments. You should see it the same way as visual arts: as a tool for expression and creative alignment.

Nowadays, most of the developments on sound will be done through some sort of Digital Audio Workstation (DAW) [134, 135]. It is relevant to have some basic familiarity with those, but consider that many composers and sound designers will have their preferred tool of choice, so regardless of your effort into learning how to operate a DAW, it is even more important to understand some of the overarching concepts of it, such as how to handle music tracks, how to apply/remove effects, how to record, etc. [133, 134, 135].

Sound in digital games will often manifest in one of these three forms:

Music: The music and ambience that plays during the game.

Sound Effects: The sound cues and effects that play as feedback for the actions that happen in the game.

Voice: The voice (acting) that plays in the game as part of dialogues, narration, and guidance.

Music

As stated before, it is recommended to have some experience with music, at least in improving your listening skills and overall musical library [134]. From my experience, it is handy to have some knowledge in music composition and mixing for my own projects, as it allows me to achieve the mood I want more clearly in a shorter time.

I often use the same basic strategy for music composition in game jams: I write and record a main track with multiple instruments and a lead instrument for the game; then I make a variation of the song without the lead instrument and variations on the harmony to be used for menus, tutorials, and other screens.

When composing those songs, I often consider the main aspects of the `Aesthetics` and the game's purpose, such as the song's intention, what music genre it is, and which instruments better reinforce the message and theme.

Sound Effects

For sound effects, the easiest start is to compile your own library of sound effects [134]. There are many websites dedicated to providing free and public domain sounds you can use, such as FreeSound.org. Given some base knowledge of working with DAWs, you should be able to tweak these sound effects and combine them to make the ones you need for your game.

Voice

For voice, consider your budget and intent. It is worth hiring voice actors with experience or dedication to their craft. Given your budget, you can ponder how extensive the use of voice is realistic and how it helps achieve your game's goal and establish the mood. Voice must also be mixed and edited with other sound tools requiring particular expertise. Moreover, from the other two, music and sound effects, voice is closer to the `Narrative` core and should take many of its points into consideration, especially in the context of voice acting and story [88].

Finally, consider that all sounds in your game should connect to your audiovisual language. Specific characters, shapes, or compositions should align with the songs and sounds. To help with that, consider using a soundboard and other interactive sound composition tools.

15.6 JUICE

Yes, juice. **Juice** is a term used to describe the extra audiovisual elements added to a game to enhance, polish, and improve it [136]. For digital games, juice often refers to special effects, particle effects, micro-interactions, post-processing effects, audiovisual feedback, etc. For physical games, juice often refers to extra details, polished assets, better-quality prints, etc.

Juice is that extra push your game needs to feel more complete, but sadly, from my experience, it is often ignored during development until it is too late to be included. That might be due to bad planning, lack of experience, or even lack of care. Contrary to many other approaches for game design and game development, I recommend you add juice to your game as soon as possible.

The sooner you add juice and include art assets in your game, the sooner their challenges become apparent. Most of the time, game development teams, especially on a smaller scale, tend to work separately on their creations and forget to combine their work. Thus, as mentioned in Chapter 4, these teams will only figure out that the work needed to combine everything is higher than expected very late in the process. The sooner you combine the work, polish it and add your juice, the sooner you can realign your plans and reconsider the next steps.

Moreover, juice greatly impacts players' perception of your game, as it provides for a better game feel [137]. It also helps the understanding of the `Mechanics` and `Economy` elements, as it provides helpful feedback. Juice can manifest as small animations that happen when a mechanic is correctly and incorrectly executed, for example.

Juice is also important for the components of Flow, as seen in Section 3.1. Juice provides better and more appropriate feedback that helps guide the player towards the expected experience. Besides that, it can help steer players towards and outwards from anxiety and boredom [138]. If a given mechanic is perceived as weak or the players themselves feel anxious in facing the game's challenges, improving the sense of strength through audiovisual means might provide the extra juice necessary to change the game's perception. In digital games, it might be in the form of louder and stronger sounds, for example, or subtle animations that make the challenge elements perceived as less threatening.

It is worth repeating. Your game will work without juice. Your players will be able to play it and even get to your game's purpose. However, juice increases all these aspects, emphasising your elements and improving the overall experience. For that, before you consider adding more gameplay elements, such as new elements for your `Mechanics`, `Economy`, and `Narrative`, consider first improving the juice of the existing gameplay elements. It is far more likely that you will achieve better results with it rather than increasing your backlog and your game's complexity with extra elements.

CHAPTER 16

UI and UX

DURING THE GAME DESIGN AND DEVELOPMENT PROCESS, the player takes the central role in most of the decision-making processes through playtest sessions. Players interact with the game using **interfaces**. An **interface** is a means by which information is exchanged either as player inputs or the game's output. Although the term interface is often associated with digital games, it applies the same to non-digital games. A card game, for example, uses the cards themselves and their positions on the table as the interface between the players and the game.

Interfaces are closely connected to both the `Aesthetics` and the `Narrative` cores, as they are tools to express the mood and message. However, as they are often associated with their visual representation, it is easier to first study them under the `Aesthetics` core. In particular, for the `Aesthetics` core, we discuss interfaces under two umbrella terms: **User Interface (UI)**, and **User Experience (UX)**.

This chapter explores and discusses important game design aspects related to UI and UX, as well as their differences and how working with them empowers the game design processes, especially in how they help achieve the game's purpose.

16.1 DIFFERENCES BETWEEN UI AND UX

UI and UX are two completely different terms, although they are often discussed together (as I am doing in this chapter) [139, 140, 141]. The simplest form of presenting their difference is with the

DOI: 10.1201/9781003351191-16

following mnemonic: **UI is what you see, while UX is how you use it.** Although not entirely correct, this mnemonic helps to differentiate what belongs to UI and what belongs to UX. Surely, some aspects will overlap. Besides, not everything related to UI is visual. UI also encompasses touch, sound, voice, and many other forms of interaction.

User Interface (UI)

According to our initial mnemonic, UI is "what you see"; for that, it is often associated with designing appealing audiovisual interface elements [141, 142]. UI design is often responsible for choosing the colour schemes and palettes, the interface grid, and the overall audiovisual style.

In the initial stages, most of the UI activities are done in **wireframes** [143], which are simplifications of how the game's interfaces will be arranged in the game's view. In the concept game `Family Tree`, for example, wireframes would be built for the cards, displaying their texts and information. Alternatively, for the concept game `Another Starry Sky`, wireframes would be built for the stargazing mechanic, placing the starry view and possible means of interaction.

Especially for digital games, UI is responsible for planning the **interface grid** that dictates how the visual elements in the game should scale as the game screen changes size [144, 145]. Consider, for example, that someone could play `Another Starry Sky` in a small screen notebook, while someone else could play it on a big TV screen. The interface grid indicates which and how the elements should scale proportionally to different display sizes.

User Experience (UX)

According to our initial mnemonic, UX is "how you use it"; for that, it is often associated with usability and accessibility, which are both part of UX[1] [141, 142, 146]. For that, UX design is often responsible for performing user interviews, user testing, designing the user journey, and creating personas, among other tasks.

[1] Accessibility is also part of UI, as we are going to discuss later.

UX is less related to how the interface elements are presented in an audiovisual manner rather than how these elements interact with each other. UX designers might, for example, handle finished pieces in the form of wireframes, which will later be polished, coloured, and illustrated by UI designers. Surely, the UX design might check on how the choice of colours and elements might impact the user experience, but they are not concerned with considering these aspects while designing.

UX designers conduct **user interviews**, which are conversations with users about topics and questions related to their experiences. In the game design process, user interviews often happen after playtest sessions to assess the game's experience.

As different players might have different goals and motivations while playing the game (consider the player typologies, for example, from Section 6.2), it is also common to separate these into different **personas** [78, 147, 148].

Personas

Personas are detailed user archetypes that are used as decision-making tools in design processes [78, 149]. For game design, a persona is an imaginary player that encompasses a set of features, characteristics, and motivations to play the game. For example, for the concept game `Family Tree`, we could design the following personas:

Lenny: Is a kid that mostly plays with their parents and enjoys adding new parts to the family tree.

Max: Is a parent that plays with their kids and partner and enjoys the negotiation aspect of the game, especially as a sort of teaching moment for the children.

Dani: Is an adult who lives with friends and mostly plays with a diverse set of friends. Enjoys the game as a relaxing leisure with friends at gatherings.

Personas are also useful for designing **user journeys**. User journeys are a sequence of steps which users (players) will follow while playing the game. It can be as general as starting from when the player started the game, to more specific, such as describing how the stargazing mechanic works in the concept game **Another Starry Sky**. Each persona might have their own user stories, as well as share some with others.

Although the user journey is more commonly part of the UX, part of it is covered by the UI, as discussed previously. In terms of game design, it is important to consider both aspects together with how they relate to the other Cores of Game Design, as follows:

`Mechanics`: Which mechanics are part of the user journey? For example, pressing buttons or drawing cards from a deck are mechanics, as they are forms of interacting with the UI and UX of the game.

`Economy`: Which resources and mechanisms are part of the user journey? For example, the numbers or icons displayed that connect elements in the UI and UX are part of your economic mechanisms.

`Narrative`: What is the meaning and information on the user journey? For example, which texts are being displayed, and what sort of message do we want to convey from them?

From my experience, while many developers often see UI and UX as mostly responsible for menus and manuals, there are plenty of games that are mostly played through menus, or that most of the mechanics are done with interfaces rather than digital avatars. Moreover, you are far more likely to deal with UX challenges as a game designer than you might expect, as these are key to how your game is perceived and played.

For example, as discussed in the previous chapter and sections, the concept game **Another Starry Sky** has a stargazing mechanic in which the players must use their notes and observe the sky to find constellations and forms of direction. But how exactly does it work? Do players only look at a vast amount of nameless stars and guess how to combine them? Do some of them are highlighted or displayed in a different light to indicate their uses? Does the game provide some sort of blueprint for constellations to guide the research?

Figure 16.1: Possible ideas for the stargazing mechanic.

Figure 16.1 shows three ideas for the stargazing mechanic. In the first one, the player sees all of the stars with no visual distinction. The second one shows a filtered version in which some stars are more prominent than others. The third one shows an example of an intended constellation (the UX constellation) connecting the stars.

While the discussion on how to approach this mechanic belongs to the `Mechanics` core, at this point, it is mostly a UX challenge. Moreover, different from usual software development UX practices, game design UX is not necessarily meant to simplify and make the players' lives easier.

As **`Another Starry Sky`** deals with grief, an overwhelming starry sky can be used as a `Narrative` element to emphasise the feeling of grief and disorientation. `Economy` mechanisms could lower the number of visible stars and narrow the options, as in overcoming grief and finding where to focus.

Furthermore, it might be part of the UX intention to add difficulties as part of the game's learning aspect. On the other hand, the UI can be used to facilitate some of these processes, especially using visual guides and **affordances** [150, 151].

16.2 AFFORDANCE

Affordance refers to the possible uses of an element and its properties, given a specific user [151]. Affordance is not a characteristic of an element but a relationship between it and the user. Stairs, for example, might afford the use of climbing up and down for some users, but not for wheelchair users. Elements can also afford multiple uses for a given user at the same time. A die, for example, can afford the idea of generating random numbers but can also act as

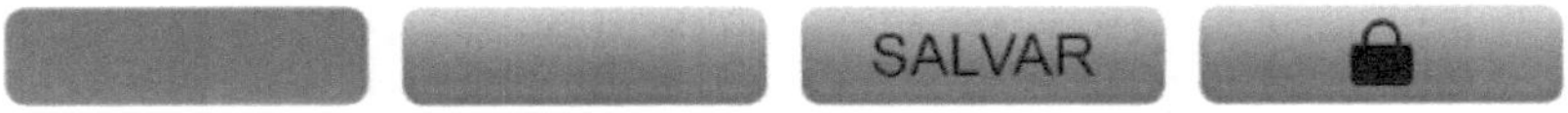

Figure 16.2: Example of affordance and signifiers on buttons.

a counter or as a (light) paperweight. A good game design exercise is to prospect gameplay possibilities by exploring the multitude of affordance relations with (game) objects.

Let's get back to the stairs example. Stairs can afford the idea of moving or progressing to able-body users, while they afford the opposite of these ideas for other users. We refer to the idea of the opposite affordance as an **anti-affordance**, the prevention of interaction [151]. In digital games, a lock is often used on top of UI elements as an anti-affordance of interaction; these locked elements are not currently available.

Affordance and anti-affordance are relations that depend on the user, and they are perceived due to the presence of **signifiers**. Signifiers communicate these possible actions (and inactions) to users, be it through marks, sounds, and any other perceivable indicators [151].

Getting back to the lock example. Let us assume that these locks all show a different key shape in front of them. Users yielding matching keys and locks can unlock their respective elements. The key shape is a signifier that affords the use of the key and, more precisely, which key to be used. At the same time, the lack of a specific key shape creates the anti-affordance – the element is locked.

Figure 16.2 shows four examples of buttons. The first one is meant to be a button, but it lacks signifiers to help it be seen as a button. It is mostly a rounded rectangle that could afford being a platform, for example, in a 2D platformer game. The lack of texts and symbols on it also prevents the affordance of being clicked on. The second one has a bevel and a gradient effect to achieve a more "squish-look", typical of digital buttons, which act as signifiers. These signifiers are enough to perceive the second element as a button, even without a text or a symbol.

The third button in Figure 16.2 plays with the idea of affordance and anti-affordance. If you can read Brazilian Portuguese, then you know what is written in button three and perceive a set of affordances. If you do not, then you might perceive it as a button, but you have no idea what it should be used for. Your lack of knowledge might prevent you from clicking the button, creating a form of anti-affordance[2].

The last button is the example discussed previously, with a lock icon on top of the button as a signifier for the anti-affordance of clicking. This button is "locked" for some reason and will not achieve any use when clicked.

While working on a game's UI, it is important to consider signifiers for the UI elements, as well as the affordances it achieves for the different users and personas. You might do it using traditional means and techniques, such as beveling buttons to add "squishiness", but also resorting to physical relations objects have, such as handles, levers, and other forms of visual interactive tools. It is also relevant to consider how the interactions with the UI will trigger audiovisual feedback, such as confirmation sounds and animations that communicate to the players that the action was successful (remember Chapter 15?). The lack of proper feedback might lead players to use the UI at first correctly but assume their usage was wrong [151].

16.3 PRACTICAL LAWS OF UX

Another useful tool to help design user journeys and the overall user experience is the laws of UX, as compiled by Jon Yablonski [146]. This section introduces and discusses some of these laws that are more relevant to the game design process, modified to suit our discussion better.

Jakob's Law

> *Players have experienced other games before and will keep their expectations and preferences and apply them to your game.*

[2]"Salvar", in Brazilian Portuguese, means "To Save", which indicates that this button saves the game progress. Without this knowledge, players might be hindered from saving their progress and losing it when closing the game.

Jakob's Law is the idea that players will come to play your game with previous experiences and knowledge that will influence how they perceive your game. If your digital game has a settings option, players might expect options to control the music volume, for example. Players might have a negative experience when their experience does not match their expectations, even if the mismatch was designed to preserve the game's purpose.

Hick's Law

> *Players will take longer to make decisions as the number and complexity of options increase.*

Hick's Law is the idea that an increase in the number and complexity of choices will scale up the player's decision-making process. The more options to consider, the more time is needed for players to feel secure with their decisions. For that, consider which options are relevant to the game's purpose, and consider removing others that do not contribute to it or that just add (unnecessary) complexity to the game.

Fitts's Law

> *The player's time to get to a target is a function of its distance and size.*

Fitts's Law sounds complex, but what it essentially boils down to is that important elements should be closer and bigger to facilitate their access. If your digital game requires the player to press a button constantly, then it should be the easiest button to press on the joystick or the keyboard, for example. Otherwise, players might get frustrated and tired of having so much trouble to achieve important and repetitive tasks.

Consider Fitts's Law also for your game design process. For example, if you expect your team to follow and update your game design document (GDD), make it as easy to access as possible. Any pain in getting to it will eventually lead people to avoid it.

Miller's Law

Players will only keep up from 5 to 9 things in their memory at once.

Miller's Law comes from a psychology experiment that showed how limited our short-term memory is [146]. In terms of game design, Miller's Law indicates that players will hold an average of 7 things in their memory while playing the game. To help players retain more information, it is wise to apply audiovisual aids, juice, and other feedback elements.

For a card game, for example, expecting players to memorise and use many cards might lead to frustration. For that, consider a smaller number of game elements and playtest them. Moreover, use mechanics to allow players to switch contexts in the game so they can "refresh" what they need to keep in mind at different moments.

Goal-Gradient Effect

Players' engagement and speed will increase as they approach the game's goals.

The Goal-Gradient Effect indicates that we tend to speed up as we approach a goal. The closer we are to succeeding at something, the more inclined we are to complete it. On the other hand, we will naturally not move faster (or slower) to activities that seem to be further from being completed.

In a digital game, for example, you might focus more intently as you see the end of a stage getting near.

Aesthetic-Usability Effect

Players often perceive more audiovisual pleasing designs and games as better and more usable than others.

Aesthetic-Usability Effect, not to be confused with the `Aesthetics`, is the idea that games with better audiovisual elements are perceived as better games. Surely, that is not particularly true for all games. You probably can name a few games with realistic graphics and amazing audiovisual elements that are not worth the time compared to other indie gems that hook you up for hours with simple graphics.

Sadly, the Aesthetic-Usability Effect still happens often, especially for indie and smaller game developers. Players will judge and play games with simpler audiovisual elements, harsher and less tolerant to errors and usability issues for the very fact that they are not as pleasing as high-budget photo-realistic games. That is not a matter of game design quality; it is merely how we act.

On the other hand, if you dedicate time to developing a nice UI and UX and add juice and other audiovisual elements to your game, you might enjoy some users being less critical of small issues and improve the quality of the feedback you get.

16.4 ACCESSIBILITY

Last but not least, **accessibility** plays a major role in all of the UI and UX discussions. Accessibility refers to how easy it is for players to access the game, which includes people with disabilities and people from diverse backgrounds and needs.

Most of this chapter has dealt with accessibility in broader terms, in how we can consider UI and UX decisions to make accessible interfaces. Moreover, deciding on a "less accessible" usability might be a game design decision to achieve the game's purpose. That can also happen as part of the `Mechanics` and `Economy` activities, such as reworking a mechanic or balancing the game.

Destructive and potentially harmful actions, such as an option to delete the game's progress in a digital game, for example, should be made less accessible by design. As the consequences of these actions are dangerous, it is important to guarantee that the player has a clear intention to perform them.

On the other hand, some functionalities might be inaccessible from the start to some players, such as players with disabilities. However, as game designers and developers are not often aware of such disabilities, common concerns and options for accessibility are lacking in many games [152, 153, 154]. To help raise awareness for some of these, this section discusses some considerations for accessibility that closely relate to UI and UX, as well as for the whole core of `Aesthetics`.

Dyslexia

Maybe one of the most common accessibility concerns is **dyslexia**, which is often described as a specific learning disability characterised by difficulties with accurate and fluent recognition of words and spelling [155, 156]. Most of the time, game designers can improve the accessibility of their games for dyslexic players by using dyslexic fonts, such as the OpenDyslexic typeface available at https://opendyslexic.org/.

Dyslexia also manifests in another form of accessibility feature: subtitles. Consider adding subtitles to your game when possible, especially when you have mechanics that depend on voice and sound. Moreover, subtitles should have a significant font size, appear on top of a high-contrast background, and have a good outline. A good rule of thumb for readable text is to use white or yellow for the font with a good, thick black outline.

Colour Blindness

Colour blindness, or **Daltonism**, is a very common disability, estimated to affect about 4% of the world's population [157]. The most common approach to deal with colour blindness is the use of colour filters that adjust the game's colours. That can help differentiate the colours in ways that improve the game's perception for players with different forms of colour blindness [158].

In more practical terms, if your game relies on the use of colours for any sort of meaning, then also include the use of textures and patterns. If red is used to denote danger, for example, use shape language and patterns (as seen in Chapter 15), such as spikes and triangles. That way, even if the colour is not perceived the same as you initially intended, the other visual elements will deliver the message.

Joystick Complexity & Physical Disabilities

On a different note, another important accessibility concern is the game's controls and forms of input, even if they are more closely associated with the `Mechanics` core. If your digital game is meant to be played on a joystick, consider how easy it is to use one. From my experience, many (digital) game designers are passionate game players who handle multiple forms of joysticks without issues. But that is not the case for all players.

Consider using fewer buttons or simplified joystick setups with redundancy, *i.e.*, having multiple buttons to serve the same purposes. A modern console joystick has about 15 buttons, directionals and sticks; by just assuming Miller's Law (see Section 16.3), that is already way more information to keep in mind than you should use.

Realistically, it might be hard to consider different types of controllers and joysticks, and many (digital) game developers will develop games for computers, which use the keyboard and mouse as the main form of input. The keyboard itself has way more buttons than a modern joystick (an average of 100 keys). Consider which buttons and layout to use.

It is even better if the player can manually remap the inputs and game functionalities. Remapping is important because it also deals with other forms of **physical disabilities** and needs. Some players might need their own layout to access buttons and functionalities better, as well as some forms of input. Constantly pressing buttons or holding them might be difficult for players with motor and other forms of disabilities, for example.

Surely, the more we discuss accessibilities, the more needs and concerns arise. This chapter has not mentioned other forms of mental disabilities, for example, related to how users might experience sounds, information, and visuals. It is imperative that we continue researching and studying how our games can embrace a larger number of players, not from a commercial point of view but from an ethical perspective. It is an instance of sharing our games and our art with others by including them.

Finally, the best form to assess your game and your solutions to improve your accessibility is to get in touch and connect with a larger variety of players and developers. You might have never considered using patterns and shapes in your colour-coded UI because you do not know anyone with colour blindness. Expand your social circle and consider how inclusive it is. Living with and knowing people with disabilities is a privilege. It's even better if you can share your games with them.

VI

Conclusion

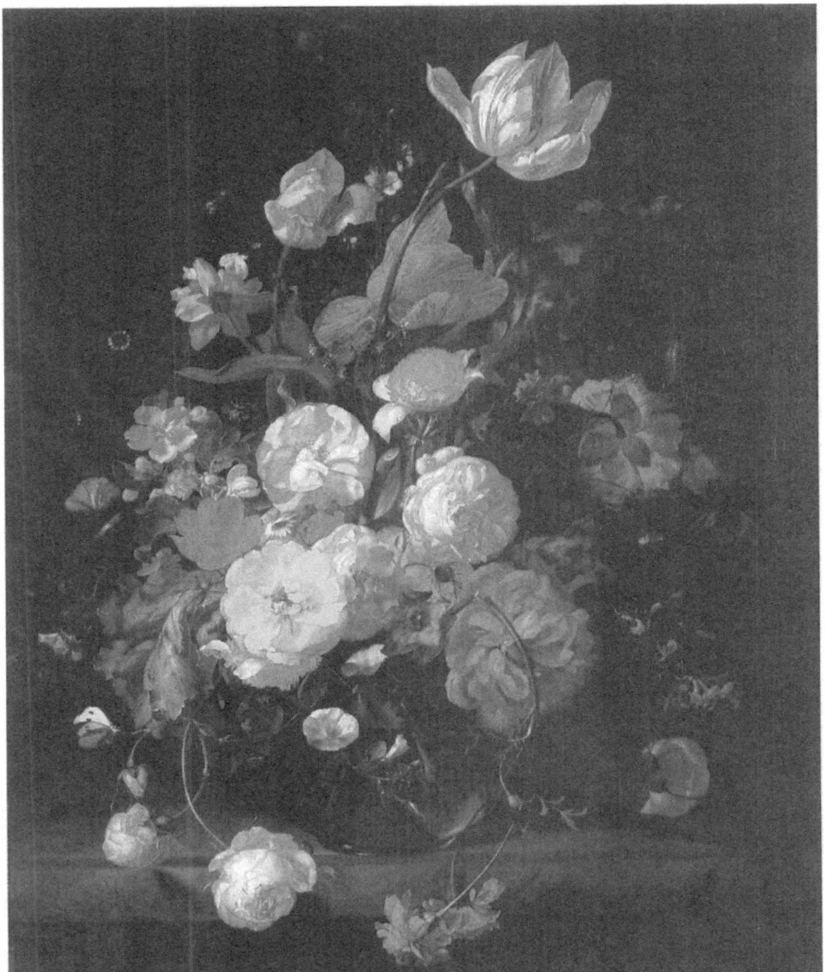

Rachel Ruysch – Roses, Tulips and Other Flowers in a Glass Vase on a Marble Ledge (1709).

CHAPTER 17

Conclusions

WELCOME TO THE END GAME. In this closing chapter, we review the main takeaways from the book and discuss other important topics related to finishing the game design process, as well as the meaning of finishing a game.

17.1 WHAT IS GOOD GAME DESIGN?

Game Design is not an exact science. Repeating the game design process with minimal changes results in widely different results. Game Design also has no exact goal in itself. Game designers have goals, and those goals are applied to their game design process to build games. Due to the unpredictability and range of game design processes and game designers' goals, it is not possible to create a single answer to what makes a good game design.

However, we can assess whether the game design process has achieved what it wanted to. We can assess if the game designer achieved the intended goal. Throughout the book, we used the term **game's purpose** to define what the game wants to achieve when played. While we cannot establish a good answer to what makes for a good game design, we can assess whether the game design process leads to the creation of a game that achieves its purpose.

The two concept games used in this book, `Another Starry Sky` and `Family Tree`, have distinct purposes. For `Another Starry Sky`, its purpose is to be entertainment. To be fun. We would assess whether `Another Starry Sky` is actually entertaining and fun by playtesting it and checking the playtester reactions.

DOI: 10.1201/9781003351191-17

As we discussed in the early chapters of the book (Section 2.1), fun is not the only possible purpose for games. Games can be made for a wider range of purposes. `Family Tree`, for example, has the purpose of teaching players about living and being happy in a community setting. Some of its mechanics and elements are designed not to be entertaining at all, as it might harm the game's purpose.

Having a clear purpose makes for a more clear and direct game design process.

Rather than thinking about what a good game design is, consider asking what the purpose of the game is and if that purpose was achieved. It might be difficult from an outside perspective when you are playing someone else's games, for example, but it is an important exercise. It helps you to consider the game design choices from a broader perspective rather than simplistic entertainment.

Moreover, we, as game designers, can search for other purposes for why we make games. What do we want with our games, and why do we make them? At the same time, it is worth considering those questions when playing other people's games and respect them for that. Some of us might make games as a hobby or self-entertainment. Others might want to raise awareness for specific issues. Others are simply using them as a means to pay their bills and live their lives with other activities unrelated to games. Those are all valid. Your reasons for making games are valid. If you feel like your process achieved your purpose, it was a valid process.

17.2 REDEFINING SUCCESS

The discussion on good game design leads to another important point: what does it mean to be a successful game designer? Or even what makes for a successful game?

While your initial instinct might be in the sense of recognition and financial success, is that what we should consider? Are the only successful games those that sold millions of copies? Or are the only successful game designers with millions of followers on social media? If so, is success only a matter of money and fame?

Particularly, I reject this view of success. If that were the case, then most of the world's population would never achieve any sense of success. Maybe you never had the experience of selling thousands of copies or being followed by the hundreds, but you certainly felt success at some point in your life. Success should not be a matter of comparison to others, especially in financial or social media standards. Success is an individual metric based on your own standards.

Finishing a game design process and making a game is already a huge struggle. Achieving your purpose with said game is another challenge. Who can tell you that you were not successful in this process? You made a game! Congratulations. Not everyone can celebrate that. It might not be all over internet forums and international broadcasts, but does it reduce the fact that you have finished your game? Every game we make should be celebrated, just as we celebrate any victory we achieve.

In many of my interviews and during my research, it was fairly common to hear stories about games that were never commercially successful, but that achieved their purposes. That caught the attention of the audience the game designers wanted, for example. I heard stories about families making games just for themselves, with elements from their daily lives, as their quality time together. There were also stories of games that were made for the game designers' communities that resulted in many positive outcomes. Even the satisfaction of watching other people playing their games made many designers feel successful and happy with their results.

Probably, the most heartwarming story was shared by one of my interviewees, Lia Fuziy. While undergoing a degree in Pedagogy, Lia had to work as an intern in a public school for young kids in the countryside of São Paulo, Brazil. Given her previous experience with computers and games, she was asked by the teachers to make educational games for the students. These games would be played in a classroom with only three working computers for 30 children between the ages of 5 and 6. Lia developed a small game for teaching the alphabet, in which the kids had to hear a word and select the word's first letter. Selecting A for Apple, for example, or P for Pizza.

Besides the fruitful educational result, the main achievement of Lia's game actually came from the game's assets. All of the art in the game featured either pictures from the actual classroom or photos of the children themselves. When they got to play the game, they saw themselves in the game and the pictures of their own school, which resulted in a higher motivation and interest. It was not just a game to learn the alphabet, which was the actual purpose of the game; it was **their** game, and they were part of it. Every time the game was played, random students appeared on the screen, which engaged them to play it more and celebrate every new appearance. It was a success from both the purpose standpoint and from a personal realisation. Having all those children cheering for the game and seeing their joy with it is a feeling that surpasses any financial and recognition gain.

Consider what success means to you and where you can find it. No matter your path and decision, I hope you are successful in your endeavours. Hopefully, the Cores of Game Design may help you with that.

17.3 CLOSING THE FRAMEWORK

Getting back to the book's main topic, the Cores of Game Design, it is good to consider how the cycle ends and the last iterations of the game design cycle.

When Is The Game Done?

The game is only done when all the intended features are present, and the game can be given to the players without interference from the developers. Consider a board game, for example; it is ready when the box is closed and sealed, ready to be given to board game fans. In digital games, nowadays, you would consider a game done when it is available online for players to access.

Notice that I used the term "intended features" instead of just "features". Your backlog, as seen in Chapter 4, is never going to be empty. However, your effort and energy to empty the backlog will reduce over time. At some points, more effort must be made to prioritise tasks to achieve the final game form. For digital games, this tends to be a more complex task as bugs and software issues might consume all the remaining energy to be fixed instead of new additions.

For that, it is always good to consider a few questions, especially in the light of the most recent playtest sessions:

1. Has the game achieved its purpose already?
2. What are the aspects needed to achieve the purpose?
3. Does the addition/modification enforce what already exists, or is it new?

If you answer point 1 with a yes, then it is very likely that your game is done and you are just polishing and working on minor improvements. If your answer is no, then consider what is still lacking. Your game is not done.

That leads to point 2. Analyse your playtest and see what is still missing the mark. That can be the case of reworking balancing elements from the `Economy` or adjusting the game mechanics (`Mechanics`). Alternatively, maybe your `Narrative` is not clear, or your mood was not set properly to achieve the aimed experience (`Aesthetics`). On a more general note, check which one of the cores and their elements could lead you closer to achieving your purpose.

Given this addition or modification you found out during the exploration of point 2, we ask ourselves point 3. Are we improving on the existing elements or creating something entirely new? From a practical standpoint, you should prefer improvements over additions. Improvements require less work and are more likely to strengthen the links between your game elements and the cores. Additions require many elements, such as considering how they are explained to the players and how they impact the game's balance and message. Surely, at some points, your only option will be to add new elements, but that is a sign that your development process is far from over.

Overcoming Perfectionism

Decades ago, it was unimaginable to make changes to released games, but currently, there are many possibilities for this. Extra updates for digital games and additional downloadable (printable) content for board games are not uncommon, for example. You do not need to worry about your final game release, as it cannot be ever improved or enhanced in the future. It certainly can.

This concern is usually one of the main factors I see new developers struggle with when releasing their games and even when planning for a release. Focus on the main aspects of your game and its purpose. Once those are set and working, you are very likely ready to release.

All the extra features and interesting ideas that could not make it for the release can be added in the future as expansions and additional content. You are not necessarily "killing your darlings", you are just postponing their execution (pun intended). Moreover, some features might need more time to be properly planned and implemented, which might happen at a better pace and in a motivated environment once the main game has been released.

Finally, this is also a matter of overcoming perfectionism. Perfectionism is an awful attribute. Perfectionists do not know when to stop and often are harmed by that. You should avoid perfectionism and its consequences as best as you can. That is not to say you should be reckless or careless with your game design activities. On the contrary, being careful and attentive to your game design process is your main task. Perfectionism is just an insecure feeling that stops you from understanding how careful and attentive you have been in the process and forces you into an unmotivated and tiresome repetitive cycle. If you want to find out if your game or your activities are good, do not judge them yourself, as that might get you into a perfectionist trap: playtest! Let others be the judge of that and trust their judgment. Accept the compliments. You deserve them.

If You Can, Add More Juice

Alternatively, it might be that you have finished your game and still have time and energy to put on it. There might be a few hours left before the end of the game jam, for example. Then, the best activity to do is to put more effort into your Juice (Chapter 15).

The Juice increases the experience and enhances all elements of the game. As a quick recap, consider how Juice can improve your game in the following aspects:

Improve the Feedback: More Juice focused on the response to events can help players better understand their outcomes. If clicking a button squishes it and makes a positive sound, players will have a better understanding that the clicking worked. If the sound has to do with the result of the button, such as gold coins sound effects when clicking a buy button, then it will emphasise the action even further.

Improve the Mood: More closely related to the `Aesthetics` core, Juice can also increment aspects of the mood, such as adding additional sound effects or atmospheric elements. Together with elements from your `Narrative`, you can create interesting environmental storytelling elements that increase the details of your game without necessarily resorting to complex and technical new additions.

Improve the Accessibility: On a more general note, you can explore multiple forms of Juice in the same context to improve accessibility. If you have sound effects for a particular moment, consider adding visual and textual elements also, for example.

17.4 GAME OVER

Throughout the book, we discussed the Cores of Game Design and the multiple forms they manifest during the game design process. Moreover, we have used the term game design process as an umbrella term that encompasses the entire game development process. That is different from other game design sources that usually limit it to the scope of planning, designing, and documenting game mechanics. From my perspective, and I hope yours too by getting here, game design is much more.

Game Design is more than the Cores of Game Design, even though I have used them as a vehicle to embrace its multiple forms. Playtesting, for example, although an important part of Game Design, is not necessarily covered by the Cores of Game Design. It is an activity that happens next to them as we cycle through the iterative game design process. The latter, in this book, is proposed as a simplified game design framework, as seen in Figure 17.1.

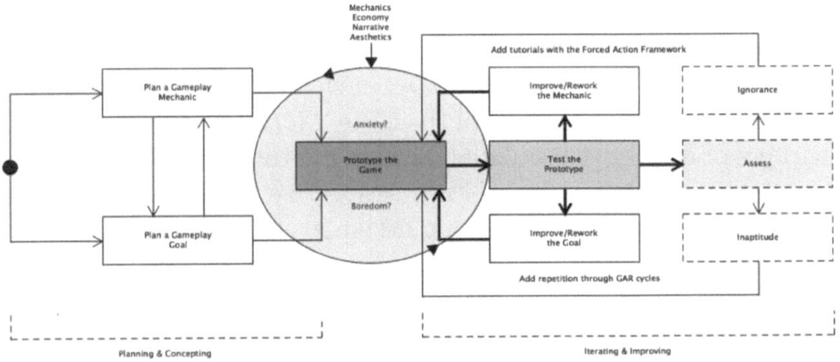

Figure 17.1: Game Design Cycle with the Cores of Game Design.

To recap, the game design cycle is composed of two interweaving moments: Planning & Concepting and Iterating & Improving. Planning & Concepting is the initial moment in a game design process in which there is no playable prototype, and all work is being put into developing the Cores of Game Design, with no particular order, until at least one game mechanic and one gameplay goal are established and implemented. The implementation of the game mechanic and the gameplay goal creates the **complete prototype**, which can then be playtested, assessed, and improved.

After achieving the **complete prototype**, the game design process moves to the Iterating & Improving moment, in which the **complete prototype** is improved with changes, additions, and removals, all of them based on the Cores of Game Design in no particular order. The improvements and iterations on the **complete prototype** continue until the game is done, as discussed in the previous sections.

In the first chapters of the book, we discussed how this cycle could be improved with the use of theoretical models, namely, the Flow Theory (Section 3.1), the Forced Action Framework (Section 3.3), and the GAR Cycle (Section 3.4). Those are used to improve the gameplay experience and also to lead the player away from the ignorance and inaptitude states (Section 3.2), which happen when the player is either unaware of what needs to be done or does not have the proper skillset required to progress in the game.

As stated previously, this entire process can start from any of the Cores of Game Design. Chapters 5, 8, 11, and 14 all present approaches and main concepts about each one of the cores and how they can be used at the start of the cycle. Moreover, the subsequent chapters of each part presented more in-depth discussions and theories related to each one of their respective cores to be applied during the iterations of the game design cycle.

Although detailed, the game design cycle presented in Figure 17.1 should be used as an overall guide on the game design process. Its main intent is to focus the process on playtest sessions that lead to incremental improvements. Each increment may be based on specific cores or a combination of multiple cores. All of them focus on improving the game until it achieves its purpose.

Use and get inspired by the game design cycle. Experiment with the cores and combine them. Make your own cores. Make your own cycles. Iterate and playtest. Make the cycle your own. Own the cycle. Make games.

17.5 THANK YOU FOR PLAYING

Finally, I want to thank you for coming through this journey with me. I hope this book has helped you expand your views on game design, as well as propose new approaches for your methods and approaches.

But, more than that, I really hope this book has motivated you to make games. There are not enough games out there, especially those made by people who love making games. I do hope that is the case for you, and I am eager to play your games.

Thank you :)

Bibliography

[1] Miguel Sicart. "Loops and Metagames: Understanding Game Design Structures." In: *FDG*. 2015.

[2] Keith Burgun. *Game design theory: A new philosophy for understanding games*. CRC Press, 2012.

[3] Ian Schreiber and Brenda Romero. *Game balance*. CRC Press, 2021.

[4] Faltin Karlsen. "Theorycrafting: from collective intelligence to intrinsic satisfaction." In: *DiGRA Conference*. 2011.

[5] Anna Anthropy. *Rise of the videogame zinesters: How freaks, normals, amateurs, artists, dreamers, drop-outs, queers, housewives, and people like you are taking back an art form*. Seven Stories Press, 2012.

[6] Lindsay Grace. *Black games studies*. Carnegie Mellon University, 2021.

[7] Bonnie Ruberg. *The queer games avant-garde: How LGBTQ game makers are reimagining the medium of video games*. Duke University Press, 2020.

[8] Saxion. *Bachelor creative media and game technologies: Saxion*. Available at https://www.saxion.edu/programmes/bachelor/creative-media-and-game-technologies. URL: `https://www.saxion.edu/programmes/bachelor/creative-media-and-game-technologies`.

[9] Ernest Adams and Joris Dormans. *Game mechanics: advanced game design*. New Riders, 2012.

[10] Joris Dormans. "Engineering emergence: applied theory for game design". In: (2012).

DOI: 10.1201/9781003351191-10

[11] Robin Hunicke, Marc LeBlanc, Robert Zubek, et al. "MDA: A formal approach to game design and game research". In: *Proceedings of the AAAI Workshop on Challenges in Game AI*. Vol. 4. San Jose, CA. 2004, p. 1722.

[12] Rogério Junior and Frutuoso Silva. "Redefining the mda framework—the pursuit of a game design ontology". In: *Information* 12.10 (2021), p. 395.

[13] Sundramoorthy Balaji and M Sundararajan Murugaiyan. "Waterfall vs. V-Model vs. Agile: A comparative study on SDLC". In: *International Journal of Information Technology and Business Management* 2.1 (2012), pp. 26–30.

[14] Clinton Keith. *Agile game development with Scrum*. Pearson Education, 2010.

[15] Jing-Wei Liu et al. "The role of Sprint planning and feedback in game development projects: Implications for game quality". In: *Journal of Systems and Software* 154 (2019), pp. 79–91.

[16] Katie Salen Tekinbas and Eric Zimmerman. *Rules of play: Game design fundamentals*. MIT Press, 2003.

[17] Janelynn Camingue, Elin Carstensdottir, and Edward F Melcer. "What is a visual novel?" In: *Proceedings of the ACM on Human-Computer Interaction* 5.CHI PLAY (2021), pp. 1–18.

[18] Dani Cavallaro. *Anime and the visual novel: narrative structure, design and play at the crossroads of animation and computer games*. McFarland, 2009.

[19] Elin Carstensdottir, Erica Kleinman, and Magy Seif El-Nasr. "Player interaction in narrative games: structure and narrative progression mechanics". In: *Proceedings of the 14th International Conference on the Foundations of Digital Games*. 2019, pp. 1–9.

[20] Jesse Schell. *The Art of Game Design: A book of lenses*. CRC Press, 2008.

[21] John Brzustowski. "Can you win at Tetris?" PhD thesis. University of British Columbia, 1992.

[22] Susie Hodge. *The short story of women artists.* Laurence King Publishing, 2020.

[23] Richard Hill-Whittall. *The indie game developer handbook.* CRC Press, 2015.

[24] Brendan Keogh. *The videogame industry does not exist: Why we should think beyond commercial game production.* MIT Press, 2023.

[25] Scott Rogers. *Level Up! The guide to great video game design.* John Wiley & Sons, 2014.

[26] Angela Tinwell, Mark Grimshaw, and Andrew Williams. "Uncanny behaviour in survival horror games". In: *Journal of Gaming & Virtual Worlds* 2.1 (2010), pp. 3–25.

[27] Tarja Susi, Mikael Johannesson, and Per Backlund. "Serious games: An overview". In: (2007).

[28] Brian J Gajadhar, Yvonne AW De Kort, and Wijnand A Ijsselsteijn. "Shared fun is doubled fun: player enjoyment as a function of social setting". In: *Fun and Games: Second International Conference, Eindhoven, The Netherlands, October 20-21, 2008. Proceedings.* Springer. 2008, pp. 106–117.

[29] DREAMFEEL. *Curtain Game.* Available at https://dreamfeel.itch.io/curtain. URL: `https://dreamfeel.itch.io/curtain`.

[30] Anthony Whitehead et al. "Exergame effectiveness: what the numbers can tell us". In: *Proceedings of the 5th ACM SIGGRAPH Symposium on Video Games.* 2010, pp. 55–62.

[31] Nina Jackson Levin et al. ""We just take care of each other": navigating 'chosen family'in the context of health, illness, and the mutual provision of care amongst queer and transgender young adults". In: *International Journal of Environmental Research and Public Health* 17.19 (2020), p. 7346.

[32] Mihaly Csikszentmihalyi. "Flow and the Psychology of Discovery and Invention". In: *HarperPerennial, New York* 39 (1997), pp. 1–16.

[33] Jeanne Nakamura and Mihaly Csikszentmihalyi. "Flow Theory and Research". In: *Handbook of Positive Psychology* 195 (2009), p. 206.

[34] Celia Hodent. *The psychology of video games.* Routledge, 2020.

[35] Ernest Adams. *Fundamentals of game design.* Pearson Education, 2014.

[36] Chanel J Larche and Mike J Dixon. "Winning isn't everything: The impact of optimally challenging smartphone games on flow, game preference and individuals gaming to escape aversive bored states". In: *Computers in Human Behavior* 123 (2021), p. 106857.

[37] Joshua D Miner. "Monitoring simulated worlds in Indigenous strategy games". In: *The Computer Games Journal* 9.3 (2020), pp. 311–329.

[38] John ER Staddon and Daniel T Cerutti. "Operant conditioning". In: *Annual Review of Psychology* 54.1 (2003), pp. 115–144.

[39] Patrick M Markey, Charlotte N Markey, and Juliana E French. "Violent video games and real-world violence: Rhetoric versus data." In: *Psychology of Popular Media Culture* 4.4 (2015), p. 277.

[40] Bennett Foddy. "Addiction: The pleasures and perils of operant behaviour." In: *N. Heather & G. Segal (Eds.), Addiction and choice: Rethinking the relationship (pp. 49–65)* (2017).

[41] Pawel Grabarczyk. "Is every indie game independent? Towards the concept of independent game". In: *Game Studies* 16.1 (2016).

[42] Leônidas S Pereira and Mauriécio MS Bernardes. "Aspects of independent game production: An exploratory study". In: *Computers in Entertainment (CIE)* 16.4 (2018), pp. 1–16.

[43] Sabine Hotho. "'Some Companies Are Fine One Day and Gone the Next': Sustaining Business in the Digital Games Industry". In: *Changing the Rules of the Game: Economic, Management and Emerging Issues in the Computer Games Industry* (2013), pp. 82–104.

[44] André Godoy and Ellen F Barbosa. "Game-Scrum: An Approach to Agile Game Development". In: *Proceedings of SBGames* (2010), pp. 292–295.

[45] Pekka Abrahamsson et al. "New directions on agile methods: a comparative analysis". In: *25th International Conference on Software Engineering, 2003. Proceedings.* Ieee. 2003, pp. 244–254.

[46] Nelsen A Rahul et al. "The Impact of Agile Methods on the Software Projects Implementation and Management". In: *American Journal of Industrial and Business Management* 13.4 (2023), pp. 183–194.

[47] Jussi Koutonen and Mauri Leppänen. "How are agile methods and practices deployed in video game development? A survey into Finnish game studios". In: *Agile Processes in Software Engineering and Extreme Programming: 14th International Conference, XP 2013, Vienna, Austria, June 3-7, 2013. Proceedings 14.* Springer. 2013, pp. 135–149.

[48] Kanban Guide. *Kanban Guide.* Available at https://kanbanguides.org/english/. URL: `https://kanbanguides.org/english/`.

[49] Kent Beck. "Embracing change with extreme programming". In: *Computer* 32.10 (1999), pp. 70–77.

[50] Krunal Bhavsar, Vrutik Shah, and Samir Gopalan. "Scrumban: An agile integration of scrum and kanban in software engineering". In: *International Journal of Innovative Technology and Exploring Engineering* 9.4 (2020), pp. 1626–1634.

[51] Jeff Sutherland and Ken Schwaber. "The Scrum Guide". In: *The Definitive Guide to Scrum: The Rules of the Game. Scrum. org* 268 (2020), p. 14.

[52] Muris Lage Junior and Moacir Godinho Filho. "Variations of the kanban system: Literature review and classification". In: *International Journal of Production Economics* 125.1 (2010), pp. 13–21.

[53] Henrik Kniberg and Mattias Skarin. *Kanban and Scrum-making the most of both.* Lulu. com, 2010.

[54] Marcos Silvano Orita Almeida and Flavio Soares Correa da Silva. "A systematic review of game design methods and tools". In: *Entertainment Computing–ICEC 2013: 12th International Conference, ICEC 2013, São Paulo, Brazil, October 16-18, 2013. Proceedings 12.* Springer. 2013, pp. 17–29.

[55] Richard Colby and Rebekah Shultz Colby. "Game design documentation: Four perspectives from independent game studios". In: *Communication Design Quarterly Review* 7.3 (2019), pp. 5–15.

[56] Heather Maxwell Chandler. *The Game Production Handbook.* Jones & Bartlett Publishers, 2013.

[57] Jane Friedhoff. "Untangling Twine: A Platform Study." In: *DiGRA Conference.* 2013.

[58] Johannes Breuer and Gary Bente. "Why so serious? On the relation of serious games and learning". In: *Journal for Computer Game Culture* 4 (2010), pp. 7–24.

[59] Lisbeth H Larsen et al. "The physical effect of exergames in healthy elderly—a systematic review". In: *GAMES FOR HEALTH: Research, Development, and Clinical Applications* 2.4 (2013), pp. 205–212.

[60] Garm Lucassen et al. "The use and effectiveness of user stories in practice". In: *Requirements Engineering: Foundation for Software Quality: 22nd International Working Conference, REFSQ 2016, Gothenburg, Sweden, March 14-17, 2016, Proceedings 22.* Springer. 2016, pp. 205–222.

[61] José Pablo Zagal, Miguel Nussbaum, and Ricardo Rosas. "A model to support the design of multiplayer games". In: *Presence: Teleoperators & Virtual Environments* 9.5 (2000), pp. 448–462.

[62] Nick Yee. *The Proteus paradox: How online games and virtual worlds change us-and how they don't.* Yale University Press, 2014.

[63] Tracy Fullerton. *Game design workshop: a Playcentric approach to creating innovative games.* CRC Press, 2014.

[64] Juho Hamari and Lauri Keronen. "Why do people play games? A meta-analysis". In: *International Journal of Information Management* 37.3 (2017), pp. 125–141.

[65] Barbaros Bostan and Digdem Sezen. "Player needs inventory (PNI): An analytical framework for analyzing player motives in video games". In: *The 23rd Annual European GAME-ON® Conference (GAME-ON®'2022) on Simulation and AI in Computer Games.* 2022.

[66] Richard M Ryan and Edward L Deci. "Self-determination theory and the facilitation of intrinsic motivation, social development, and well-being." In: *American Psychologist* 55.1 (2000), p. 68.

[67] Richard Bartle. "Hearts, clubs, diamonds, spades: Players who suit MUDs". In: *Journal of MUD Research* 1.1 (1996), p. 19.

[68] Ji-Won Moon and Young-Gul Kim. "Extending the TAM for a World-Wide-Web context". In: *Information & Management* 38.4 (2001), pp. 217–230.

[69] Catherine Potard et al. "Video game players' personality traits: An exploratory cluster approach to identifying gaming preferences." In: *Psychology of Popular Media* 9.4 (2020), p. 499.

[70] Torill Elvira Mortensen. "WoW is the new MUD: Social gaming from text to video". In: *Games and Culture* 1.4 (2006), pp. 397–413.

[71] Richard A Bartle. *Designing virtual worlds*. New Riders, 2004.

[72] Nick Yee. "Motivations for play in online games". In: *CyberPsychology & Behavior* 9.6 (2006), pp. 772–775.

[73] Kurt D Squire and Constance A Steinkuehler. "Generating cyberculture/s: The case of Star Wars galaxies". In: *Cyberlines* 2 (2006), pp. 177–198.

[74] Yu-kai Chou. *Actionable gamification: Beyond points, badges, and leaderboards*. Packt Publishing Ltd, 2019.

[75] Nick Yee. *The 9 Quantic Gamer Types - Quantic Foundry*. [Accessed 06-08-2023]. 2015. URL: `https://quanticfoundry.com/gamer-types/`.

[76] Lennart E Nacke, Chris Bateman, and Regan L Mandryk. "BrainHex: preliminary results from a neurobiological gamer typology survey". In: *Entertainment Computing–ICEC 2011: 10th International Conference, ICEC 2011, Vancouver, Canada, October 5-8, 2011. Proceedings 10*. Springer. 2011, pp. 288–293.

[77] Jukka Vahlo et al. "Digital game dynamics preferences and player types". In: *Journal of Computer-Mediated Communication* 22.2 (2017), pp. 88–103.

[78] Tomasz Miaskiewicz and Kenneth A Kozar. "Personas and user-centered design: How can personas benefit product design processes?" In: *Design Studies* 32.5 (2011), pp. 417–430.

[79] John Feil and Marc Scattergood. *Beginning game level design*. Thomson Course Technology, 2005.

[80] Christopher W Totten. *Architectural approach to level design*. CRC Press, 2019.

[81] Mark Hendrikx et al. "Procedural content generation for games: A survey". In: *ACM Transactions on Multimedia Computing, Communications, and Applications (TOMM)* 9.1 (2013), pp. 1–22.

[82] Robert Yang. *The Level Design Book*. [Accessed 19-08-2023]. 2022. URL: `https://book.leveldesignbook.com/`.

[83] David Milam and Magy Seif El Nasr. "Design patterns to guide player movement in 3D games". In: *Proceedings of the 5th ACM SIGGRAPH Symposium on Video Games.* 2010, pp. 37–42.

[84] Jaakko Stenros. "The game definition game: A review". In: *Games and Culture* 12.6 (2017), pp. 499–520.

[85] Jonne Arjoranta. "How to define games and why we need to". In: *The Computer Games Journal* 8.3-4 (2019), pp. 109–120.

[86] Machinations.io. *What is Machinations.* [Accessed 27-08-2023]. 2021". URL: `https://machinations.io/docs/home/`.

[87] Róbert Szilágyi et al. "Development of Farm simulation application, an example for gamification in higher education". In: *Journal of Agricultural Informatics* 8.2 (2017).

[88] Hannah Nicklin. *Writing for games: Theory and practice.* CRC Press, 2022.

[89] Tobias Heussner et al. *The game narrative toolbox.* CRC Press, 2023.

[90] Flint Dille and John Zuur Platten. *The ultimate guide to video game writing and design.* Lone Eagle, 2008.

[91] B Mitchell Peck, Paul R Ketchum, and David G Embrick. "Racism and sexism in the gaming world: Reinforcing or changing stereotypes in computer games". In: *Journal of Media and Communication Studies* 3.6 (2011), pp. 212–220.

[92] TV Tropes. *TV Tropes.* [Accessed 18-09-2023]. 2023. URL: `https://tvtropes.org/pmwiki/pmwiki.php/Main/Tropes`.

[93] Stephanie Rennick and Seán G Roberts. "Improving video game conversations with trope-informed design". In: *Game Studies* 21.3 (2021).

[94] TV Tropes. *TV Tropes: Evil Overlord.* [Accessed 18-09-2023]. 2023. URL: `https://tvtropes.org/pmwiki/pmwiki.php/Main/EvilOverlord`.

[95] Robert C Allen. *To be continued...: soap operas around the world*. Routledge, 2002.

[96] TV Tropes. *TV Tropes: The Tropeless Tale*. [Accessed 27-09-2023]. 2023. URL: `https://tvtropes.org/pmwiki/pmwiki.php/JustForFun/TheTropelessTale`.

[97] Syd Field. *Screenplay*. Delacorte New York, 1982.

[98] Lisa Cron. *Story Genius: How to Use Brain Science to Go Beyond Outlining and Write a Riveting Novel (before You Waste Three Years Writing 327 Pages that Go Nowhere)*. Ten Speed Press, 2016.

[99] Joseph Campbell. *The hero with a thousand faces*. Vol. 17. New World Library, 2008.

[100] Christopher Vogler. *The Writer's journey*. Michael Wiese Productions Studio City, CA, 2007.

[101] Glenda Hambly. "The not so universal hero's journey". In: *Journal of Screenwriting* 12.2 (2021), pp. 135–150.

[102] Sarah Stang and Aaron Trammell. "The ludic bestiary: Misogynistic tropes of female monstrosity in Dungeons & Dragons". In: *Games and Culture* 15.6 (2020), pp. 730–747.

[103] Emma Vossen. "There and back again: Tolkien, gamers, and the remediation of exclusion through fantasy media". In: *Feminist Media Histories* 6.1 (2020), pp. 37–65.

[104] Tanner Higgin. "Blackless fantasy: The disappearance of race in massively multiplayer online role-playing games". In: *Games and Culture* 4.1 (2009), pp. 3–26.

[105] Helen Young. *Race and popular fantasy literature: Habits of whiteness*. Routledge, 2015.

[106] Nicholas David Bowman, Daniel Schultheiss, and Christina Schumann. ""I'm attached, and I'm a good guy/gal!": How character attachment influences pro-and anti-social motivations to play massively multiplayer online role-playing games". In: *Cyberpsychology, Behavior, and Social Networking* 15.3 (2012), pp. 169–174.

[107] Albert Bandura. "Moral disengagement in the perpetration of inhumanities". In: *Personality and Social Psychology Review* 3.3 (1999), pp. 193–209.

[108] Albert Bandura. "Mechanisms of moral disengagement". In: *Insurgent Terrorism.* Routledge, 2017, pp. 85–115.

[109] TV Tropes. *TV Tropes: Character Alignment.* [Accessed 07-12-2023]. 2023. URL: `https://tvtropes.org/pmwiki/pmwiki.php/Main/CharacterAlignment`.

[110] Gary Gygax and Dave Arneson. *Dungeons & Dragons.* Vol. 19. Tactical Studies Rules Lake Geneva, WI, 1974.

[111] Bernard Gert and Joshua Gert. "The definition of morality". In: (2002).

[112] Andre Dowsett and Mervyn Jackson. "The effect of violence and competition within video games on aggression". In: *Computers in Human Behavior* 99 (2019), pp. 22–27.

[113] Patrick M Markey and Charlotte N Markey. "Vulnerability to violent video games: A review and integration of personality research". In: *Review of General Psychology* 14.2 (2010), pp. 82–91.

[114] Craig A Anderson et al. "Screen violence and youth behaviour". In: *Pediatrics* 140.Supplement_2 (2017), S142–S147.

[115] M Gallagher. *Entertainment Software Association: ESSENTIAL FACTS ABOUT THE COMPUTER AND VIDEO GAME INDUSTRY 2011.* 2011.

[116] Kellie Vella et al. "A sense of belonging: Pokémon GO and social connectedness". In: *Games and Culture* 14.6 (2019), pp. 583–603.

[117] Christopher John Ferguson. "The good, the bad and the ugly: A meta-analytic review of positive and negative effects of violent video games". In: *Psychiatric Quarterly* 78 (2007), pp. 309–316.

[118] Zhaojun Teng, Yujie Li, and Yanling Liu. "Online gaming, internet addiction, and aggression in Chinese Male students: The mediating role of low self-control". In: *International Journal of Psychological Studies* 6.2 (2014), p. 89.

[119] Greg Blackburn and Erica Scharrer. "Video game playing and beliefs about masculinity among male and female emerging adults". In: *Sex Roles* 80 (2019), pp. 310–324.

[120] Tracy Cassidy. "The mood board process modelled and understood as a qualitative design research tool". In: *Fashion Practice* 3.2 (2011), pp. 225–251.

[121] Nuno Neto et al. "Development of an inclusive multiplayer serious game for blind and deaf". In: *2020 15th Iberian Conference on Information Systems and Technologies (CISTI)*. IEEE. 2020, pp. 1–6.

[122] Marcella Mandanici, Antonio Rodà, and Marco Ricca. "The task of walking straight as an interactive serious game for blind children". In: *EAI Endorsed Transactions on Serious Games* 5.16 (2018).

[123] Alex Jaffe. *GDC 2019: Cursed Problems in Game Design.* [Accessed 18-12-2023]. 2019. URL: `https://www.gdcvault.com/play/1025756/Cursed-Problems-in-Game`.

[124] Greg Lobanov. *GDC 2022: Gamifying Creativity in Chicory: A Colorful Tale.* [Accessed 18-12-2023]. 2022. URL: `https://www.gdcvault.com/play/1028033/Gamifying-Creativity-in-Chicory-A`.

[125] Chris Solarski. *Drawing basics and video game art: Classic to cutting-edge art techniques for winning video game design.* Watson-Guptill, 2012.

[126] Alphonso Dunn. *Pen & ink drawing: A simple guide.* Three Minds Press New Jersey, 2015.

[127] Sam R Kennedy. *How to become a video game artist: The insider's guide to landing a job in the gaming world.* Watson-Guptill, 2013.

[128] Robin P. Williams. "The Non-designers Design Book: Design and Typographic Principles for the Visual Novice. Non Designer's Design Book". In: *Peachpit Press Publications* (2005).

[129] Scott Robertson. *The Skillful Huntsman.* 2005.

[130] Marianne Roland Michel and Ursula Korneitchouk. "A Basket of Plums". In: *The Bulletin of the Cleveland Museum of Art* 60.2 (1973), pp. 52–59.

[131] Jos van den Broek. *Visual Language: Perspectives for both makers and users.* Eleven International Publishing, 2012.

[132] Roy R Behrens. "Art, design and gestalt theory". In: *Leonardo* 31.4 (1998), pp. 299–303.

[133] Melanie Fritsch and Tim Summers. *The Cambridge companion to video game music.* Cambridge University Press, 2021.

[134] Aaron Marks. *The complete guide to game audio: For composers, musicians, sound designers, game developers.* Routledge, 2012.

[135] GW Childs. *Creating music and sound for games.* Course Technology Press, 2006.

[136] Tero Koskela. "Choosing Juice: Enabling Fun in Games through Better Visual Design". In: (2015).

[137] Steve Swink. *Game feel: a game designer's guide to virtual sensation.* CRC Press, 2008.

[138] Takashi Nakamura and Kazunori Miyata. "Influence of audiovisual Feedback on player behavior and performance in response to video game failure". In: *International Workshop on Advanced Imaging Technology (IWAIT) 2021.* Vol. 11766. SPIE. 2021, pp. 318–323.

[139] Khairul Yusri Zamri. "The Effects of 10 User Interface (UI) Elements on Game Design Process". In: *EDUCATUM Journal of Science, Mathematics and Technology* 9.2 (2022), pp. 82–90.

[140] Dedy Prasetya Kristiadi et al. "The effect of UI, UX and GX on video games". In: *2017 IEEE International Conference on Cybernetics and Computational Intelligence (CyberneticsCom)*. IEEE. 2017, pp. 158–163.

[141] Gourisha Goel, Poonam Tanwar, and Shweta Sharma. "UI-UX design using user-centred design (UCD) method". In: *2022 International Conference on Computer Communication and Informatics (ICCCI)*. IEEE. 2022, pp. 1–8.

[142] Andreas Kurniawan, Nunnun Bonafix, Hendri Hartono, et al. "Design UI/UX Mobile Games for Left-Hand Dominant People". In: *Journal of Games, Game Art, and Gamification* 5.2 (2020), pp. 48–53.

[143] MJ Hamm. "Wireframing Essentials: An Introduction to User Experience Design". In: *Preuzeto* 4 (2014), p. 2020.

[144] Ellen Lupton. *Thinking with type: A critical guide for designers, writers, editors, & students*. Chronicle Books, 2014.

[145] Niraj Ramesh Dayama et al. "Grids: Interactive layout design with integer programming". In: *Proceedings of the 2020 CHI Conference on Human Factors in Computing Systems*. 2020, pp. 1–13.

[146] Jon Yablonski. *Laws of UX: Using psychology to design better products & services*. O'Reilly Media, 2020.

[147] Anders Tychsen and Alessandro Canossa. "Defining personas in games using metrics". In: *Proceedings of the 2008 Conference on Future Play: Research, Play, Share*. 2008, pp. 73–80.

[148] Alessandro Canossa and Anders Drachen. "Play-personas: behaviours and belief systems in user-centred game design". In: *Human-Computer Interaction–INTERACT 2009: 12th IFIP TC 13 International Conference, Uppsala, Sweden, August 24-28, 2009, Proceedings, Part II 12*. Springer. 2009, pp. 510–523.

[149] Alan Cooper, Robert Reimann, and David Cronin. *About face 3: the essentials of interaction design*. John Wiley & Sons, 2007.

[150] James J Gibson. "The theory of affordances". In: *Hilldale, USA* 1.2 (1977), pp. 67–82.

[151] Don Norman. *The design of Everyday Things: Revised and expanded edition.* Basic Books, 2013.

[152] Bei Yuan, Eelke Folmer, and Frederick C Harris. "Game accessibility: a survey". In: *Universal Access in the Information Society* 10 (2011), pp. 81–100.

[153] Michael Heron. "Inaccessible through oversight: the need for inclusive game design". In: *The Computer Games Journal* 1 (2012), pp. 29–38.

[154] Renata Pontin M Fortes et al. "Game accessibility evaluation methods: a literature survey". In: *Universal Access in Human-Computer Interaction. Design and Development Approaches and Methods: 11th International Conference, UAHCI 2017, Held as Part of HCI International 2017, Vancouver, BC, Canada, July 9–14, 2017, Proceedings, Part I 11.* Springer. 2017, pp. 182–192.

[155] G Reid Lyon, Sally E Shaywitz, and Bennett A Shaywitz. "A definition of dyslexia". In: *Annals of Dyslexia* 53 (2003), pp. 1–14.

[156] Richard K Wagner et al. "The prevalence of dyslexia: A new approach to its estimation". In: *Journal of Learning Disabilities* 53.5 (2020), pp. 354–365.

[157] MP Simunovic. "Colour vision deficiency". In: *Eye* 24.5 (2010), pp. 747–755.

[158] Mateus Pinheiro, Windson Viana, and Ticianne de Gois Ribeiro Darin. "Why Should Red and Green Never Be Seen? Exploring Color Blindness Simulations as Tools to Create Chromatically Accessible Games". In: *Proceedings of the ACM on Human-Computer Interaction* 7.CHI PLAY (2023), pp. 165–196.

Index